D0948261

Thoreau of Walden

THE MAN AND
HIS EVENTFUL LIFE

BY

Henry Beetle Hough

ARCHON BOOKS
1970

PS
3053
H6
1970

FIRST PUBLISHED 1956 SIMON AND SCHUSTER, INC.
© 1956 BY HENRY BEETLE HOUGH
REPRINTED 1970 WITH PERMISSION
IN AN UNALTERED AND UNABRIDGED EDITION

SBN: 208 00929 9
LIBRARY OF CONGRESS CATALOG CARD NUMBER: 77-103988
[REPRODUCED FROM A COPY IN THE YALE UNIVERSITY LIBRARY]
PRINTED IN THE UNITED STATES OF AMERICA

For Betty, with Appreciation

CONTENTS

❧ ❧

1

INTRODUCTORY

1. To Walden

(In Thoreau's journals these two words—"To Walden"—recur like a repeated stage direction, an invitation on a guidepost, or perhaps like a theme in music.)

THE FIRST-REMEMBERED GREATNESS of Henry David Thoreau is that he wrote a book named after a pond near Concord, Massachusetts. It is a book as native as the huckleberry bushes that reddened the Concord hills in fall, and as ancient as the sacred writings of the Hindus.

Thoreau was pungently impolite to the generality of his fellow men and to most of their ideas. He wrote, "I have a great deal of company in my house; especially in the morning, when nobody calls."

He liked to enlarge upon this theme: "Society is commonly too cheap. We meet at very short intervals, not having had time to acquire any new value for each other . . . we live thick and are in each other's way, and I think that we thus lose some respect for one another. . . . It would be better if there were but one inhabitant to the square mile, as where I live. The value of a man is not in his skin, that we should touch him."

One of his contemporaries remarked that he "had the right

1

to saunter at will in the fields and woods of Concord, though he need not have spent so much time there." Thoreau himself was the best judge of this and other necessities of his life. He found most of his best minutes and hours and even years in the fields and woods, but when he wrote of his experience he was not addressing the woodpeckers and squirrels but the spirit of man. Some of his fellow citizens never have understood that sufficiently.

Thoreau in his time appeared as an eccentric with a prominent nose, brusque ways, and the attire of a rustic. He wrote that "the mass of men lead lives of quiet desperation," and the fashion was not so much to refute the statement as to resent it and exclaim that of course it was not so. Some time and reflection were necessary to appreciate what he meant by living.

"I did not wish to live what was not life," he wrote, "living is so dear; nor did I wish to practice resignation, unless it was quite necessary. I wanted to live deep and suck out all the marrow of life, to live so sturdily and Spartan-like as to put to rout all that was not life, to cut a broad swath and shave close, to drive life into a corner, and reduce it to its lowest terms, and if it proved to be mean, why then to get the whole and genuine meanness of it, and publish its meanness to the world; or if it were sublime, to know it by experience, and be able to give a true account of it in my next excursion."

He asked not only himself but the friends with whom he corresponded and all the rest of the literate world, "Will you live? or will you be embalmed? Will you live, though it be astride of a sunbeam; or will you repose safely in the catacombs for a thousand years?"

He was not afraid of demanding too much of life, but he wanted to be "up to the occasion which it is." He said he would be sorry to remember that he was in the world and noticed nothing remarkable—"not so much as a prince in disguise; lived in the golden age a hired man; visited Olympus even, but fell asleep after dinner, and did not hear the conversation of the gods. I lived in Judaea eighteen hundred years ago, but I never knew there was such a one as Christ among my contemporaries!"

If most lives in and about Concord, and elsewhere too, fell as short as it was obvious they did, then he thought it should be considered whether the men and women who lived them were trying for distance in the wrong things and on the wrong scale.

"A man must find his occasions in himself, it is true. . . . I had this advantage, at least . . . that my life was become my amusement and never ceased to be novel. It was a drama of many scenes and without an end."

He found early and beyond a doubt that the plainest things were not the meanest, and he did a great deal of exploring of the inexhaustible resources of plainness and simplicity, as for instance "the dear wholesome color of shrub-oak leaves, so clean and firm, not decaying, but which have put on a kind of immortality. . . . Emblem of my winter condition." He came to know the face, grain, and temper of the natural world so well that he seemed to rediscover it, but all this might have been of minor importance had he not rendered his account in a new style of his own.

His words were natural and not likely to fade in weather or with time. His sentences leaped with tang and fertility, as streams flow and breezes rustle.

Thoreau's aware and alertly stubborn mind particularly relished freedom, nonconformity, dissent, as when he wrote, "I wish my countrymen to consider that whatever the human law may be, neither an individual nor a nation can ever commit the least act of injustice against the obscurest individual without having to pay the penalty for it."

It was always in his determination and manner of life that "we should be men first and subjects afterward," nor was he less abrupt with the lip service of the respectable church people. He quoted some of the noblest teachings of Jesus and went on: "Think of this, Yankees! . . . Think of repeating these things to a New England audience! thirdly, fourthly, fifteenthly, till there are three barrels of sermons! . . . Who, without cant, can hear them and not go out of the meeting-house? They never *were* read, they never *were* heard. Let but one of these sentences be rightly read, from any pulpit in the land, and there would not be left one stone of that meeting-house upon another."

He declared that "the ways by which you get money almost without exception lead downward" and observed likewise that "nature is really very kind and liberal to all persons of vicious habits. . . ."

He was never a reformer—and some of his finest invective was applied to reformers who came to his house—but he asked, "If I could help infuse some life and heart into society, should I not do a service?"

His Concord neighbors saw that what he said was inextricably intertwined with how he lived and what he did, but most of them did not know what to make of either.

Critics, teachers, philosophers, writers can no more avoid turning to Thoreau than they can refrain from opening a window on a warm spring day—but when they speak of his life, most of them remark sooner or later, and many at the outset, that it was uneventful. Precisely at this early crossroads, before the narrower, twisting way begins, sun-spattered through the leaves of oaks or swamp maples, they part company with their subject, with him who might have been, despite his lifetime avoidance of too much society, a friend.

Thoreau's life uneventful?

". . . I will build my lodge on the southern slope of some hill, and take there the life the gods send me."

"Many a day spent on the hilltops waiting for the sky to fall, that I might catch something."

"Go forth and hear the crickets chirp at midnight. Hear if their dynasty is not an ancient one and well founded."

"What need to travel? There are no sierras equal to the clouds in the sunset sky."

"Once it chanced that I stood in the very abutment of a rainbow's arch, which filled the lower stratum of the atmosphere, ringing the grass and leaves around, and dazzling me as if I looked through colored crystal. It was a lake of rainbow light. in which, for a short while, I lived like a dolphin."

If Thoreau's life was uneventful, the earth might as well be all neon lights and pavement, and the time of man appointed in a subway. To say that it was uneventful is to disclose an unbelief in what he experienced and wrote, and to fend him off with closed-room words.

Clouds gather quickly. The sunlight is obscured by smoke and haze of cities. Despite their scholarly attainments, it is certain that critics such as these will never arrive at Walden Pond.

2. Giant-Size Truth

Anyone who wishes to know Henry David Thoreau should read *Walden*, and anyone who desires to know him better should read *Walden* again—and then again, and so on, between times perhaps accompanying him afoot on the sands of Cape Cod or by small boat to the headwaters of the Concord and Merrimack. Yet sooner or later a reader will wonder to what extent he has come to know a man and to what extent a book; he will, of course, know both, but the book is greater by Thoreau's deep design.

"I, too, would fain set down something besides facts. Facts should be only the frame to my pictures; they should be material to the mythology which I am writing; not facts to assist men to make money, farmers to farm profitably, in any common sense; facts to tell who I am, and where I have been or what I have thought; as now the bell rings for evening meeting, and its volumes of sound, like smoke which rises from where a cannon is fired, make the tent in which I dwell. My facts shall be falsehoods to the common sense. I would so state facts that they shall be significant, shall be myths or mythologic. Facts which the mind perceived, thoughts which the body thought— with these I deal. I, too, cherish vague and misty forms, vaguest when the cloud at which I gaze is dissipated quite and naught but the skyey depths are seen."

Something besides facts. Not the idiom of the early grades of common school carried forward into adult life, not the disguise of the obvious, not that shorthand of the senses employed to facilitate an escape from or a compromise with the world around—none of these, but, standing alive and monumental, all brave and glistening in the sunlight, a giant-size truth. Truth with an extra atomic weight to excite and attract, not to avoid, the mysterious reactions of life for the man who lives it. A New England mythology which should soar high and far, which should bring back, like morning, the heroic ages, which should be at the same time common and cosmical.

Thoreau wrote in his journal: "Some incidents in my life have seemed far more allegorical than actual; they were so significant that they plainly served no other use."

He did not mistake the stature of man in the world. By the shore of Walden Pond in the early morning he listened to the hum of a mosquito that "was Homer's requiem; itself an Iliad and Odyssey in the air, singing its own wrath and wanderings."

He was certain of his own purpose and method. "I fear only lest my expressions may not be extravagant enough—may not wander far enough beyond the narrow limits of our ordinary insight and faith, so as to be adequate to the truth of which I have been convinced. I desire to speak somewhere without bounds, in order that I may attain to an expression in some degree adequate to the truth of which I have been convinced. From a man in a waking moment to men in their waking moments."

That behind the myth and extravagance there should be a lesser and everyday truth with only the long-familiar atomic weight is hardly a great discovery for a critic or a biographer. As much credit should go to a child who, having seen a Concord house ruddily tinted by an autumn sunset, should later discover and announce that this house was, in reality, a sober white, painted so by a townsman named Buttrick or Hosmer. More than this is needed to expunge a sunset glow.

A man in a waking moment may, as part of a grand design, listen to the hum of a mosquito and hear it as an *Iliad* and *Odyssey* in the air, but no man in a waking moment may hear an *Iliad* and *Odyssey* and put it down as the humming of a mosquito.

2

THE SUN ROSE CLEAR

❧ ☙

1. *Thoreau's on Long Wharf*

THE PRONUNCIATION of the name is out of Concord, not out of St. Helier; the accent is on the first syllable. Sophia Hawthorne supplied a guide when she was newly residing in the Old Manse and, before knowing him well, wrote in a letter: "Mr. Thorrow was here." He had not made too favorable an impression on the first encounter, but the second was much better.

One July day in 1851, Henry Thoreau, having made one of his journeys afield from Concord, reached the seacoast town of Cohasset and called on an old salt-water man who remembered his grandfather. Indeed, the old man remembered fishermen who had "fitted out at Thoreau's" on Long Wharf in Boston.

John Thoreau, sometime merchant and outfitter, was born at St. Helier, on the Island of Jersey in the English Channel, in April 1754, the son of Philippe Thoreau and Marie Le Gallais. Philippe and Marie were only names in the haze-drifted background of family origins. Henry gazed now and then into even bluer distances, as when he wrote: "Perhaps I am descended from the Northman named 'Thorer, the Dog-footed,' " mentioned in the sagas. The ocean-ranging spirit of the Vikings appealed to him, and he felt an essence of antiquity within himself derived from yet broader sources: ". . . I have not changed an opinion one iota from the first. As the stars looked to me when I was a shepherd in Assyria, they look to me now, a New Englander."

Observing a mirage when he was walking the outer beach of Cape Cod, Henry recalled the tale of Thorfinn's expedition to Vinland in 1007, and added, "But whether Thor-finn saw the mirage here or not, Thor-eau, one of the family, did; and perchance it was because Leif the Lucky had, in a previous voyage, taken Thor-er and his people off the rock in the middle of the sea, that Thor-eau was born to see it."

But all this was cut off from present view, whereas John, Henry's grandfather, could still be discerned as a moving figure above the horizon, though for a little while only before he too must surely vanish. As a young man he had left his native Jersey and voyaged westward. "I do not know at what time he emigrated to this country," wrote Henry's Aunt Maria long afterward, "but have been told he was shipwreck'd on the passage and suffered much. I think he must have left a large family circle, as Uncle Peter in his letters refers to aunts and cousins, two of which, aunts Le Capelain and Pinckney, resided in London, and a cousin, John Thoreau, was an officer in the British army."

There were only a few letters from Uncle Peter, addressed to Henry's Aunt Elizabeth at "Concord, near Boston," the last of them dated in April 1806, after which it was assumed the old gentleman must have died.

So much for the Thoreaus of the Island of Jersey and the Old World, and if Henry retained any recognizable inheritance from them it was perhaps an odd way of pronouncing his "R's," a mannerism that might have been French—as his friend Ellery Channing suggested—or, equally, might have been Scotch, or his own.

Boston was not only an inviting gateway to America but also a hive of commerce where it was believed any man could get on even if he had only his two hands to start with. Henry's grandfather found work with a cooper who was busy supplying casks for the needs of the port's trade, but then came the Revolution and a sudden halt to American commerce on the seas. The cooper called his men together and told them he had nothing for them to do. So John Thoreau shipped aboard the American privateer *General Lincoln*—which was at once an adventurous and practical thing to do. Yet there was more to his Revolutionary experience than this, for he was to tell his son, Henry's father, of being stationed at some defenses, and of a cannonball that came close, with the compliments of the British, spilling sand over him and his companions.

The surrender of the British at Yorktown in 1781 marked both an ending and a beginning, and in that year John Thoreau married Jane Burns, of Scottish and Quaker background, in Boston. Long afterward, Mrs. William Monroe of Concord provided a child's-eye glimpse, remembered across the years, of this Jennie Burns. Henry noted the reminiscence in his journal: "She says she was only 3 or 4 years old, and that she went to school with Aunt Elizabeth and one other child, to a woman named Turner, somewhere in Boston, who kept a spinning wheel a-going while she taught these three little children. She remembers that one sat on a lignum vitae mortar turned bottom up, another on a box, and a third on a stool."

To this primitive schoolroom came Jennie Burns Thoreau, leading her little daughter who was "so small that she could not tell her name distinctly, but spoke thickly and lispingly—'Elizabeth Orrok Thoreau.' " The mother of Jennie Burns was Sarah Orrok, and when she was courted by Jennie's father "he was obliged to doff his rich apparel of gems and ruffles and conform to the more simple garb of his Quaker bride."

Mrs. Monroe remembered Henry's paternal grandfather,

also. John Thoreau was "taller than Father, and used to ride out to their house [so Henry noted]—she was a Stone and lived where she and her husband did afterward, now David Merriam's—when they made cheeses, to drink the whey, being in consumption."

John Thoreau, his first stock in trade a single hogshead of sugar, had gone into business for himself on Long Wharf. It was remembered of him that he was strong for his size and would ask or tolerate no help in handling a barrel of molasses that might need to be shifted or set on its head. But the Long Wharf enterprise was presently succeeded by a shop on Boston's King Street, later rechristened State.

As John's health became more precarious, he acquired a house at Concord, twenty miles from Boston, and there he died of consumption at the age of forty-seven in the year 1801. His wife, Jennie Burns, had already died in 1796 at the age of forty-two. Their children were Elizabeth, Jane, John, and Maria. John, at the time of his father's death, was twelve.

2. Near Trillium Wood

So the drift of family and circumstances was arranging a rare setting for Henry, who could be born within easy reach of such places as Trillium Wood, Hubbard's Close, Well Meadow Head, Hosmer's Meadow, Brister's Spring, Money Digger's Shore, Pinxter Swamp—and Walden.

But the Thoreau history was only half in any case and, as Henry's temperament was to prove later, perhaps less than half. Henry's mother was Cynthia Dunbar, a granddaughter of ruddy and fleshy Elisha Jones, whose lands, two slaves, and otherwise large fortune had been bound up with the British rule. Elisha had served as a colonel of militia in the pre-Revolutionary days, when it was a case of British against Indians and disorder. He sat in the General Court, aired his Tory opinions, and was trusted by General Gage, who was running into trouble in Boston.

Elisha's children numbered fourteen sons and a daughter, Mary, who married Reverend Asa Dunbar, then a young minister at Salem and on the opposite side of the ditch from his father-in-law over politics and the rights of man. Mary's brother Josiah got the patriots after him when his father, whom General Gage had appointed forage commissioner, put him aboard the sloop *Polly* as supercargo on a mission to bring hay to Boston. Josiah and a companion were taken to Arundel, now Kennebunkport, and handed over to the local committee.

From there they were sent back to Concord and lodged in jail. Meantime Salem had been blockaded, and Mary Dunbar was living at her father's home in Weston, handily within reach of Concord. On the very day of the battle of Bunker Hill (or Breed's Hill), Mary went to visit Josiah, carrying a basket of cherries from the Jones orchard. Beneath the cherries she had hidden a number of files through the use of which her brother and his comrade were soon free of the Concord jail.

Mary had set a rendezvous at her father's cider mill, deserted and forgotten at that time of year, where she had food and clothing in readiness, as well as a horse and carriage to convey the fugitives to Falmouth, the modern Portland, from where they could reach Nova Scotia. Asa Dunbar suffered some embarrassment because of Mary's Tory activities.

Asa, Henry Thoreau's maternal grandfather, was born in the town of Bridgewater in 1745 and became a graduate of Harvard in 1767. He preached at Bedford—which was near Concord—and settled in Salem in 1772. Just as the Revolution was ending, he resigned his pastorate and moved to Keene, New Hampshire, where he practiced as a lawyer until his death in 1787. It was during the final year of his life that his daughter Cynthia, Henry's mother, was born.

Though Asa's death left Mary Jones Dunbar a widow, there

was life aplenty in her still, and she took for her second husband Jonas Minott, who had been a Revolutionary captain at the fight in Concord when the embattled farmers had turned on the British. This marriage brought Mary and her daughters, Cynthia and Louise, to the Minott house in Concord.

It was, in the words of Ellery Channing, "a perfect piece of our New England style of building, with its gray, unpainted boards, its grassy, unfenced dooryard." The roof reached nearly to the ground in the rear. The Virginia Road, beside which it stood, was "an old fashioned, winding, at-length-deserted pathway, the more smiling for its forked orchards, tumbling walls, and mossy banks. About the house are pleasant, sunny meadows, deep with their beds of peat, so cheering with its homely, hearthlike fragrance; and in front runs a constant stream through the center of that great tract sometimes called 'Bedford levels'—this brook a source of the Shawsheen River."

The Shawsheen, like the Concord, was a tributary of the Merrimack, but reached the larger stream by a different course.

Sometimes on warm, music-filled nights in the country summer, Cynthia got out of bed at midnight or after and sat on the doorstep of her mother's house, listening to the sounds of the insects and feeling the mystery of the stars.

Cynthia had reached Concord a little ahead of that twelve-year-old boy, John Thoreau, who was to become her husband. John was sent to Lexington Academy for a year or so, then went to work as a clerk in Deacon White's store at the northwest end of the Concord green, and there learned the give-and-take, the buy-and-sell of commerce. He advanced into the dry-goods business in a store in Salem, then returned to Concord and when he was about twenty-one opened a store for himself on a corner where the town house was later built.

On Sundays John played the flute in the Congregational church where Dr. Ezra Ripley had succeeded the pastor of 1775, Reverend William Emerson, for whom the Old Manse had been built. Dr. Ripley not only lived in the house but he married Reverend William Emerson's widow and became step-father of another Reverend William Emerson who was to become pastor of the First Church in Boston.

John Thoreau, as he was shorter in stature than Cynthia, so otherwise seemed the lesser in their marriage. She was gifted with opinions, curiosity, a racing interest matched by a ready flow of talk. She was a natural-born participant, even if vicariously, in all the affairs about her. As a "stirring" person, she felt proprietorship in gossip, feuds, church affairs, village hopes and despairs. In short, she was equipped by temperament and energy to become a housewife and mother in a New England town, and to manage, and, when she could not manage, to engage in running commentary upon the unfolding times of her family and of Concord.

John was overshadowed. He was grave, habitually silent, and as the years passed he became deaf. Whether by accident or whether the relationship was implicit in his attraction to Cynthia, he was just the sort of husband and father who could live contentedly among female relatives—and boarders—listening to their prattle, interests, prejudices, sharing some, especially matters of family pride, letting the rest pass by. He became a good deal of an onlooker.

But when he and Cynthia were married in 1812, he was still in his early twenties, his mind fertile and hopeful with youth. They went to live in the house on the Virginia Road, and here their first child, Helen, was born that same year, and John, their second, in 1814.

Henry, long afterward, noted in his journal the facts of his own arrival: "Born July 12, 1817, in the Minott House, Virginia Road, where Father occupied Grandmother's thirds, carrying on the farm. The Catherines the other half of the house. Lived there about 8 months . . ."

Henry's uncle, David Dunbar, for whom he was named, died

when he was six weeks old. He had been baptized in the old Concord meetinghouse by Dr. Ripley (who had been known as "Holy" Ripley at Harvard) and did not cry—a fact which the family preserved fondly, along with other such memories and the baby clothes put away in a chest in the attic. Henry was christened David Henry Thoreau, but he himself changed the arrangement when he was at Harvard and in many assorted ways taking charge of his own life.

3. *Uncle Charles*

It is hardly possible to understand a New England town—a Yankee town—as it was then or is now unless one can appreciate a character such as Uncle Charles. Charles Dunbar, Cynthia Thoreau's brother, was lusty and nonconforming, a common and at the same time a most uncommon man. A small boy on the coast of Maine heard Uncle Charles hail a passing ship with so mighty a bellow that when the boy was man-grown he still remembered the voice and, because of it, Uncle Charles himself.

Big of frame and powerful of muscle, Uncle Charles took to expressing himself through his strength, and he had a gay heart and gusty humor too. He was at home in a tavern, where he liked a warming tipple of gin, but his head was as strong as his body and he was never known to get drunk. He never used tobacco, except for a borrowed pinch of snuff now and then, and he was not profane—but he was earthily vulgar.

Uncle Charles would take a twelve-foot ladder, run up one side while it balanced excitingly—for the spectators—then run down the other side, kicking the ladder from behind with a fine gesture as he was done with it. When he carted logs to Barrett's mill, he had been known to leap over the yoke of oxen and then back again for the entertainment of the boys and no doubt as a testimony of the overflowing vigor that was in him.

Henry made many notes about his Uncle Charles, especially after the old gentleman's death, when his exploits were being reviewed in town talk.

"People are talking about my uncle Charles. George Minott tells how he heard Tilly Brown once asking him to show him a peculiar inside lock in wrestling. 'Now don't hurt me—don't throw me hard.' He struck his antagonist inside his knees with his feet, and so deprived him of his legs.

"Edmund Hosmer remembers his tricks in the bar-room, shuffling cards, etc.; he could do anything with cards, yet he did not gamble. He would toss up his hat, twirling it over and over, and catch it on his head invariably. He once wanted to live at Hosmer's, but the latter was afraid of him."

The talk between the two went like this:

"Can't we study up something?" asked Uncle Charles.

Hosmer invited him into the house and brought out apples and cider.

"You!" said Uncle Charles. "I burst the bully of Haverhill."

He wanted to wrestle and Hosmer could not put him off. "Well, we won't wrestle in the house."

So they went out into the yard and a crowd gathered.

"Come, spread some straw here," said Uncle Charles. "I don't want to hurt him."

He threw Hosmer at once. They tried again, and Uncle Charles called for more straw. Then he "burst" Hosmer.

"Uncle Charles used to say that he hadn't a single tooth in his head. The fact was they were all double, and I have heard that he lost about all of them by the time he was twenty-one. Ever since I knew him he could swallow his nose. . . ."

A man who moved to Concord and became one of Henry's biographers, F. B. Sanborn, wrote that one of Uncle Charles's tricks was "to swallow all the knives and forks and some of the plates at the tavern table, and then offer to restore them if the landlord would forgive him the bill. I remember this worthy in his old age, an amusing guest at his brother-in-law's table, where his nephew plied him with questions."

It was Uncle Charles who was referred to in *Walden* as going to sleep shaving himself, and as being obliged to sprout potatoes in a cellar Sundays in order to keep awake and keep the Sabbath.

On a trip to New York, Uncle Charles stepped across the gangplank from steamboat to wharf and noticed some birds in the water that were strange to him. He called out to a bystander to ask what birds these were, and just then his hat blew off.

"Mister, your hat is off," said the bystander.

"Blast you, sir," retorted Uncle Charles, "I want to know what those birds are."

Henry recorded this annal, with the note that by the time Uncle Charles had got his information he had got his hat back too from the hand of a sailor.

The conventional record of almost any man's family background is ritualistic, usually a history of the family name only, ignoring the fact that the most alien and surprising influences may have been smuggled in by marriage, generation after generation. But sometimes a family turns up elements of character and temperament that perhaps serve as signs of what is to come; and so it was with Cynthia Thoreau and her brother Charles. As he brimmed over with his wrestling and gay eccentricities, she brimmed over with talk and with the shrewdness and strength necessary for raising a family and keeping a boarding-house.

Henry was, they said, "clear Dunbar." He took after his mother's side, and of course she was part Jones, deriving from the active Mary and the nonconforming sons of old Elisha. There were many "stirring" people in the line that Henry favored, and from these he may have drawn a significant part of his natural endowment.

And, of course, it was characters such as Uncle Charles who did much to fix the tone of Yankee towns, prodigies of one kind

and another—shouters of religion, gusty liars, strong men, ped-
dlers, ingenious tinkers with strange inventions, seers, mixers
of herbs, walkers in the moonlight. Yankee life could not have
been so sober and level in its precepts if there had not been
these foils to provide balance and perspective. Yankees generally praised God, but they did not quarrel with Nature; they
saw that in the long run Nature was God's way too. Many of
them took advantage of the fact to contrive satisfactions of
their own.

4. Shops, Farms, and Hearthstones

It was no longer necessary for farmers to turn out with mus-
kets to fight either redskins or British. The old exploits had been
written into history, and Dr. Ripley, who had performed the
wedding ceremony for John and Cynthia Thoreau and felt
himself to be custodian of tradition—one of the duties of a New
England minister—was agitating for a monument of commemo-
ration of the Concord fight. Men and women of the town were
free to go about their own business, for the great tasks had been
done. It was almost two centuries since Reverend Peter Bulkeley and his companions had pushed through swamps, brush,
and forest to settle the place, a journey of some twenty miles
that, for the description of its wildness and difficulties, might
have been to the Pacific Coast; and now Concord was a town
where it was commonplace for men and women to spend all
their lives. George Minott, for instance, had been to Boston
only once, having walked there when it appeared that fighting
men would be needed during the War of 1812.

The inhabitants of Concord had a right to say, if they cared
to, that their region was a completed place, because they or
their kinsmen had seen the completion accomplished. The result lay open to view. The countryside was tamed to civility
with stone walls, pastures, orchards, roads that led to neighbor-

ing hamlets and to Boston, Salem, or Worcester. Anyone could look on this and see the comeliness of the town and the outlying fields, farmsteads, hills. Yet for all its civility, the countryside still held a brimming store of nature that could be drawn upon by the inhabitants at will.

Concord, like all New England, had not undertaken and finished off its new business in America without developing also a point of view. From here on there would be pretty much more of the sort of life now established—more of the same liberty, now securely won, more of the same thrift and husbandry, more of the New England style and pattern spreading over the nation as a whole. These were people who were nothing if they were not possessive.

The future of the social order was hazier than the rest of the prospect, but little worrying was done about that in most New England households. Whatever the future turned out to be, it was assured. It was safe, favored by Providence. Those who wrestled with it would do so mostly for exercise, out of stubbornness, or from self-indulgence. The real and immediate concern was with the relationship between men and their environment rather than with that between men and other men; but one of the advantages of the settled prospect was that there were all the time and opportunity in the world for those who wished to chase matters of the intellect, including social theory and philosophy, into some convenient fence corner.

New England was a singularly appropriate region. It had fallen into a natural harmony. What a man did, as a rule, was becoming to him: the farmer deserved credit for being a farmer, the shopkeeper for being just that, and even so with the tinker, the shoemaker, and the town character—for he was part of New England and was demonstrating something natural that had to be indulged even if, in theory, it was deplored.

Concord lived by farming and by trade. The traveled road from New Hampshire farms ran through Concord to Boston.

Long lines of teams loaded with produce drew up in front of the taverns, and sometimes the drivers bought and sold in the Concord square. On the return journey from Boston to the up-country regions, it was the same story but with different stuff for sale—rum, known as "West India goods," hardware, manu-factured products. As the nineteenth century opened, "there were five stores and three taverns in the middle of the town where intoxicating liquors were sold by the glass to any and every body; and it was the custom, when a person bought even so little as fifty cents' worth of goods, to offer him a glass of liquor, and it was generally accepted."

Dr. Ezra Ripley had been graduated from Harvard College at Concord, for the college was forced out of Cambridge that year by business of the Revolution. So Concord lived by other means as well as farming and trade; it lived by statesmanship and its own importance. And it was a seemly town, though Henry Thoreau wrote later that to him no town was beautiful; beauty was of a different order. Here were the square and the white-painted meetinghouse, and close by was the confluence of the Assabet and Sudbury rivers to form the Concord, the old name of which, relished by Henry, was the Musketaquid, or Grass-ground River.

"It will be Grass-ground River as long as grass grows and water runs here, it will be Concord River only while men lead peaceable lives on its bank. To an extinct race it was grass-ground, where they hunted and fished; and it was still peren-nially grass-ground to Concord farmers, who own the Great Meadows, and get the hay from year to year."

Concord had settled, shaped, completed itself without the aid of Ralph Waldo Emerson, though a contrary impression became established later. Reverend William Emerson, descend-ant of Reverend Peter Bulkeley, settler of the town, had been the Revolutionary pastor and became Ralph's grandfather; but Dr. Ezra Ripley was now both pastor and patriarch. Characteristic Concord names were Hosmer, Buttrick, Barrett, Hoar, Heywood, Minott, Pratt—and others as little associated with literature.

Squire Hoar represented the legal profession as well as immense dignity and probity; he and Deacon White put a stop to travel past their homes on Sunday. He, with Colonel Whiting and Squire Brooks, started the Concord Academy in 1820. Similar academies were being established elsewhere in Massachusetts, to flourish until public high schools later took their places. The town clerk was Dr. Heywood, this office having run in his family from father to son for a century. It was he who had cried the banns of Cynthia Dunbar and John Thoreau in the meetinghouse.

Though these were the names of Concord, it was true that no Emerson could ever be a stranger or a newcomer. Through Reverend Peter Bulkeley and Reverend William Emerson the chain was laid like a fuse, and after Dr. Ezra Ripley married William Emerson's widow, he made it known to the Emerson family that they would ever be welcome at the Old Manse. As an Emerson biographer has written, "Concord was the key to Emerson family history," though Concord did not exist for that purpose and no doubt would have existed otherwise.

Ralph Waldo Emerson's father was another Reverend William Emerson, pastor of the First Church at Boston; and when he died, Dr. Ripley sent out a cow from Boston, and Ralph ran barefoot behind her on summer days, taking her to and from pasture on the common.

As for Henry Thoreau, in his memory no one was more closely identified with Concord, and no one more accurately embodied the spirit of the town, than his father. As he looked backward from the vantage point of later years, but still with the eye of childhood, that was what he saw: John Thoreau on Concord Street and in the square.

With a differently appraising eye, Henry was to observe less finish and perfection in the Concord prospect than did his fellow citizens. He wrote:

"I observed that the vitals of the village were the grocery, the bar-room, the post office, and the bank; and, as a necessary part of the machinery, they kept a bell, a big gun, and a fire engine, at convenient places; and the houses were so arranged as to make the most of mankind, in lanes and fronting one another, so that every traveller had to run the gauntlet, and every man, woman and child might get a lick at him. Of course, those who were stationed nearest to the head of the line, where they could most see and be seen, and have the first blow at him, paid the highest prices for their place; and the few straggling inhabitants in the outskirts, where long gaps in the line began to occur, and the traveller could get over walls or turn aside into cowpaths, and so escape, paid a very slight ground or window tax. Signs were hung out on all sides to allure him; some to catch him by the appetite, as the tavern and victualling cellar; some by the fancy, as the dry goods store and the jeweller's; and others by the hair, or the feet, or the skirts, as the barber, the shoemaker, or the tailor."

People who lived in Concord had never seen themselves as Henry came to see them:

"I aspire to be acquainted with wiser men than this our Concord soil has produced, whose names are hardly known here. Or shall I hear the name of Plato and never read his book? As if Plato were my townsman and I never saw him—my next door neighbour and I never heard him speak or attended to the wisdom of his words. . . . We are underbred and low-lived and illiterate; and in this respect I do not make any very broad distinction between the illiterateness of my townsmen who cannot read at all, and the illiterateness of him who has learned to read only what is for children and feeble intellects."

This was not how Henry saw Concord when he was a boy —the point of view was one he grew into with years—but this is the way the town must have been then too: not so wise as it believed, nor so ambitious, nor half so secure in the progression of real culture.

When Ralph Waldo Emerson presented an "Historical Discourse" as the address of the occasion when Concord rounded the turn into its third century as an incorporated town on September 12, 1835, his view was loftier and more generous. "For the most part," he said, "the town has deserved the name it wears. I find our annals marked with a uniform good sense. I find no ridiculous laws, no eavesdropping legislators, no hanging of witches, no ghosts, no whipping of Quakers, no unnatural crimes. . . .

"Of late years the growth of Concord has been slow. Without navigable waters, without mineral riches, without any considerable mill privileges, the natural increase of her population is drained by the constant emigration of youth."

He went on: "Humble as is our village in the circle of later and prouder towns that whiten the land, it has been consecrated by the presence and activity of the purest men. Why need I remind you of our Hosmers, Minotts, Cummings, Barretts, Beattons, the departed benefactors of the town? . . . I have had much opportunity of access to anecdotes of families, and I believe this town to have been the dwelling-place, in all times since its planting, of pious and excellent persons, who served God and loved man, and never let go the hope of immortality."

Emerson's discourse also brought out that Concord, in 1830, had a population of 2,020. The town's public expenses were $4,290, of which about $1,800 went for public schools and $800 for the Concord poor.

5. *A Family*

Jonas Minott, who had married Henry's grandmother in her widowhood, used to roast wild apples in a long red row on the hearth while the coals glowed, and when he went to bed he took with him a glass of country milk from which he would drink as he waked during the night. Once, at the last, he failed to turn and reach out his hand; the glass stood full, and his wife, Henry's grandmother, found he was dead. This was in 1813, and in 1815 Mrs. Minott applied to the Grand Lodge of Masons in Massachusetts for financial aid, with Dr. Ripley's endorsement. Her first husband, Asa Dunbar, had been a good Mason, and there was none better than Dr. Ripley. The application was entirely proper, but it was a measure of Mrs. Minott's circumstances.

"In the Red House, where Grandmother lived, we had the west side until October, 1818. ...."

John Thoreau experienced difficulty in milking cows and, all in all, farming did not appeal to him. He had taken in a man named Isaac Hurd as partner in his store, "to his injury," as Henry recorded later. "They soon dissolved, but could not settle without going to law, when my father gained the case, bringing his books into court. Then, I think, he went to Bangor and set up with Billings, selling to Indians (among others) ... lived in Boston; writes thence to aunts at Bangor in 1815 with John on his knee; moved to Concord (where I was born), then to Chelmsford."

Dr. Ripley wrote a letter to help John Thoreau obtain a liquor license: "Understanding that Mr. John Thoreau, now of Chelmsford, is going into business in that place, and is about to apply for a license to retail ardent spirits, I hereby certify that I have been long acquainted with him, that he has sustained a good character, and now view him as a man of integrity, accustomed to store-keeping, and of correct morals."

In Chelmsford, "Father kept shop and painted signs." There Henry's younger sister Sophia was born in 1819; she was to have, in Sanborn's words, "along with her mother's lively and dramatic turn, a touch of art."

Henry later condensed a stock of family reminiscences: "Father complained of the powder in the meeting-house garret at town meeting, but it did not get moved while we lived there." The meetinghouse was next door to the Thoreaus, and churches in those days were usual repositories for gunpowder —arsenals of righteous warfare on earth, as of the heavenly combat involving sin. Probably it was Cynthia who put John up to complaining.

In Chelmsford Henry's father "painted over his old signs for guideboards, and got a fall when painting Hale's (?) factory. Here the bladder John was playing with burst on the hearth. The cow came into the entry after pumpkins. I cut my toe and was knocked over by a hen with chickens, etc. etc."

Next the family moved to Boston, where John Thoreau tried teaching; but in 1823, his inheritance gone and his prospects not improved, he returned to Concord for good. By this time the Monroes, who lived in Concord, had established the business of pencil-making there, and John at length settled into this craft with gradually increasing assistance from his family. In 1826 he moved for a year to a house next door to Squire Hoar's, and then moved again.

The stories of Henry's childhood illumine the pride of his family, mostly that of his female relatives, more than they contribute to a picture of him. They might have been drawn from a common stock kept in some attic chest for the storage of all remembered infancies and early childhoods. Two biographers who knew the Thoreaus and were friends of Henry's in later life recorded the sort of incidents that mothers and aunts liked to tell, and still do. Sanborn evoked the family atmosphere:

"When he was three or four years old, at Chelmsford, on being told that he must die, as well as the men in the New England primer, and having the joys of heaven explained to him, he said, as he came in from coasting, that he did not want to die and go to heaven, because he could not carry his sled to so fine a place; for, he added, 'the boys say it is not shod with iron and not worth a cent.' "

"He also had the firmness of the Indian, and could repress his pathos," wrote Ellery Channing, "as when he carried (about the age of ten) his pet chickens to an innkeeper for sale in a basket, who thereupon told him 'to stop' and for convenience' sake took them out one by one and wrung their several pretty necks before the poor boy's eyes, who did not budge. He had such seriousness at the same age that he was called 'judge.' " This was Squire Hoar's nickname for Henry. "His habit of attending strictly to his own affairs appears from this, that being complained of for taking a knife belonging to another boy, Henry said, 'I did not take it'—and was believed. In a few days the culprit was found, and Henry then said, 'I knew all the time who it was, and the day it was taken I went to Newton with father.' 'Well, then,' of course was the next question, 'why did you not say so at the time?' 'I did not take it,' was his reply."

Channing saw this anecdote as a key to many traits in Henry's character. "A school-fellow complained of him because he would not make a bow and arrow, his skill at whittling being superior. It seems he refused, but it came out after that he had no knife. . . . When he had grown to an age suitable for company, and not very fond of visiting, he could not give the common refusal—that it was not convenient, or not in his power, or he regretted—but said the truth—'I do not want to go.' "

These were the memories, copybook style, that helped later to show how the Thoreaus had been a family in spacious and narrow senses alike. Such fragments reflected credit on Henry but left him stiff and unrecognized, lacking the interest there must have been in his boyish nature. The family of a statesman or general, given time in later years, could usually recall some prophetic incident of his childhood; and so with Henry Thoreau it should have been noticed, for later remembrance, that he was discovering remarkable commonplaces in the countryside around Concord, that nature was more to him than to other children. But most adults, except for Henry's mother, had never discovered the Concord countryside for themselves, so how could they appreciate Henry's early ventures?

6. *Childhood Memories*

Henry's own recollections naturally took another turn. Walden was in them almost from the beginning:

"Twenty-three years since, when I was five years old, I was brought from Boston to this pond, away in the country—which was then but another name for the extended world for me—one of the most ancient scenes stamped on the tablets of my memory, the oriental Asiatic valley of my world, whence so many races and inventions have gone forth in recent times. That woodland vision for a long time made the drapery of my dreams. That sweet solitude my spirit seemed so early to require that I might have room to entertain my thronging guests, and that speaking silence that my ears might distinguish the significant sounds. Somehow or other it at once gave the preference to this recess among the pines, where almost sunshine and shadow were the only inhabitants that varied the scene, over that tumultuous and varied city, as if it had found its proper nursery."

But by this time, though he wrote with tenderness and clear vision, Henry was engaged with his mythology.

"Ah, that life that I have known! How hard it is to remember what is most memorable. We remember how we itched, not how our hearts beat. I can sometimes recall to mind the quality, the immortality of my youthful life, but in memory is the only relation to it."

Yet the shafts of sunlight struck backward at times through clear and quiet air.

"I think that no experience which I have today comes up to,

or is comparable with, the experiences of my boyhood. And not only is this true, but as far back as I can remember, I have unconsciously referred to the experiences of a previous state of existence. . . . My life was ecstasy. In youth, before I lost any of my senses, I can remember that I was all alive, and inhabited my body with inexpressible satisfaction; both its weariness and refreshment were sweet to me. The earth was the most glorious musical instrument, and I was audience to its strains."

His memory sought the simpler themes that matured and flowed in his later life: "I remember how glad I was when I was kept from school a half a day to pick huckleberries on a neighboring hill all by myself to make a pudding for the family dinner. Ah, they got nothing but the pudding, but I got invaluable experience beside! A half a day of liberty like that was like the promise of life eternal. It was emancipation in New England."

From the beginning, of course, he knew the basic and primitive round of both country and village. He remembered how the river froze in December and how the sedge looked through the ice over the meadows that had been flooded by fall rains. It was long before he applied himself to any botany, but from the beginning he knew the old-fashioned tansy and myrtle, chickadees, skunk cabbage, sunflowers, lilacs, plowed and planted fields. He knew the smell of freshly scrubbed floors and of wet coats in the post office at mailtime and of the different winds that blew. He knew the stillness of sanctity in the meetinghouse, and the voice of the choir and of Dr. Ripley preaching.

He was sent on errands to the stores. He watched the gunners and fishermen, and by the age of ten he was both himself, following his admired brother John, with whom he had started life in a trundle bed, out to the riverbank, to the marshes, or into the woods. He picked not only huckleberries but cranberries and wild apples and wild grapes.

Man-grown, he copied into his journal a page of day-book

entries showing how a Concord angler had bought daily rum and sugar, as well as an occasional cod line. "I can faintly remember to have seen this same fisher in my earliest youth, still as near the river as he could get, with uncertain, undulatory step, after so many things had gone downstream, swinging a scythe in the meadow, his bottle like a serpent hid in the grass; himself as yet not cut down by the Great Mower."

Henry remembered another "old brown-coated man" who fished the river. "A straight old man he was, who took his way in silence through the meadows, having passed the period of communication with his fellows; his old experienced coat, hanging long and straight and brown as the yellow-pine bark, glittering with so much smothered sunlight, if you stood near enough. . . . I often discovered him unexpectedly amid the pads and the gray willows when he moved, fishing in some old country method—for youth and age then went a-fishing together—full of incommunicable thoughts, perchance about his own Tyne and Northumberland. He was always to be seen in serene afternoons haunting the river. . . . I think nobody else saw him; nobody else remembers him now, for he soon after died, and migrated to new Tyne streams. His fishing was not a sport, nor solely a means of subsistence, but a sort of solemn sacrament and withdrawal from the world, just as the aged read their Bibles."

These fragments came back to Henry, but though he must have remembered Squire Hoar also, he had no recollections of the squire that coaxed to be put down in his journal. The men and scenes that won his sympathy and understanding were not of the town or of the copybook.

When he and John set out on their river journey, he recalled the occasional canal boats that had reached Concord when commerce followed the natural tracks of the waterways, even such placid and minor streams, and reproduced the quality and feeling of old river scenes. This was the sort of thing that appealed to him as a child and later as a man.

"The news spread like wildfire among us youths, when formerly, once in a year or two, one of these boats came up the Concord River, and was seen stealing mysteriously through the meadows and past the village. It came and departed as silently as a cloud, without noise or dust, and was witnessed by few. One summer day this huge traveler might be seen moored at some meadow's wharf, and another summer day it was not there. Where precisely it came from, or who these men were who knew the rocks and soundings better than we who bathed there, we could never tell. We knew some river's bay only, but they took rivers from end to end. They were a sort of fabulous rivermen to us. It was inconceivable by what sort of mediation any mere landsman could hold communication with them. Would they heave to, to gratify his wishes? No, it was favor enough to know faintly of their destination, or the time of their possible return. I have seen them in the summer, when the stream ran low, mowing the weeds in mid-channel, and with hayers' jests cutting broad swaths in three feet of water that they might make a passage for their scow, while the grass in long windrows was carried down the stream, undried by the rarest haying weather. We admired unwearyingly how their vessel would float, like a huge chip, sustaining so many casks of lime, and thousands of bricks, and such heaps of iron ore, with wheelbarrows aboard, and that, when we stepped on it, it did not yield to the pressure of our feet. It gave us confidence in the prevalence of the law of buoyancy and we imagined to what infinite uses it might be put. The men appeared to lead a kind of life on it, and it was whispered that they slept aboard. Some affirmed that it carried sail, and that such winds blew here as filled the sails of vessels on the ocean; which again others much doubted. They had been seen to sail across our Fair Haven bay by lucky fishers who were out, but unfortunately others were not there to see."

As a boy, too, Henry played baseball in the russet fields toward Sleepy Hollow when spring was in the air and the snows were melting. He was full of the concerns of boyhood and with a boy's awareness of the precepts and patterns of Concord life. He knew Concord first of all—Concord, where people went on temperance picnics, fishing, huckleberrying, and where they picked flowers and took "a very few walks in the woods"; Concord, where men groaned over their labors, submitted to the will of God, borrowed money at the bank, and made a necessary habit of the succession of their days from youth to toothless old age. He knew all this, but even then he subscribed only to the fringe of it.

7. *A Mess of Learning*

Henry wrote in his first book: "Scholars are wont to sell their birthright for a mess of learning."

But before he came to this he had first to get acquainted with learning and find out where the mess of it was, and where the choice part that a man could profit by and employ for his own increase and delight in the world. He must know books in order to arrive at his own opinion concerning them: "Books, not which afford us a cowering enjoyment, but in which each thought is of unusual daring; such as an idle man cannot read, and a timid one would not be entertained by, which even make us dangerous to existing institutions—such I call good books."

The public schools were nothing much in Henry's childhood. Some threadbare youth or worn exemplar of book words, figures, and moral sentiments, who could meet the approval of a bargaining school committee and who would also accept their terms as to salary, was employed to lift each new generation up to the necessities imposed by the older generations that were still alive, and in some degree to the requirements of the times.

Like winter, these schools fulfilled a traditional and necessary role in the life of boys and girls who escaped as soon as possible into the brighter and easier opportunities of spring.

The aspiration of learning was always something over and above this, and that was why Squire Hoar and the others founded the Concord Academy where Greek and Latin were taught, and retained as its master Phineas Allen, who boarded for a while with the Thoreaus and was later to run for the office of town clerk against Mr. Heywood, showing that his interests were not exclusively with the classics.

To visit the academy at a time when David Henry Thoreau (his name not yet turned around) was very likely one of the pupils came Charles Chauncy Emerson, favorite brother of Ralph Waldo and some five years his junior. Charles had been graduated from Harvard in 1828, and in 1830, while a student of the law, he stopped for a time with Dr. Ripley at the Old Manse.

"Mr. George Bradford and I attended the Exhibition yesterday at the Academy," Charles wrote. "We were extremely gratified. To hear little girls saying their Greek grammar and young ladies read Xenophon was a new and very agreeable entertainment."

Charles Chauncy did not mean to be patronizing. He was twenty-two that year and afflicted with a "pallid brow" and "slight figure," besides having won all sorts of honors at Harvard. "He was like a young Greek in Plato's Academy—straight as an arrow, with clear blue eyes, crisp hair, and a fair complexion." A few years later he was to move into the Old Manse with the Ripleys, pay court to Squire Hoar's daughter Elizabeth, and occupy a desk in the squire's law office. Elizabeth Hoar was sixteen in 1830 and may have been one of the young ladies whose Greek delighted Charles upon the occasion of his visit to the academy.

Concord had come in a rush from muskrats to Xenophon, so

that now the two themes overlapped, and Henry Thoreau was concerned with both. Book learning was, however, elevated and apart in the general scheme. It was both means and goal of a new enlightenment, and of a new respectability as well. The learning was an end in itself in these times, and even men and women who did not or could not have much of it themselves leaned toward it when possible.

Besides the academy, there was the Concord Lyceum, likewise new and characteristic of the year and of the people. The lyceum movement had started in 1826 over in Millbury, a town just south of Worcester, and the seed was wafted on the wind to Concord; lecturers were to nourish the general intelligence and the special functions of citizenship with information concerning arts, sciences, and public affairs. One trouble was that good lecturers were hard to get without cost, or even for normal fees, unless they lived close by, and Concord experienced a plethora of ready-tongued congressmen, governors, and others who had a special interest in being heard—until the Emerson influence arrived to tip the scale of values.

Henry Thoreau, when he reached the age of twelve, was eligible to attend the lyceum. He did not record any comments as to lyceum or school then, but when he had grown well away from these experiences he wrote: "I was fitted or rather made unfit for college at Concord Academy, mainly by myself, with the countenance of Phineas Allen, Preceptor." This seemed to indicate that Henry had followed his own bent pretty much as to books and reading, and that Phineas Allen had been filtered through the Thoreau temperament.

As readily, later on, Henry could refer to the pap dispensed at Harvard. He professed to be surprised when he was told that he had studied navigation there. He was pointing to the "mess of learning" as if it were something unhappily left on a rug, but at the time it served him well. His debt to schools was never to turn out as the conventional one, yet how else but for the

Concord Academy and Harvard could he have been equipped
to read Homer and Vergil and do translations of Persius, Aes-
chylus, Cato, Aristotle, Pindar, Anacreon, and Pliny, or have
been attracted into the exploration of less obvious poets of old
England, along with Chaucer, Milton, and Ossian? How could
he have come to know books well enough to define for himself
which were the good ones?

8. *Harvard*

That Henry was able to go to Harvard involved a good deal
of scraping and sacrifice. His father could supply part of the
money, and his sister Helen, who was now a schoolteacher,
contributed both money and the prideful encouragement to
ambition that was characteristic of her profession and also of
her place in the family. His aunts helped him, too. He did what
he could for himself, and there was a stipend, though a small
one, from the beneficiary fund of the college, obtained through
the good offices of that old Harvard graduate, Dr. Ripley, and
later continued with the helpful intercession of Ralph Waldo
Emerson of the class of 1821 and at this time of Concord.

Henry was sixteen when he entered Harvard on September
1, 1833, with the warm autumn days coming on and golden sunshine falling gently on the college yard. From Concord to Cambridge had become a far easier and shorter journey than when
Reverend Peter Bulkeley had first made it on foot. Henry was
to make it on foot, too, when he chose, as that time when he
walked from Concord to Boston to hear Emerson lecture and
then walked home again. None of the Thoreaus, not even
Henry himself, suspected in this late summer that the journey
from Concord to Cambridge would be less important in the
long run than the return journey from Cambridge to Concord.

At sixteen, essentially a country boy, equipped with the ambition explicit in the lives of men like Squire Hoar or Dr. Rip-

ley, but as yet with few supporting experiences and no course shaped beyond the acquiring of knowledge, Henry brought no new excitement to Harvard. The college ground on, unchanged, Henry slipped into a convenient obscurity, and only occasional oddities were noticed about him—as when he wore his green homespun coat to chapel instead of the black coat the rules prescribed. Although this defiance of custom and authority grew from his lack of means, it helped him appreciate that rules were not necessarily to be respected and that many worked as well or better in reverse.

Henry was reserved but not solitary. He shared a room in Hollis, one of the dormitories, and ate cheaply in the company of his fellows at the college commons. Later on he was to exchange letters with classmates or friends in which he entered freely into the idiom of undergraduate comradeship.

Between times he explored Boston somewhat, but went most often to the end of Long Wharf to smell the sea and to feel kinship with his grandfather, who had opened business there with a hogshead of sugar. But books were most important, and he read consistently, usually taking notes, intending to cover the ground completely the first time without having to retrace his steps.

The courses he took were in mathematics, rhetoric, Latin, and Greek, and a definitive modern biographer, Dr. Henry Seidel Canby, says there were "approaches toward science" in lectures for the whole class, sometimes with real experiments. Always there was the Harvard Library, in which Henry began to follow his own inclination as to reading. In his senior year he enrolled for a course in German with Henry Wadsworth Longfellow, then an unwhiskered thirty years, but did not continue long. He learned some French, some Spanish, and Italian.

Edward Tyrrell Channing, uncle of Ellery Channing who later became Henry's Concord friend and walking companion, was teaching rhetoric at Harvard. In his classes had sat Emer-

son, and in them were to sit James Russell Lowell, Edward
Everett Hale, Charles Sumner, and Oliver Wendell Holmes.
But Edward Tyrrell Channing saw little promise in Thoreau.
Dr. Canby reports that the distinguished teacher's favorite of
that class was a youth named Horace Morison, who in later life
published a book of children's stories called *Pebbles from the
Sea Shore.*

When he could look back on Harvard from a safe distance,
Henry wrote to Dick Fuller, brother of Margaret Fuller, who
is to be mentioned a good deal later on: "What I was learning
in college was chiefly, I think, to express myself, and I see now,
that as the old orator prescribed, 1st, action; 2d, action; 3d, action; my teachers should have prescribed to me, 1st, sincerity;
2d, sincerity; 3d, sincerity. The old mythology is incomplete
without a god or goddess of sincerity, on whose altars we
might offer up all the products of our farms, our workshops,
and our studies. . . . I mean sincerity in our dealings with ourselves mainly; any other is comparatively easy."

A classmate of Henry's, Reverend John Weiss, tried to bring
the Thoreau college career into perspective. But it was not
until three years after Henry's death that Weiss wrote, referring to the "reserve and unaptness" of his life at Harvard: ". . .
he passed for nothing, it is suspected, with most of us; for he
was cold and unimpressible. The touch of his hand was moist
and indifferent, as if he had taken up something when he saw
your hand coming, and caught your grasp upon it. How the
prominent, gray-blue eyes seemed to rove down the path, just
in advance of his feet, as his grave Indian stride carried him
down to University Hall!

"He did not care for people; his classmates seemed very remote. This reverie hung always about him, and not so loosely
as the odd garments which the pious household care furnished.
Thought had not yet awakened his countenance; it was serene,
but rather dull, rather plodding. The lips were not yet firm;

there was almost a look of smug satisfaction lurking around
their corners. It is plain now that he was preparing to hold his
future views with great setness, and personal appreciation of
their importance. The nose was prominent, but its curve fell
forward without firmness over the upper lip; and we remember
him as looking very much like some Egyptian sculptures of
faces, large-featured, but brooding, immobile, fixed in a mystic
egotism. Yet his eyes were sometimes searching, as if he had
dropped or expected to find, something. It was the look of Nature's own child learning to detect her wayside secrets; and
those eyes have stocked his books with subtile traits of animate
and inanimate creation which had escaped less patient observers.
For he saw more upon the ground than anybody suspected to
be there."

Henry's tone, his old classmate wrote, "was very confident,
as of an opinion that had formed from granitic sediment, but
also very level and unflushed with feeling. The Sphinx might
have become passionate and excited as soon."

The advantage of considerable hindsight shows in some of
this language, and there were others who knew Henry at Harvard who disputed Weiss and said that he was really one of the
boys. Sanborn thought it likely that Henry got on well in the
recognized collegiate fashion; unable to cite anything of
Henry's own to bear out his opinion, he fell back on a letter
addressed to Henry by a young Harvard acquaintance named
Peabody, who described some of the larking of the Davy Club,
an undergraduate group.

The club "got into a little trouble, the week before last, from
the following circumstances: H. W. gave a lecture on Pyro-
techny, and illustrated it with a parcel of fireworks he had prepared in the vacation. As you may imagine, there was some
slight noise on the occasion. In fact, the noise was so slight that
Tutor B. heard it at his room in Holworthy. This worthy
boldly determined to march forth and attack the 'rioters.'

Accordingly, in the midst of a grand display of rockets, etc., he stepped into the room, and, having gazed round him in silent astonishment for the space of two minutes, and hearing various cries of 'Intrusion!' 'Throw him over!' 'Saw his leg off!' 'Pull his wool!' etc., he made two or three dignified motions with his hand to gain attention, and then kindly advised us to 'retire to our respective rooms.' Strange to say, he found no one inclined to follow this good advice, and *he* accordingly thought fit to withdraw."

If Henry had not shared the undergraduate state of mind, Sanborn argued, young Peabody would hardly have sent him, in some temporary absence, quite so enthusiastic and lively an account of an episode resulting in public admonition of the ringleaders. Henry was certainly not present—or noticed—at most of the skylarking and upheavals that marked those Harvard years, but this might have been because he had no money to waste and was forced to rule himself closely. The responsibilities of Concord were always tugging on him.

Following an accepted custom, Henry was permitted to take time off from college in his sophomore year to teach school for a while and thus earn money to help pay for his tuition. In December 1835, at the age of eighteen, he went to the town of Canton, south of Boston, to assume charge of a class of seventy pupils for a term of six weeks or more. He was directed to the Reverend Orestes A. Brownson for examination as to his fitness, and the two stayed up until midnight in lively conversation. Mr. Brownson not only certified Henry to the Canton school committee as competent and desirable, but took the boy to board at his home. They began at once to study German and to share the stimulus of their respective personalities.

It was Brownson, of course, whose mind, an extraordinarily active one, nourished their discourse, while Henry's responded as if touched by aptly slanting sunlight at exactly the right moment. Brownson was a big-framed man from Vermont, then thirty-two, and getting on with his "New Views of Christianity, Society and the Church," which were to be published as a book of this title the following year. At first a Presbyterian, then a Universalist, then a Unitarian, Brownson had freed himself of doctrine for a sort of crusading nonconformity; he was seeking valiantly for what could not yet be found.

But his direction then was socialistic. He had seen and abhorred injustices of the times, and he had aided the new Workingmen's Party. He was a Vermont-bred Utopian in full onslaught, with banners, unafraid. He would shoot at conformity as far away as he could see it, so long as his cause was moral and political reform, and it mattered not what church systems or fatted calfs might be wounded in the fray. Religion had to be an active force among men in their lives on earth or it was not the real thing at all.

When Harvard was behind him, Henry wrote to Brownson: "I have never ceased to look back with interest, not to say satisfaction, upon the short six weeks which I passed with you. They were an era in my life—the morning of a new Lebenstag. They are to me as a dream that is dreamt, but which returns from time to time in all its original freshness. Such a one as I would dream a second and a third time, and then tell before breakfast."

When he returned to his classes, Henry had something even more important than the money he had earned at Canton. His weeks with Brownson were a preparation for later associations, such as those with Emerson, Bronson Alcott, and others. And Emerson now was looming like an aurora in the sky.

That next year, 1836, saw the publication of a small but by no means slight volume called *Nature*, offered to the public anonymously at first. Here was Ralph Waldo Emerson's initial philosophic utterance between covers, product of contemplation, study, travel, and of his straying across the old fences as he was bound to do; it was also the prophecy of Emerson's essays to come. The importance of *Nature* was little recognized, though it was attacked for its departures from orthodoxy. Only a few hundred copies were sold at the time, but one came to Henry Thoreau's hand, and there was no doubt of its importance there.

Emerson offered rhapsodic words about nature that made some readers think he was writing poetry in prose, but his theme revolved about the concept of man, not solely as a part of nature which, if this were so, would be nothing more than fate, or bondage, but, if he could grasp the active role, as part of the cause.

"Build, therefore," Emerson wrote, "your own world. As fast as you conform your life to the pure idea in your mind, that will unfold its grand proportions. A correspondent revolution in things will attend the influx of the spirit."

Apart from the philosophic content, there were phrases and sentences in *Nature* that Henry Thoreau could read with sensitive appreciation; Emerson too had walked beside Walden Pond.

"There is a property in the horizon that no man has but he whose eye can integrate all the parts, that is, the poet. This is the best part of these men's farms, yet to this truth their warranty-deed gives no title."

"Give me health and a day, and I will make the pomp of emperors ridiculous. The dawn is my Assyria; the sunset and moonrise my Paphos, and unimaginable realms of faerie; broad noon shall be my England of the sense and understanding; the night shall be my Germany of mystic philosophy and dreams."

Thus Emerson in *Nature*. Henry was drawn yet more from the accumulated habits of Harvard College. He had been ill in his senior year—a sinister omen of pulmonary weakness that was a family trait—and likewise had shown an increasing indifference to matters that did not engage his own special interest, now assuming nicer sharpness and direction.

Emerson was in Concord, and though he had not yet seen Henry, he wrote to Josiah Quincy, President of Harvard, in Henry's behalf. Emerson's help may have been asked by Dr. Ripley or by the Thoreaus directly. Quincy's reply straddled neatly:

MY DEAR SIR,

Your view concerning Thoreau is entirely in consent with that which I entertain. His general conduct has been very satisfactory, and I was willing and desirous that whatever falling off there had been in his scholarship should be attributable to his sickness. He had, however, imbibed some notions concerning emulation and college rank which had a natural tendency to diminish his zeal, if not his exertions. His instructors were impressed with the conviction that he was indifferent, even to a degree that was faulty, and that they could not recommend him, consistent with the rule by which they are usually governed in relation to beneficiaries. I have always entertained a respect for and interest in him, and was willing to attribute any apparent neglect or indifference to his ill health rather than to wilfulness. I obtained from the instructors the authority to state all the facts to the Corporation, and submit the result to their discretion. This I did, and that body granted twenty-five dollars, which was within ten, or at the most fifteen, dollars of any sum he would have received, had no objection been made. There is no doubt that, from some cause, an unfavorable opinion has been entertained, since his return after his sickness, of his disposition to exert himself. To what it has been owing may be doubtful. I appreciate very fully the goodness of his heart and the strictness of his moral principle; and have done as much for him as, under the circumstances, was possible. Very respectfully, your humble servant,

JOSIAH QUINCY

Henry was certainly straying from the reservation, and with his eyes open. In August 1837 he was graduated; and that same month Emerson delivered a famous Phi Beta Kappa oration on "The American Scholar":

"The scholar is that man who must take up into himself all the ability of the time, all the contributions of the past, all the hopes of the future. He must be an university of knowledges. If there be one lesson more than another which should pierce his ear, it is, The world is nothing, the man is all; in yourself is the law of all nature, and you know not yet how a globule of sap ascends; in yourself slumbers the whole of Reason; it is for you to know all; it is for you to dare all. Mr. President and Gentlemen, this confidence in the unsearched might of man belongs, by all motives, by all prophecy, by all preparation, to the American scholar. We have listened too long to the courtly muses of Europe. The spirit of the American freeman is already suspected to be timid, imitative, tame. Public and private avarice make the air we breathe thick and fat. The scholar is decent, indolent, complaisant. See already the tragic consequence. The mind of this country, taught to aim at low objects, eats upon itself. . . ."

It seems likely that Henry Thoreau was present to hear this address, and if he was, he listened with sensitivity already awakened and a surging disposition to believe the speaker. His spirit was not timid, and he had begun to breathe fresh and heady air.

The Harvard years completed, Henry went back to Concord, though he was not yet sure he would stay there. During his senior year at college he had gone on a camping trip with a classmate, Charles Stearns Wheeler, whose home was in Lincoln, a township adjoining Concord, in which lay Flint's Pond. Near this pond Wheeler had built a shack in the woods for a retreat and study, and he and Henry spent some weeks there, sleeping on straw in rudely built bunks.

9. *Ventures in Nonconformity*

At the commencement exercises, Henry went on the program with Henry Vose, another Concord boy, in what was called a conference on "The Commercial Spirit." No one much recalls what Henry Vose said, but Henry Thoreau struck out trenchantly with words prophetic of the life he was to live:

"Let men, true to their natures, cultivate the moral affections, lead manly and independent lives; let them make riches the means and not the end of existence, and we shall hear no more of the commercial spirit. The sea will not stagnate, the earth will be as green as ever, and the air as pure. This curious world which we inhabit is more wonderful than it is convenient; more beautiful than it is useful; it is more to be admired and enjoyed than used. The order of things should be somewhat reversed; the seventh should be man's day of toil, wherein to earn his living by the sweat of his brow; and the other six his Sabbath of the affections and the soul—in which to range this widespread garden, and drink in the soft influences and sublime revelations of Nature."

These were the words of a young man who had found already that most timeworn precepts of the world would work as well or better if they were turned around backward. Against the pompous, much-preached, unquestioned generalizations he presented the challenge of an obstinate and deliberate simplicity. One of his final essays as a Harvard senior was on the subject of "whether moral excellence tends directly to increase intellectual power."

"With by far the greater part of mankind," he wrote, "religion is a habit, or rather, habit is religion, their views of things are illiberal and constricted, for the very reason that they possess not intellectual power sufficient to attain to moral excellence. However paradoxical it may seem, it appears to me that to reject religion is the first step towards moral excellence;

at least, no man ever attained to the highest degree of the latter by any other road. Could infidels live double the number of years allotted to other mortals, they would become patterns of excellence."

From the same attitude, as he stood in the role of onlooker watching the peculiar conduct of man, and the odd disparity between man's professions and man's behavior, came these later lines which he called "A Prayer":

> Great God, I ask for no meaner pelf
> Than that I may not disappoint myself,
> That in my action I may soar as high
> As I can now discern with this clear eye.

> And next in value, which thy kindness lends,
> That I may greatly disappoint my friends,
> Howe'er they think or hope that it may be,
> They may not dream how thou'st distinguished me.

10. *Emerson at Concord*

It was not exactly predestined that Ralph Waldo Emerson should go to live at Concord, although this did seem a divinely appointed arrangement in later years. The boy who had rolled a hoop on Boston Common and helped pasture there the cow that Dr. Ezra Ripley had sent in had gone through Harvard without disclosing the brilliance of his mind. It was as if he had held his fire for later salvos.

He had studied at the Harvard Divinity School, taken a trip south for his health, and begun to preach from pulpits here and there. He preached twice at Concord, New Hampshire, then sometimes known as New Concord, the second time for the sake of his brother Edward, two years his junior, who had come through a mental crisis and was thought to need changes of scene. From New Concord, on December 24, 1828, Waldo—

as he signed himself—wrote exciting news to his older brother William:

"I have the happiness to inform you that I have now been for one week engaged to Ellen Louisa Tucker, a young lady who, if you will trust me, is the fairest and best of her kind. She is the youngest daughter of the late Beza Tucker, a merchant of Boston. . . . It is now just a year since I became acquainted with Ellen . . . but I thought I had got over my blushes and my wishes when I determined to go into that dangerous neighborhood on Edward's account. But the presumptuous man was overthrown by the eyes and the ear, and surrendered at discretion. He is now as happy as it is safe in life to be. She is seventeen years old, and very beautiful, by universal consent."

But Ellen already was "raising blood"; she was wasting with tuberculosis, a disease that had stricken other members of her family, though Waldo made himself believe she would recover. While her health hung poised between hope and less-than-hope, he was chosen assistant pastor of the Old North Church, Unitarian, with the prospect of advancement. In September 1829 he and Ellen were married, and he invited his mother to live with them.

Among those who heard him preach in the Old North Church was Margaret Fuller, precocious daughter of a Boston lawyer, then nineteen and already teeming with zeal and learning. On the whole she approved of Emerson because his sermons were not all words. But Emerson's marriage and ministry were both appointed for brief terms.

Ellen died in 1831 and in 1832 Emerson resigned from the church because he had come to dislike the ministry and because he was unable to regard the Lord's Supper as a sacrament. He had other doubts and unorthodoxies too: he did not believe that God was personal; he thought that Calvinism was, to say the least, an imperfect version of the moral law, but so was Unitarianism in the hands of many teachers; and he believed

that "the highest revelation of God is in every man"—a faith
that to many of the devout was a lack of faith.

Charles Chauncy Emerson wrote to their aunt, Miss Mary
Moody Emerson, the remarkable and diminutive lady who always said she had been "in arms" at the Concord fight because
quite literally she had been, who had helped make the match
between their father and mother, and later on had helped bring
up the Emerson boys: "Waldo is sick. His spirits droop; he
looks to the South, and thinks he should like to go away. I
never saw him so disheartened. When a man would be a reformer, he wants to be strong. . . . One does not want to feel
that there is any doom upon him."

On Christmas Day 1832, Waldo was sailing from Boston
for a sojourn abroad that would fill him with the wonder of
Old World cathedrals, bring him close to Carlyle, Coleridge,
and Wordsworth, and give him much to think about as to the
difference between Reason and Understanding. He came home
in the late winter of 1833—but where was home now?

His mother had been staying at Newton, near Boston, and
he joined her there. He wrote to his brother Edward: "One of
these days, if we may believe the lawyers, I am to be richer
for Ellen's estate; and, whenever that day arrives, I hope it
will enable me to buy a hearth somewhere to which we pious
Aeneases may return with our household gods."

Waldo had just visited Concord, where Charles Chauncy
had lectured to the lyceum on the subject of Socrates. By the
next spring the Tucker estate was so far settled that the philosophic widower was sure of an income of about twelve hundred dollars, with more to come later, on the strength of which
he suggested that he and Edward and their mother might "retreat into Berkshire." But Edward died in the early autumn of
1834, and in July 1835 Waldo was at Bangor writing to a ministerial friend, "I am almost persuaded to sit down on the banks
of this pleasant stream, and, if I could only persuade a small

number of persons to join my colony, we would have a settlement thirty miles up the river, at once."

Bangor, however, proved just one more way station on the
roundabout route to Concord and old scenes. Dr. Ripley invited Waldo and his mother to live in the Old Manse, and in
October they arrived there. The decision was reached because
Charles Chauncy was taking over the law office of Squire Hoar,
who was Washington bound as a member of Congress, and
moreover had got himself engaged to Elizabeth Hoar. Waldo
was drawn by the wish to be near his brother, drawn too by
many old memories of Concord, where so often as a child he
had driven out with Dr. Ripley or played in the grounds of the
Old Manse that ran to the riverbank, and where he had been
treated with burdock tea to cure an eruptive disease of the skin.

At the Manse, Emerson settled comfortably into Dr. Ripley's old chair that had an arm fixed for writing, and here
completed his first book, *Nature*.

He continued to preach and lecture here and there. Opportunities took him to Plymouth, where one of his listeners,
Lydia Jackson, was presently surprised, while in the commonplace act of going upstairs, by a mystical vision of herself in
bridal attire descending those same stairs with Emerson at her
side. After a later Plymouth visit, he wrote a proposal of marriage and sent it by post; just before it arrived, Lydia seemed
to see his face and gaze intent on hers for a fleeting, significant
instant.

Emerson was thirty-one, eight months younger than Lydia.
When personal conversation had cemented their engagement,
he told William that his feeling was one of "a very sober joy,"
a state of mind quite different from that which had led him to
write Ellen, his first love, the burning words, "I am enamoured
of thy loveliness, lovesick with thy sweet beauty." He and
Lydia, however, enjoyed an "unexpected community of sentiment & speculation."

Charles Chauncy Emerson wrote of Waldo's fiancée: "The lady is a sort of Sybil for wisdom—She is not beautiful anywise that I know, so you look at the outside alone. . . ." Since nineteen, when she had not recovered satisfactorily from scarlet fever, Lydia had experienced ill health and had gone in for fads that did not remove the threat of later invalidism. She took cold baths, slept with the windows open, and tried exercises both mental and physical.

Even after their marriage she usually referred to her husband as Mr. Emerson or, in letters, as Mr. E. He had been at the Manse a year when he wrote to William: "I hope to hire a house and set up a fireside. . . . Perhaps Charles also; and, a year hence, shall we not build a house on grandfather's hill, facing Wachusett, Monadnoc, and the setting sun?" Wachusett, a bit over 2,000 feet high, and Monadnock (the modern spelling), a thousand feet higher, across the New Hampshire line, were mountains that Henry Thoreau already knew and loved. Emerson admired them from afar, and as for the Concord River at the foot of the Old Manse grounds, he thought it was "like God's love journeying out of the gray past into the green future."

Lydia would have preferred to live at Plymouth, where she owned a comfortable colonial house, but though Emerson had considered many another retreat, Plymouth would not do; to him it was "streets." At Concord he prized "a sunset, a forest, a snow-storm, a certain river view" which were "more to me than many friends, and do ordinarily divide my day with my books."

But instead of building on the hillside opposite the Manse—called Peter's fields or Caesar's woods, from the freed slaves who had once lived there—Emerson bought the old Coolidge house at Concord, which he described as a "mean place" until "trees and flowers give it a character of its own. But we shall crowd so many books and papers, and, if possible, wise friends into it, that it shall have as much wit as it can carry."

The prospect of many intellectual visitors pleased Lydia too. Meantime Emerson had lectured in Boston on Michelangelo, Luther, Milton, and so on, and had addressed the American Institute of Education on "the best mode of inspiring a correct taste in English literature," in the course of which he was accused of inserting disparaging words concerning prayer.

On September 12, 1835, came the Concord address on the town's second anniversary, with some of the minutemen occupying seats of honor beside him. It could be said that he graced the occasion; and the occasion graced him, too. His effort was a major one, long in preparation. Two days later he drove to Plymouth for his marriage to Lydia and brought her to the home he had prepared; he brought also her favorite plants from her Plymouth garden, which she proceeded to set out in the new soil. Waldo liked outdoor work too, and while he was puttering about among his vegetables the next spring a townsman complained to him of a stray pig; thus he discovered that he had been elected hogreeve, this office being a traditional Concord tribute to the newly married.

Charles Chauncy was to marry Elizabeth Hoar that September, but while it was only March he rode on top of a stagecoach from Boston to Concord and developed what they said was a cold but really meant a worsening of tuberculosis. Waldo hastened back from lecturing at Salem to take his brother to a milder climate. From South Brookfield he wrote to Lidian—for so he had renamed her in the interest of euphony—expressing regret at his absence and alluding to her as "wifey," one of the few words in his letters that was not addressed to the ages as well as to the immediate recipient.

Charles Chauncy, as it turned out, was already doomed. He got as far as New York only and died there. "And so, Lidian,"

Waldo wrote out of his sorrow, "I can never bring you back
my noble friend, who was my ornament, my wisdom, and my
pride. . . . I determined to live in Concord, as you know,
because he was there. . . . I am thankful, dear Lidian, that you
have seen and known him to the degree you have. I should not
have known how to forgive you an ignorance of him, had he
been out of your sight."

This may have seemed a narrow squeak for the new wife; she
might easily have missed Charles Chauncy as he sloped down
the western sky in his Apollo chariot, and in that case, what?

Waldo went on: "And you must be content henceforth with
only a piece of your husband; for the best of his strength lay
in the soul with which he must no more on earth take counsel."
At home once more, Waldo developed his elegiac theme: "My
brother, my friend, my ornament, my joy and pride has fallen
by the wayside; or rather has risen out of this dust. . . . The
eye is closed that was to see nature for me and give me leave
to see."

Dr. Ripley announced to his congregation that "This event
seems to me loud and piercing, like thunder and lightning.
Whilst many aged and burdensome are spared, this beloved
youth is cut down in the morning."

One result of the death of Charles Chauncy was that Elizabeth Hoar, to use Waldo's words, became a sister to him. She
was to have a share in many a gathering at his house even
though, like Henry Thoreau, she had been born at Concord
and had not arrived by stage like the inspired philosophers and
poets.

Already the yeasting minds had begun to assemble in Bos-
ton: Emerson; George Ripley, another literary Unitarian who
was soon to be president of the Utopian colony of Brook Farm;
James Elliot Cabot, who spoke to these others as well as to
God; presently Theodore Parker, newly out of Harvard
Divinity School and bent on social reform; Stearns Wheeler,

Thoreau's classmate who was now a Harvard tutor; A. Bronson Alcott, peddler, clockmaker, founder of a new kind of school at Boston; Miss Elizabeth Peabody, who had put Alcott's school principles and experiences into a book; and the fire-driven and knowledgeable Margaret Fuller.

Soon the group was meeting at Emerson's house at Concord, where Lidian was employing three maids and now entertained Margaret Fuller for three weeks. Margaret seemed to know every intellectual worth knowing. She stirred things up, stirred Emerson too, and would have stirred him more if she had been able. It was he who was now putting Concord in the way of greater fame even than had come through the fight at the bridge. Here was the home of transcendentalism.

The term had come from Germany, but the Concord version was divorced from Old World definitions and used variously and conveniently. James Elliot Cabot said that the transcendental was "whatever lay beyond the stock notions and traditional beliefs to which adherence was expected because they were generally accepted by sensible persons." An irreverent contemporary said that the transcendentalists were "a race who dove into the infinite, soared into the illimitable, and never paid cash." Transcendental ideas flew about like pigeons when Emerson's house, by his wish and Lidian's, was so stocked with effervescing wit and wisdom, and not all of them flapped to the same rhythm or were capable of mating.

One of the early visitors at the Emerson house was, in the terms then used, crazy, but was little handicapped on that account. He was Jones Very, some four years older than Thoreau, who had entered Harvard in February 1834 as a second-term sophomore and for a time had been Thoreau's classmate and his tutor in Greek. Tall, slender, and hollow-cheeked, Very looked the part of a poet, and poet he was. Cabot considered him to have "an abnormal acceleration of the whole mental machinery; a psychical intoxication." Emerson wrote:

"Very has been here lately, and stayed a few days; confounding us with the question whether he was insane. At first sight and speech you would certainly pronounce him so. Talk with him a few hours, and you will think all insane but he." Among Very's interesting notions was that it was an honor for him to wash his own face. Odder still, he believed he had been raised from the dead.

Emerson's *Nature* was the first of the transcendental scriptures, for it let the other world go and opened the more immediate vista of heavenly life on earth, should man make use of his opportunities in ways worthy of the godlike faculties with which he was endowed. Surely this lay beyond the current "stock notions and traditional beliefs."

No one accounted it significant, when the lights were glowing in Emerson's house on some of those conversational evenings when the company was transcendentally distinguished, that Henry Thoreau was likewise present at Concord as a matter of plain circumstance after taking his Harvard degree. Emerson, of course, had become an American planet, an aristocrat of the intellect, already a philosopher, already pervadingly important. He was dispensing a new sort of luminosity over an old scene, and Henry was part of the scene, hardly more.

Up to now, New England had been a rugged mixture of changeable weather, stone walls, the autumn blazing of maples and oaks, farms with grazing sheep and cattle, plowed furrows and huckleberry thickets, wild-apple taciturnity and shrewdness, and all the rest, with a good measure of leathery theology thrown in. Now it became also words—literary words put together in resonant, flowing sentences, or even in the rhyme and cadence of poetry. Emerson was not solely responsible, but his sunlight seemed to shine most warmly through the least cloud, shedding radiance itself but no less importantly disclosing radiance where it fell. He, too, more than anyone else, had put New England into the world market of philosophy.

No one would be able to think long of the region again without thinking of literature. When Emerson wrote of the Concord that had become his, despite those impulses to settle elsewhere, his prose had style: "... I did not know what a bargain
I had in the bluebirds, bobolinks, and thrushes, which were
not charged in the bill. As little did I guess what sublime mornings and sunsets I was buying, what reaches of landscape. ..."
He transcendentalized nature. Other people had enjoyed sun-
rises and sunsets, but Emerson's were different, once he had
put them into his personal scripture.

The new titan and hogreeve of Concord was thirty-four in
May 1837, tall, thin, his most prominent feature a long and
forthright yet scholarly nose, the very New England essence
in a philosopher's face, especially considered with the lines
that ran from it to the corners of his mouth. In him were paired
the qualities of sensitivity and intellectual strength. His long
hair was generally disordered, scholar fashion. He was still
youthful yet authoritatively mature, impressive on the lecture
platform, possessor of a lean nobility and a prophet's leadership that did not need to assume so much because it came armed
with a sight draft on the accounts of those who were aware
enough to see and to listen.

11. "My Young Friend"

Emerson must have known the Thoreaus, and probably he
had known something about the family for a long time. Anyone who had seen a good deal of Dr. Ripley, as Emerson had
from boyhood, would have been well introduced to all Concord.

"I remember, when a boy," Emerson wrote, "driving about
Concord with him, and in passing each house he told the story
of the family that lived in it, and especially he gave me
anecdotes of the nine church members who had made a divi-

sion in the church in the time of his predecessor, and showed me how every one of the nine had come to bad fortune or to a bad end."

Either the old minister or Mrs. Thoreau or the two together had got Emerson to write his letter in behalf of Henry to President Quincy of Harvard. But whether Emerson and Henry had met, save perhaps passing on the street or in some casual, inadvertent way, is uncertain up to the spring of 1837.

Emerson had married Lidian, one of the Jackson girls, but there was another, a sister older by almost four years, Lucy, who had married a Boston commission merchant named Charles Brown. Brown, finding himself financially submerged, absconded to Europe from where he wrote pious letters warning against Emerson's unorthodoxy.

Lidian Emerson felt toward Lucy with special sisterly affection and sympathy. To Lucy she described a typical day in the Emerson household: "We have prayers in the morning a little before 7—breakfast at 7—then I hold a consultation with Nancy about dinner and can go to my work reading or writing without further care. We dine exactly at one—Mr. E. & myself then set about writing letters if there are any to write or finish—for the mail at 3—then I take a nap—and then my walk with Mr. E. or to see Aunt Mary—or she comes here—or I sit down to my occupations. . . . We drink tea at six—half an hour before which Mr. E. issues forth from his sanctum to sit the blind-man's-holiday with me. In the evening he brings down his work and I take mine and after talking a bit we 'make a mum' and keep it till 9 o'clock when we call the girls and have prayers."

In the fall of 1836 Lucy came for a long visit at the Emerson house. About this time the brother of Lucy and Lidian, Dr. Charles Thomas Jackson, was experimenting with ether at his chemistry laboratory in Boston and had already—so he maintained later—mentioned ideas about telegraphy to Samuel F. B.

Morse which, he said, Morse stole. The Jackson family was an interesting one, but little is remembered about Lucy except her sweetness as a woman, and Henry Thoreau was largely responsible for that gracious memory.

After visiting Lidian, Lucy boarded for a time at the Thoreau house, and there one day she talked about a lecture prepared by her distinguished brother-in-law. Helen Thoreau exclaimed that her brother Henry had put down some of the same thoughts in his diary. The coincidence was regarded as remarkable, and Helen brought Henry's diary from upstairs to show it to Lucy Brown. That Helen was familiar with the diary and knew just where it was kept is another revealing family fact—the older Thoreaus shared closely in Henry's life and observed it intimately.

Of course Lucy spoke to Emerson of the parallel between his thoughts and Henry Thoreau's, and Emerson asked to have Henry come to Coolidge Castle—that had become a usual term for the Emerson house, perpetuating the ring of former ownership—for a talk. The first sequel was followed by a second, for the philosopher's interest was kindled and it was only a question of time before Henry would become a sort of back-door attendant at the transcendental conversations.

Henry's thoughts were running in the practical direction of a career, or at least of a livelihood. Though his college record had somewhat disappointed the family, it had really been a pretty creditable one. In any case, his parents and sisters were as proud of him as ever, and the women were flutteringly concerned with the decision that was held in balance.

One of the family tales was of how, while he was still at Harvard, Henry asked his mother what profession she would advise him to choose. "She replied that he could buckle on his knapsack and roam abroad to seek his fortune in the world. The tears rose to his eyes at this suggestion, and his sister Helen, who was standing by, tenderly put her arm around him and said, 'No, Henry, you shall not go; you shall stay at home and live with us.' "

This annal, often repeated in later years, was taken as a sort of prophecy. Yet at the time there was a ready and natural choice for a young man's calling: school teaching seemed appointed for the learned and ambitious who did not happen to be drawn to the law or the ministry. Teaching, in any case, was broader and more aptly suited to the New England character and the mode of the times than almost anything else. If Henry was not ambitious in a worldly sense, which was by no means certain as yet, teaching represented the way of least resistance and would please the family. The family!

Channing wrote of Henry: "In his own home he was one of those characters who may be called household treasures; always on the spot with skilful eye and hand to raise the best melons in the garden, plant the orchard with the choicest trees, act as extempore mechanic; fond of pets, the sister's flowers, or sacred Tabby, kittens being his favorites—he would play with them by the half-hour." Henry was a family man in this sense, and he could not have been so free in his relationship to the world without this safe harbor from which to take bearings and voyage outward.

In 1836 he had made a trip to New York with his father, "peddling," as he recorded later, which must have meant selling the family product of pencils; but there was no thought of entering Henry, fresh from Harvard, into any branch of commerce. And so he was chosen to teach the Concord grammar school that first fall after his return. The engagement lasted only two weeks.

Deacon Cyrus Stow of the school committee was the man who put a stop to it. He observed that Henry did not punctuate teaching with corporal punishment. Henry had no idea of doing so, for he believed in moral influences only—though he

did not go so far as Bronson Alcott, who punished himself, as
the teacher, when the pupils did wrong. Rebuked by the deacon, however, Henry administered the ferrule to a half-dozen
youngsters, one of them a girl who did domestic work at his
mother's house, and walked out of the school for good. At
least one of the pupils thus punished held a grudge against
Henry throughout his life on that account. He did not feel
honored that he was included in an ironic demonstration.

Meantime Henry had written a poem, tied it with a bouquet
of violets, and tossed it into Lucy Brown's room through the
window. The tribute was one of inner and poetic confiding, a
self-revelation, to a woman who would understand, not to a
woman loved—Lucy Brown was not only married but advanced in her thirties—yet the episode was romantic too, perhaps more genuinely romantic than a lyric of calf love could
have made it.

When Henry later put the lines into a book, he introduced
them with an allusion to the circumstances: "I have seen a
bunch of violets in a glass vase, tied loosely with a straw, which
reminded me of myself."

He called the poem "Sic Vita," and it ran:

> I am a parcel of vain strivings tied
>   By a chance bond together,
> Dangling this way and that, their links
>   Were made so loose and wide
>   Methinks,
>   For milder weather
>
> A bunch of violets without their roots,
>   And sorrel intermixed,
> Encircled by a wisp of straw
>   Once coiled about their shoots,
>   The law
>   By which I'm fixed.

And so on. Mrs. Brown showed the poem to Emerson.

Henry, having run through the town school in record time, let his intentions more or less drift until spring. To Helen, who was at Taunton, he wrote: "Please you, let the defendant say a few words in defense of his long silence. You know we have hardly done our own deeds, thought our own thoughts, or lived our own lives hitherto. For a man to act himself, he must be perfectly free; otherwise he is in danger of losing all sense of responsibility or of self-respect. Now when such a state of things exists, that the sacred opinions one advances in argument are apologized for by his friends, before his face, lest his hearers receive a wrong impression of the man—when such gross injustice is of frequent occurrence, where shall we look, and not look in vain, for men, deeds, thoughts? As well apologize for the grape that it is sour, or the thunder that it is noisy, or the lightning that it tarries not."

Helen had been overanxious about the impression Henry might make on men and women in the practical world. Womanlike, she could see that a grape must be sour, but not that Henry must be sour or hasty or assertive of controversial opinions. He had set her right. But the cruel, incurable truth of the relationship between them was that she was older than he.

Henry Vose, Henry Thoreau's commencement partner, wrote to him: "You envy my happy situation, and mourn over your fate, which condemns you to loiter about Concord and grub among the clamshells. . . ." This complaint may have been rhetorical, or an expression of uncertainty. Presently Henry Thoreau was off to Maine, where his mother had relatives, to apply for a teaching job. He took with him a letter from Dr. Ripley, addressed "To the Friends of Education" and concluding with a note of apology for the handwriting: "N. B. It is but justice to observe here that the eyesight of the writer is much impaired."

Henry also had a letter written by Emerson recommending him as "an excellent scholar, a man of energy and kindness." Nevertheless, he did not get the job in Maine, nor one that Josiah Quincy tried to put him in the way of at Alexandria, Virginia.

Henry had written to Orestes Brownson for help "in obtaining employment":

"Perhaps I should give some account of myself. I could make education a pleasant thing both to the teacher and the scholar. This discipline which we allow to be the end of life, should not be one thing in the schoolroom, and another in the street. We should seek to be fellow-students with the pupil, and we should learn of, as well as with him, if we would be most helpful to him. But I am not blind to the difficulties of the case; it supposes a degree of freedom, which rarely exists. It hath not entered into the heart of man to conceive the full import of that word—Freedom—not a paltry republican freedom, with a *posse comitatus* at his heels to administer it in doses as to a sick child—but a freedom proportionate to the dignity of his nature—a freedom that shall make him feel that he is a man among men, and responsible only to that reason of which he is a particle, for his thoughts and actions.

"I have ever been disposed to regard the cowhide as a nonconductor—methinks that, unlike the electric wire, not a single spark of truth is ever transmitted through its agency to the slumbering intellect it would address. I mistake, it may teach a truth in physics, but never a truth in morals."

At length, finding himself still without a school to teach in, Henry started one of his own, at the Thoreau house, and presumably his remarks to Orestes Brownson were part of its otherwise unwritten charter.

Meantime Henry had delivered a lecture on "Society" at the Concord Lyceum, had attended a meeting of Sunday-school teachers—this was one of Lidian's enterprises—at the Emerson house, and was advancing to a higher degree of acceptance with the transcendental circle. Emerson was referring to him as "my young friend."

Reverend D. G. Haskins, who had known Thoreau at Harvard, was surprised and a good deal put out when he visited Concord and found Henry in the company of the elect. "Meeting Mr. Emerson one day, I inquired if he saw much of my classmate, Mr. Henry D. Thoreau, who was then living in Concord. 'Of Thoreau?' replied Mr. Emerson, his face lighting up with a smile of enthusiasm. 'Oh yes, we could not do without him. When Mr. Carlyle comes to America, I expect to introduce Thoreau to him as *the* man of Concord.' "

Mr. Haskins was surprised and chagrined, for he had no such good opinion of Henry. Later, watching Henry at the Emerson house, he made a discovery that others were to mention as well:

"I was quite startled by the transformation that had taken place in him. His short figure and general cast of countenance were of course unchanged; but in his manners, in the tones of his voice, in his modes of expression, even in the hesitations and pauses of his speech, he had become the counterpart of Mr. Emerson. Thoreau's college voice bore no resemblance to Mr. Emerson's, and was so familiar to my ear that I could have readily identified him by it in the dark. I was so much struck by the change that I took the opportunity, as they sat together talking, of listening with closed eyes, and I was unable to determine with certainty which was speaking. I do not know to what subtle influence to ascribe it, but after conversing with Mr. Emerson for even a brief time, I always found myself able and inclined to adopt his voice and manner of speaking."

Here too came young James Russell Lowell, exiled from Harvard for being a bad boy, farmed out in Concord to be tutored by Dr. Ripley's assistant, Reverend Barzillai Frost, and to write the class ode which, because of his suspension, he could not deliver in person at the college exercises.

Lowell did not appreciate the tranquil aspect of Concord. "It appears a decent sort of place, but I've no patience with it," he wrote. "I'm homesick and all that sort of thing." He had letters of introduction to Emerson and was one of several undergraduate guests invited to dinner on the Fourth of July— an opportunity he used to gather material for lines of satire against Emerson in the class poem.

He wrote in one letter, "I met Thoreau last night, and it is exquisitely amusing to see how he imitates Emerson's tone and manner. With my eyes shut, I shouldn't know them apart."

Emerson himself was noting many observations about Henry Thoreau in his journal, such as these, now and a little later:

"I delight much in my young friend, who seems to have as free and erect a mind as any I have ever met."

"My good Henry Thoreau made this solitary afternoon sunny with his simplicity and clear perception. How comic is simplicity in this double-dealing, quacking world. Everything that boy says makes merry with society, though nothing can be graver than his meaning."

"Montaigne is spiced through with rebellion, as much as . . . my young Henry Thoreau."

"My Henry Thoreau will be a great poet for such a company, & one of these days for all companies."

Emerson was "delighted in being led to the very inner shrines of the wood gods by this man, clear-eyed and true and stern enough to be trusted with their secrets."

Emerson had good right to the joy of recognition and a discoverer's special rights, but he made a mistake in the possessive pronoun; even now, and in spite of all appearances that misled Lowell and others, the young man of Concord was not Emerson's Henry Thoreau.

12. *"They Loved John"*

As Henry, in his physical and temperamental endowment, took after his mother's family and was "clear Dunbar," so his older brother John took after his father's people and was "clear Thoreau." He had neither Henry's reserve nor Henry's native inclination to contradiction and dissent. He made quicker and easier adjustments. John was described as "a clear and flowing spirit," as "earnest and lovable." The difference between the two brothers was enough to account for the strong attachment that existed between them, since the quality of unlikeness is apt to be a bond in families. But Henry, as the younger by three years, had looked up to John from the beginning, followed his leadership, learned from him the prowess that comes more quickly from companionship and emulation, especially in a country boyhood.

It was with John that Henry learned to fish and hunt and to explore the Concord countryside. Now John had become a teacher at a school in Taunton, and Henry wrote a letter to him in mock Indian style, not the usual sort of thing for a Harvard graduate, but long ago he had called John "Sachem Hopeful of Hopewell." "Brother: it is many suns that I have not seen the print of thy moccasins by our council-fire: the Great Spirit has blown more leaves from the trees."

There was a good deal of this, so much that John might have had enough some minutes before he reached the end. But four months later Henry wrote in a more practical vein: "I have a proposal to make. Suppose by the time you are released we should start in company for the West, and there either establish a school jointly, or procure ourselves separate situations. Suppose, moreover, you should get ready to start previous to leaving Taunton, to save time."

Then followed the words of declaration: "Go *I* must, at all events . . ."

Dr. Edward Jarvis, formerly of Concord, had written from Kentucky that there was a good prospect in that region for teachers. Henry's letter ended with this passage: "The bluebirds made their appearance the 14th day of March; robins and pigeons have also been seen. Mr. Emerson has put up the bluebird box in due form. All send their love. From your aff. br. H. D. Thoreau."

The bluebird box was made for Emerson by John and was of more than trifling moment; Emerson remembered it as characteristic of John's kindness.

"Go *I* must, at all events . . ."

Here, rising to the crest of a current of more or less ordinary and familiar news, was a new flare, signal of Henry's spirit. He was young and at a crossroads. His classmates were settling into livelihoods and adjustments here and there; the world was moving on. The very moment urged him, and the West was a symbol of freshness and difference, of much that he recognized more minutely later on. But John said no, and Henry lingered at Concord. In July he wrote: "Now I wish you to write and let me know exactly when your vacation takes place, that I may take one at the same time. I am in school from 8 to 12 in the morning, and from 2 to 4 in the afternoon. After that I read a little Greek or English, or, for variety, take a stroll in the fields. . . . Report says that Elijah Stearns is going to take the town school. I have four scholars, and more engaged."

Henry wrote also of the good blueberry year and reported his identification of a rush sparrow that he had known by note and not by name.

From Taunton, John went to West Roxbury, teaching still, and then he made up his mind to return to Concord and join Henry. In September 1838 the brothers were installed as masters of the Concord Academy, where soon they had an enrollment of twenty-five, and a waiting list, with some of the out-of-town children boarding at the Thoreau house. Business was therefore doubly good.

John, at twenty-three, took the post of principal. He taught English and arithmetic and warmed the smaller children with a personality that always won affection. Henry taught Latin, Greek, and higher mathematics, yet he gave Helen advice by letter—she was now at Roxbury—as to instruction in mental philosophy. This, he said, "is very like Poverty which, you know, begins at home. . . ."

"As for themes," he wrote to Helen, "say first 'Miscellaneous Thoughts.' Set one up to a window, to note what passes in the street, and make her comment thereon; or let her gaze in the fire, or into a corner where there is a spider's web, and philosophize, moralize, theorize, or what not. What their hands find to putter about, or their minds to think about, that let them write about."

Henry sounded sage and professional—and modern—but John was the better teacher. The school program included talks by both brothers, outdoor walks of instruction and just plain discovery, and the suggestion of corporal punishment never arose. Among the pupils, after a while, were Louisa May Alcott and her sister, for their father had moved to Concord, where he was to make the Platonic world "as solid as Massachusetts" to Emerson—though he was also a "tedious archangel." Later on, Henry Thoreau was to remark that Alcott was the best-natured man he had ever met; "the rats and mice make their nests in him." The good-natured and tedious archangel proceeded from idea to idea, morning, noon, and night, without a backward glance. Massachusetts was never solid to him but remained the cloud land that the Platonic world might have continued to be for Emerson.

"With regard to the private school of John and Henry Thoreau," wrote James Elliot Cabot in 1883, "I collected the testimony some twenty years since, of such of the scholars as I could find, and all but one (who was not very bright and had been among the younger pupils) had remembered it as a privilege of their lives; they loved John and respected Henry."

Edward Waldo Emerson, the great Emerson's son, who likewise inquired and whose childhood was colored by memories and traditions concerning the Thoreau brothers, wrote that Henry was then in a "green apple stage." He was not loved. He was conscientious and rigid. When he told stories to the children he seemed to be fending them off, abashed by his young charges.

3

A MAN HAS NOT EVERY-
THING TO DO

ᵕᵌ ᵎᵂ

1. *Henry and the Church Tax*

THE UNEVENTFUL PART of Henry's career was almost over,
though no one, not even he, was aware of the way that
wind blew. He was earning a livelihood in the traditional New
England fashion, and if he talked against some of the trite,
respectable folkways, it was no more than others did who were
young, contrary, or eccentric.

He had begun his journal in 1837: "Oct. 22. 'What are you
doing now?' he asked. 'Do you keep a journal?' So I make my
first entry today."

The "he" was Emerson, and thus Henry founded many volumes of his writings and observations that were to run for years,
on Emerson's suggestion. But later Henry copied what he
chose from this early journal into another, entitling the new
volume *Gleanings or What Time Has Not Reaped of My
Journal,* and discarded the original. He kept mostly the jot-
tings of epigrams, allusions, thoughts, and so on, that presumably he might use one day in some writing or other, and did
not keep much that concerned the ordinary course of his own
life.

No one thinks much of his early epigrams nowadays, for they were bookish, juvenile, contrived, hardly characteristic or original enough to have made a stir at Emerson's.

"Men are constantly dinging in my ears their fair theories and plausible solutions of the universe, but ever there is no help, and I return again to my shoreless, islandless ocean, and fathom unceasingly for a bottom that will hold an anchor, that it may not drag."

He paid his respects to the women of the Thoreau household: "Here at my elbow sit five notable, or at least noteworthy, representatives of this nineteenth century—of the gender feminine. One a sedate, indefatigable knitter, not spinster, of the old school, who had the supreme felicity to be born in days that tried men's souls. ... Opposite, across this stone hearth, sits one of no school, but rather one who schools, a spinster who spins not, with elbow resting on the book of books, but with eyes turned towards the vain trumpery of that shelf—trumpery of sere leaves, blossoms and waxwork, built on sand, that presumes to look quite as gay, smell quite as earthy, as though this were not by good rights the sun's day."

Even then it was the genuine Henry Thoreau, though young and unformed, who was writing.

"Nov. 5. Truth strikes us from behind, and in the dark, as well as from before and by broad daylight."

"Nov. 12. I yet lack discernment to distinguish the whole lesson of today; but it is not lost—it will come to me at last. My desire is to know *what* I have lived, that I may know *how* to live henceforth."

"Homer. March 3. Three thousand years and the world so little changed! The Iliad seems like a natural sound which has reverberated to our days."

The reverberations that others in Concord were aware of did not seem to trace from the *Iliad*, though some might have been Biblical in their source. Poor old Dr. Ripley, survival of an ear-

lier age, was approaching the end of his pastorate. He had settled in the town at the age of twenty-nine in the year 1778 when
to be a Unitarian was to be not only modern but advanced; he
had never considered that the material was in him for the making of an old fogy. But, at the end, this sad fact was implicit
in Emerson's tribute: "It was a pity that his old meeting house
should have been modernized in his time. I am sure all who remember him will associate his form with whatever was grave
and droll in the old, cold, unpainted, uncarpeted, square-pewed
meeting house, with its four iron-gray deacons in their little
box under the pulpit—with Watts's hymns, with long prayers,
rich in the diction of ages; and not less with the report like mus-
ketry from the movable seats."

Dr. Ripley had been required by circumstance to withstand
anti-Masonic assaults and a violent recrudescence of Trini-
tarianism which had trolled deserters from his church, among
them Henry's mother and her sisters and sisters-in-law. But
Mrs. Thoreau had returned later to Dr. Ripley's congregation.

Now it was Henry who caused the old clergyman some pain,
for when the church tax was collectible, Henry would not pay
it. The dispute was with the civil authorities, since church and
state were not then separate, but Dr. Ripley was perforce a
witness of the stubborn revolt of a young man he had baptized,
whose family he had shepherded through the years, and for
whom he had written references. Henry's account of the episode was set down later, and so it has accents of his mythology;
yet it is a good account, and the plain reality shows through:

". . . the State met me in behalf of the Church, and com-
manded me to pay a certain sum toward the support of a clergyman whose preaching my father attended, but never I myself.
'Pay,' it said, 'or be locked up in the jail.' I declined to pay. But,
unfortunately, another man saw fit to pay it. I did not see why
the schoolmaster should be taxed to support the priest, and not

the priest the schoolmaster; for I was not the State's schoolmaster, but I supported myself by voluntary subscription. I did not see why the Lyceum should not present its tax-bill, and have the State to back its demand, as well as the Church. However, at the request of the selectmen, I condescended to make some such statement in writing:—'Know all men by these presents, that I, Henry Thoreau, do not wish to be regarded as a member of any incorporated society which I have not joined.' This I gave to the town clerk; and he has it. The State, having thus learned that I did not wish to be regarded as a member of that church, has never made a like demand on me since; though it said that it must adhere to its original presumption that time. If I had known how to name them, I should then have signed off in detail from all the societies which I never signed on to; but I did not know where to find a complete list."

There were surely lively discussions of this affair at the Thoreau home, and it must have distressed the family to see Henry making himself conspicuous and to some people offensive through his studied nonconformity. Majority feeling in New England was always against "scenes" and this was a "scene" of a kind. Yet Henry's position was taken on principle, and all the Thoreaus could understand principle and uphold it. Family loyalty, too, was firmly rooted.

It was likewise true that if Henry had taken the first step, and perhaps a few more steps too, toward being a town "character," he bore no resemblance to the stock figure of village infidel. He was making his own mold.

He already had in mind and before long was to write of the New Testament, "I love this book rarely, though it is a sort of castle in the air to me, which I am permitted to dream." He had been prejudiced against it, he said, by the church and the Sabbath school, "yet I early escaped from their meshes. It was hard to get the commentaries out of one's head and taste the true flavor." Christ, he declared, was "the prince of Reformers and Radicals" and the New Testament was remarkable for its pure morality.

But he also wrote, "What are time and space to Christianity, eighteen hundred years, and a new world?—that the humble life of a Jewish peasant should have force to make a New York bishop so bigoted."

Henry may have taken some of these ideas to Emerson's and he may have brought some of them away. When the Sunday-school teachers were meeting there, and Henry had joined them but was not of them, Edmund Hosmer, a Concord farmer on weekdays, argued that Christ was identifiable with the human mind, but soon took flight from the venturesome idea in a traditionalist panic. Henry observed dryly that Hosmer had kicked the pail over, and this pleased Emerson enough to make an entry of it in his journal.

Some of the old Concord was slipping away. Emerson, ushering in the new, gave hallowed and literary indulgence to what was passing. It was he who held attention in the town and in the outer world—rightly so, for his fine intelligence was sweet and mellow with understanding and the capacity to appreciate humanity's full spectrum; he doubted his own sincerity, in a sense, since he realized that the views he uttered one day would be revised or replaced on another—this was surely the quintessence of openmindedness—yet he seemed to speak and write from a platform securely and rightly anchored. He seemed to embody, and apparently without half trying, the point of view of a new day—whatever it happened to be at the hour he was expressing it.

As for Henry Thoreau, the chances were that he would be cutting out a new washer for the kitchen pump, or mending a latch on the shed door. Or perhaps he was alone in his room: "I sit here . . . looking out on men and nature from this that

I call my perspective window, through which all things are seen in their true relations. This is my upper empire, bounded by four walls, viz., three of boards, yellow-washed, facing the north, west, and south respectively, and the fourth of plaster, likewise yellow-washed, fronting the sunrise—to say nothing of the purlieus and outlying provinces, unexplored as yet but by rats."

2. *Lovely Ellen Sewall*

On July 20, 1839, the stage drove into Concord and discharged a young girl passenger named Ellen Devereux Sewall, who had come from Scituate with her mother for three weeks' visit with Ellen's grandmother, Mrs. Joseph Ward, and her aunt Prudence Ward, who were boarding at the Thoreau home. The Wards had been good friends of Aunt Maria Thoreau's in Boston.

Ellen Sewall was seventeen, a magic age, and her face and figure were kindled and kindling with fresh youth, both eager and tender, her fine nose slightly upturned as if by way of accent, her hair soft and lovely, her lips and chin as delicate as a girl's should be. If it was Henry who carried in the luggage, it is likely that he blushed—for one of the girls who did domestic work at the Emerson house said later that he never passed through the kitchen where they were without coloring.

A year earlier Henry had been somewhat enraptured by Ellen's younger brother Edmund, eleven, who had also stayed with the Thoreaus and had been taken on journeys of exploration in the countryside by John and Henry. The rapture was such that it produced a poem which Henry entitled "Sympathy," with expressions of a nature that led at least one biographer to believe he had really written it about Ellen. She, however, had not then risen as a star in his sky.

The poem began:

> Lately, alas, I knew a gentle boy
> Whose features all were cast in Virtue's mould,
> As one she had designed for Beauty's toy,
> But after named him for her own stronghold.

The final lines were:

> If I but love that virtue which he is,
> Though it be scented in the morning air,
> Still shall we be truest acquaintances,
> Nor mortals know a sympathy more rare.

Edmund later on was embarrassed by the poem, but apparently Henry never was, nor needed to be, except for its literary shortcomings. It was a kind of transcendental punctuation mark in his line of progress. Emerson said the poem was "the purest strain, and the loftiest, I think, that has yet pealed from this unpoetic American forest." Emerson could find the right words for saying anything, but he was much too generous in his judgment.

A time came when Edmund entered the school kept by John and Henry, and by then he was an entirely prosaic character. John and Henry had met Ellen, and it was she who made both their hearts leap far beyond a pure and lofty strain of sympathy.

Exactly five days after Ellen's arrival, Henry wrote this single line in his journal: "There is no remedy for love but to love more."

He saw Ellen across the dining table; he spoke to her and watched the changing expression in her eyes and the motion of her body. Out in the summer sunlight that could give so tropic a fertility to austere New England, he was aware of Ellen's radiance—and so it went. She had altered Concord for him that summer, and altered much else too.

What would come of this romance he could only dream and

wonder; and so things stood when he and John set out on the last day of August for a river trip they had planned for a long time.

3. *River Journey*

"Made seven miles," Henry wrote in his journal that night, "and moored our boat on the west side of a little rising ground which in the spring forms an island in the river, the sun going down on one hand, and our eminence contributing its shadow to the night on the other. . . ."

The river, of course, was Henry's beloved Musketaquid, or Concord, but for the spirit of this enterprise of the Thoreau brothers it might have been the Euphrates or the Zambesi, and the village yonder might have been the encampment of a strange race of savages instead of tame old Billerica. The whole account of the 1839 expedition was to appear in Henry's first book, *A Week on the Concord and Merrimack Rivers.*

"Here we found huckleberries still hanging upon the bushes, where they seemed to have slowly ripened for our especial use. Bread and sugar, and cocoa boiled in river water, made our repast, and as we had drank in the fluvial prospect all day, so now we took a draft of the river with the evening meal to propitiate the river gods. . . .

". . . when we had pitched our tents on the hillside, a few rods from the shore, we sat looking through its triangular door in the twilight at our lonely mast on the shore just seen above the alders, and hardly yet come to a standstill from the swaying of the stream; the first encroachment of commerce on this land. There was our port, our Ostia. That straight, geometrical line against the water and the sky stood for the last refinements of civilized life, and what of sublimity there is in history was there symbolized."

John and Henry had built their boat that spring; it had cost them a week's labor, Henry said. It "was in form like a fisher-man's dory, fifteen feet long by three and a half in breadth at the widest part, painted green below, with a border of blue, with reference to the two elements in which it was to spend its existence." This craft they had named *Musketaquid*.

In it they voyaged the grass-ground river and by noon on Sunday, their second day afloat, "were let down into the Mer-rimack through the locks at Middlesex, just above Pawtucket Falls, by a serene and liberal-minded man, who came quietly from his book. . . . By this man we were presented with the free-dom of the Merrimack. . . ."

The river widened and the harbors of Chelmsford and Dra-cut "lay as smooth and fairy-like as the Lida, or Syracuse, or Rhodes." Encamped under some oaks at Tyngsboro that night, Henry ascertained his latitude and longitude as a good voyager should. Then "instead of the Scythian vastness of the Billerica night, and its wild musical sounds, we were kept awake by the boisterous sport of some Irish laborers on the railroad, wafted to us over the water, still unwearied and unresting on this sev-enth day, who would not have done with whirling up and down the track with ever-increasing velocity and still reviving shouts, till late in the night."

On Monday morning "a million crisped waves came forth to meet the sun" and the brothers pressed onward through early fog before the sun was fairly out. "All that is told of mankind, of the inhabitants of the Upper Nile, and the Sunderbunds, and Timbuctoo, and the Orinoko, was experienced here." At a sandy place the voyagers bathed in the river and lay under some buttonwoods to rest and talk. That night they camped under a pine wood near Nashua.

"Far in the night, as we were falling asleep on the bank of the Merrimack, we heard some tyro beating a drum incessantly, in preparation for a country muster, as we learned. . . . We could have assured him that his beat would be answered. . . .

Fear not, thou drummer of the night, we too will be there. And still he drummed on in the silence and the dark. . . . No doubt he was an insignificant drummer enough, but his music afforded us a prime and leisure hour, and we felt that we were in season wholly."

Before sunrise they were moving again, passing a canal boat unseen in the fog but listening to its "few dull, thumping, stertorous sounds." As part of their equipment, the brothers had brought wheels with which to maneuver their boat around such river obstructions as falls; but they passed Cromwell's Falls by means of the locks, waiting to give canal boats first turn.

"In the forward part of one stood a brawny New Hampshire man, leaning on his pole, bareheaded and in shirt and trousers only, a rude Apollo of a man, coming down from that 'vast up-landish country' to the main; of nameless age, with flaxen hair, and vigorous, weather-beaten countenance, in whose wrinkles the sun still lodged, as little touched by the heats and frosts and withering cares of life as a maple of the mountain; an undressed, unkempt, uncivil man, with whom we parleyed awhile, and parted not without a sincere interest in one another. His humanity was genuine and instinctive, and his rudeness only a manner. He inquired, just as we were passing out of earshot, if we had killed anything, and we shouted after him that we had shot a *buoy*, and could see him for a long time scratching his head in vain to know if he had heard aright."

Past Thornton's Ferry and Naticook Brook, past Litchfield and up the river the brothers rowed the *Musketaquid*, and during the heat of the day they rested on an island and boiled rice for a noon meal. They caught a pigeon and saved it for supper; Henry had not yet become a vegetarian, though he and John were both unable to go through with eating some squirrels they had killed and skinned. "With a sudden impulse we threw them away, and washed our hands and boiled some rice for dinner."

That afternoon they tried their sail as long as the wind favored, then rowed again and made camp just before sundown at what seemed a retired place but turned out to be squarely across a path used by workmen. On Wednesday they embarked and rowed in leisurely fashion past open country and wooded islands, locking themselves around falls, and coming at last to Manchester. They locked themselves past the greater falls of Amoskeag, "surmounting the successive watery steps of this river's staircase in the midst of a crowd of villagers, jumping into the canal, to their amusement, to save our boat from upsetting, and consuming much river water in our service."

At evening they procured a loaf of homemade bread and both watermelons and muskmelons from a farmhouse. Rain was falling when they awoke Thursday morning, and since they had almost reached the limit of easy navigation for their craft, they proceeded by foot. "We managed to keep our thoughts dry, however, and only our clothes were wet." Their land journeying took them to Concord and Plymouth, New Hampshire, to Franconia, and Conway, for a full week's introduction to the mountain country, whither Henry was to journey again many years later; then they regained their boat and were embarked upon the return voyage.

"We had made about fifty miles this day with sail and oar, and now, far in the evening, our boat was grating against the bulrushes of its native port, and its keel recognized Concord mud, where some semblance of its outline was still preserved in the flattened flags which had scarce yet erected themselves since our departure; and we leaped gladly on shore, drawing it up, and fastening it to the wild apple tree, whose stem still bore the mark which its chain had worn in the chafing of the spring freshets."

What had been, in a certain diminished realistic sense, a boys' holiday excursion of no remarkable aspects held yet the proportions of a world journey across adventurous frontiers.

There were two truths—the outer and plainer one, and the inner one of Henry's awakened mind. Here, already, was one of the patterns chosen for his life.

4. *Spring, Summer, Romance*

Ellen Sewall was no longer at Concord when the brothers returned from their trip, and John hastened to pay her a visit at Scituate. In December, John and Henry both went to Scituate with Ellen's Aunt Prudence Ward. Henry presented Ellen's father with a copy of a volume of poems by Jones Very so that he too might wonder if Very was really crazy.

The rest of the winter there were only letters and messages. By correspondence, Henry persuaded Ellen to give up both coffee and tea as an experiment—an odd method of pressing a romance. But he sent her original poems too.

When spring stirred, he felt the urging of unrest. In his journal that March he wrote: "The world is a fit theatre today in which any part may be acted. There is this moment proposed to me every kind of life that men lead anywhere, or that imagination can paint. By another spring I may be a mail-carrier in Peru, or a South African planter, or a Siberian exile, or a Greenland whaler, or a settler on the Columbia River, or a Canton merchant, or a Robinson Crusoe in the Pacific, or a silent navigator of any sea. So wide is the choice of parts, what a pity if the part of Hamlet be left out!"

He needed verse, too, to express that spring emotion in the tantalizing warmth of which the part of Hamlet held fascination:

> Two years and twenty now have flown;
> Their meanness time away has flung;
> These limbs to man's estate have grown,
> But cannot claim a manly tongue.

Amidst such boundless wealth without
I only still am poor within;
The birds have sung their summer out,
But still my spring does not begin.

In June, Ellen came again to Concord, and Henry was glad
of the opportunities of companionship. The time of year was all
on the side of tenderness; Ellen was as freshly beautiful as ever.

"The other day," Henry wrote, "I rowed in my boat a free,
even lovely young lady, and, as I plied the oars, she sat in the
stern, and there was nothing but she between me and the sky."

But Henry said nothing to Ellen of his yearning, and again
she went home to Scituate. John had taken her out too, and
now again he followed her, this time for the purpose of making
a proposal of marriage. The Thoreaus always believed that
Henry sacrificed his own love so that the brother he had adored
might have first chance, and this must have been the occasion.
Dr. Canby concludes, and convincingly, that John told Henry
what he was about, and Henry kept silent, deliberately standing aside.

John then had Ellen all to himself at Scituate, and the two
took walks which he made the opportunity for courtship.
When he offered his avowal, she accepted him, but it seemed
later to her and to others that she had been surprised into com-
pliance. At any rate, her mother soon persuaded her that the
engagement was unsuitable. That was a time when Henry's
reputation for unorthodoxy and contrariness may have hurt
John, but Ellen could not have cared for him or she would not
have broken the engagement so promptly. In a few weeks she
was off to Watertown, New York, to visit an uncle.

Henry had never spoken of his love to Ellen, and might never
have spoken in words, but now that he could do so without
interfering with John—who had already lost—he sat down and
wrote a proposal of his own. The month was November, a time

of cold omen. Ellen in Watertown sent on news of the proposal
to her father, who "wished me to write immediately in a *short
explicit* and cold manner to Mr. T. He seemed very glad I was
of the same opinion as himself in regard to the matter."

She went on: "I wrote to H. T. that evening. I never felt so
badly at sending a letter in my life. I could not bear to think
that both these friends whom I have enjoyed so much with
would now no longer be able to have the free pleasant intercourse with us as formerly. My letter was very short indeed.
But I hope it was the thing. . . .

"I do feel so sorry H. wrote to me. It was such a pity. Though
I would rather have it so than to have him say the same things
on the *beach* or anywhere else. If I could only have been at
home so that Father could have read the letter himself and have
seen my answer, I should have liked it better. But it is all over
now. . . ."

Henry had loved, but he had not believed in professions of
love. Soon he was writing in his journal of "the inexpressible
privacy of a life."

"My truest, serenest moments are too still for emotion; they
have woollen feet. In all our lives we live under the hill, and if
we are not gone we live there still."

Later, in his essay on friends and friendship, he wrote with
eloquence and deep feeling:

"I never asked thy leave to let me love thee—I have a right.
I love thee not as something private and personal, which is *your
own*, but as something universal and worthy of love, *which I
have found*. Oh, how I think of you! You are purely good—
you are infinitely good. I can trust you forever. I did not think
that humanity was so rich. Give me an opportunity to live.

"You are the fact in a fiction—you are the truth more strange
and admirable than fiction. Consent only to be what you are.
I alone will never stand in your way.

"This is what I would like—to be as intimate with you as our

spirits are intimate—respecting you as I respect my ideal. Never
to profane one another by word or action, even by a thought.
Between us, if necessary, let there be no acquaintance.

"I have discovered you; how can you be concealed from me?"

This, Henry wrote, was the address "the true and not de-
spairing friend would make to his Friend." But he was speaking
too of love and lovers. Had he written in such deeply felt words
to Ellen Sewall, or was he now addressing her after the event—
for he said later that the memory of her had influenced his life?

"Friendship," he went on, "is never established as an understood relation. Do you demand that I be less your Friend that
you may know of it? . . . Let me never have to tell thee what I
have not to tell. Let our intercourse be wholly above ourselves,
and draw us up to it.

"The language of Friendship is not words, but meanings. . . ."

This was not theory but the fact of Henry's mind and heart.
The understood relationship, apart from words, in defiance of
words, was one of the touchstones of his life.

Meantime the Sewing Circle was meeting at the Thoreau
home, just the same and yet not at all the same, as the transcen-
dentals met at Emerson's. Sam Black, the Thoreau pet cat, was
ailing. Henry turned his hand to the necessary tasks of the
household. He looked the part of a tinker or mender, plain and
Yankee-competent. When he was traveling by rail, perhaps on
that journey to Maine in search of a teaching job, he applied
himself to the shutting of a car window after other passengers,
even as most of the human race, had wrestled with it and admitted defeat. For Henry, the window went shut. Observing
this, one of his train companions offered him a job in a factory,
implementing the offer with assurance as to wages and working
hours.

"Farmers have asked me to assist them in haying when I was
passing their fields," Henry wrote. "A man once applied to me
to mend his umbrella, taking me for an umbrella-mender, be-

cause, being on a journey, I carried an umbrella in my hand while the sun shone. Another wished to buy a tin cup of me, observing that I had one strapped to my belt, and a sauce-pan on my back."

This was how he went about on his explorations, and this was how he appeared to fellow citizens and neighbors.

5. Words and Huckleberries

One of the first projects of the transcendentalists had been the launching of a journal to project their ideas and contributions to a new and yeasting era in the time of man, an era they were themselves piloting through the channel to a broad and unknown sea. The essence of so many conversations was a requirement that they become something more, that they take on permanence and the authority of essays on a printed page. Accordingly, the first issue of a transcendental quarterly, *The Dial*, appeared in July 1840.

Emerson's name and prestige were, of course, attached to it, but Margaret Fuller, more driving and effective in action than the rest of them, was editor. As for the Emerson prestige, it was great enough and growing, but no longer starched with the hallowing tradition of the ministry; he had turned the respectable church upside down with an address at the Harvard Divinity School, and the Harvard doors had been closed after him with a bang. As lecturer, writer, and philosopher he was in greater harmony with himself and the outer world. Thanks to him, the first issue of *The Dial* contained Henry Thoreau's poem, "Sympathy," which had been inspired by Ellen Sewall's young brother Edmund.

Margaret Fuller was an exacting editor with a tendency to reject Henry or ask changes in his text. The next time round she wished to substitute the word "relume" for the phrase "doth have" in a poem of his. When Emerson reported this to

Henry, he boggled at the alteration, so much so that Emerson wrote to Margaret, ". . . our tough Yankee must have his tough verse," adding, "you need not print it if you have anything better."

The first issue of *The Dial* also contained the first of Bronson Alcott's "Orphic Sayings," of which a Boston newspaper remarked that they were like a train of fifteen coaches with only one passenger.

On the strength of a poem Henry had addressed to his favorite mountains and submitted to her, Margaret Fuller wrote not only a rejection and criticism but something of a character analysis of Henry as well: he was, she judged, "healthful, rare, of open eye, ready hand and noble scope. He sets no limit to his life, nor to the invasions of nature; he is not willfully pragmatic, cautious, ascetic or fantastical. But he is as yet a somewhat bare hill, which the warm gales of Spring have not visited. . . ."

Margaret was no stranger to the powers of divination like those of an ancient sybil. In her precocious childhood, stuffed with Latin and advanced reading, she had tossed with dreams and nightmares, blown her thoughts and emotions too to incandescent heat and strange exhalations, nor had she ever cooled or hardened. At the trick of opening the Bible or a volume of poems and by apparent chance or inner power turning up a prophetic or significant passage, she was adept. The *sortes vergilianae* this was called, and she was its mistress.

Therefore Margaret's words concerning Henry Thoreau held some touch of lightning flame or clarity; yet to see him as a "somewhat bare hill" should not have called for clairvoyance, only for a particular point of view.

His soil, she said, was "not a soil for the citron and the rose, but for the whortleberry, the pine, or the heather." Here she did not know the natural things of Concord as well as he, but she was mainly correct. "The unfolding of affections, a wider and deeper human experience, the harmonizing influences of other natures, will mould the man and melt his verse. He will seek thought less and find knowledge the more. I can have no advice or criticism for a person so sincere; but, if I give my impression of him, I will say, 'He says too constantly of Nature, she is mine.' She is not yours till you have been more hers. Seek the lotus, and take a draught of rapture."

Then, toward the end, she wrote, "Let me know whether you go to the lonely hut, and write to me about Shakespeare, if you read him there." Already he had talked of a woodland retreat.

She signed herself Margaret F. This was she at the age of thirty-one writing sybilline advice to him at twenty-four. Henry referred to her as Miss Fuller.

To Emerson she wrote differently: "Let no cold breath paralyze my hope that there will be a noble and profound understanding between us." She appreciated his "serene and elevated nature" and came near to ignoring Lidian, her Concord hostess, both socially and intellectually. Emerson had to fend her off with serene and elevated but carefully protective letters.

In October 1841 George Ripley, resigned like Emerson from the ministry, with Margaret Fuller and Bronson Alcott, met at Emerson's home to discuss the plan of a pioneering ideal community, Brook Farm, to be established at West Roxbury and directed by Ripley. The community would be inhabited by the intellectuals, all of whom would do some work with their hands and learn a way to escape any share in the evils of industrialism. Emerson felt much attraction for the plan, but for him it would have meant too great a surrender of his stature and free movement as an individual; he became spectator rather than participant.

Alcott did not become a Brook Farmer, either. At the moment, he was going through an interlude of hard times, having been, in a manner of speaking, cashiered out of his Temple

School by respectable Boston, shocked that he should have conversed with young children about the birth of Christ and other
matters best understood—or misunderstood—in proper silence.

Even lacking Emerson and Alcott, however, Brook Farm
found enough recruits. "Institute of Agriculture and Education," home of "plain living and high thinking," the enterprise
was incorporated as a joint stock company with twenty-four
shares of a value of $500 each. The farm comprised 192 acres
and no one ever knew how much intellect and aspiration. Soon
it was fairly launched under George Ripley and his wife Sophia,
symbol of an urge of the times.

But Henry Thoreau's thoughts were running in other directions, as when he wrote in his journal: "Would it not be a
luxury to stand up to one's chin in some retired swamp for a
whole summer's day, scenting the sweet-fern and bilberry
blows, and lulled by the minstrelsy of gnats and mosquitoes?
A day passed in the society of those Greek sages, such as
described in the 'Banquet' of Xenophon, would not be comparable with the dry wit of decayed cranberry vines, and the
fresh Attic salt of the moss beds. Say twelve hours of genial
and familiar converse with the leopard frog. The sun to rise
behind alder and dogwood, and climb buoyantly to his merid-
ian of three hands' breadth, and finally to sink to rest behind
some bold western hummock. To hear the evening chant of
the mosquito from a thousand green chapels and the bittern
begin to boom from his concealed fort like a sunset gun! Surely,
one may as profitably be soaked in the juices of a marsh for one
day, as pick his way dry-shod over sand. . . ."

Henry had listened a great deal to the grand talk about Brook
Farm, but he still hankered after the swamp. "As for these communities," he wrote, "I think I had rather keep bachelor's hall
in hell than go to board in heaven."

His own unrest with the times was different but it was real
enough, and the proof became clear when he and John an-

nounced in March 1841 that their school was to close. They
were doing well with it, and as a successful teacher and earner
of a sufficient livelihood from this profession Henry held his
only claim to the confidence and respect of Concord's prosaic
people. Otherwise he was slanting more and more into the
status of town character, as some heavy object slides down a
pitched roof.

John had some reason to stop the school, for his health was
not good; he felt an approaching exhaustion of that energy
without which his teaching would fail. This was reason enough
for anyone, but Henry's was less open to understanding. He
did not care much for teaching and still felt the call of so many
other roles that might be more interesting, including that of
Hamlet.

"Life looks as fair at this moment as a summer's sea. . . .
Through this pure, unwiped hour, as through a crystal glass, I
look out upon the future, as a smooth lawn for my virtue to
disport in. . . . I see the course of my life, like some retired road,
wind on without obstruction into a country maze."

Not so long before, wondering what he could do for a living,
Henry had "thought often and seriously of picking huckleberries; that surely I could do, and its small profits might suf-
fice, so little capital is required, so little distraction from my
wonted thoughts. . . ." He had considered that "I might gather
the wild herbs, or carry evergreens to such villagers as loved
to be reminded of the woods, and so find my living got."

These possibilities rejected, teaching now resigned, he relin-
quished none of his appreciation of swamps and huckleberries;
yet he played with the notion of buying a farm, the Hollowell
place, where he might farm a little and in his own fashion while
he was living and writing much, also in his own fashion. He
went so far as to pay ten dollars down, but the owner's wife
was sharper than her husband and would not put her signature
to a deed that brought so small a down payment. The Hollowell

Farm, as Henry saw its future, was an early, imperfect groping
for the Walden hut and would not have been an agricultural
enterprise save for some efforts at subsistence.

Henry cast about in other directions too, but property was
not for him, then or later. He was not upset when none of the
schemes took concrete form. Most of his creative attention was
fixed on words. Whatever else he might do, it was ordained
from within that he would write, and perhaps it had been so
ordained from the beginning.

6. *In Emerson's House*

Brook Farm was not for Emerson, nor for Henry, but the
whetted spring breeze of such ideas touched all philosophers
who were then alive.

Bronson Alcott, dreamer, characterized by Emerson as
"world-builder" and all the same a ne'er-do-well, had been living in Concord since 1840, drawn there by Emerson's presence
and the natural wandering progress of his nature. In Concord,
Alcott and his family were just as hard up as they had been elsewhere, and Emerson proposed that they move into his house
with him and Lidian for a year's venture in "labor & plain living." This might seem a long descent from the bold, stirring,
soul-calls of the intellectuals for economic and social reform,
yet a household containing the Emersons and the Alcotts would
be a small-scale experiment, with its share of pioneering and
plain nobility.

Already Emerson and Lidian had arranged to have Louisa
and Lydia, their maid and cook, sit at table with them for meals;
Louisa accepted the notion in a spirit of sacrifice, but Lydia remained unconverted. The plan bobbed about uneasily, then
sank. Nor would the Alcotts accept the invitation proffered to
them. Floundering about in family straits, as he called them,
Alcott read more great and dimly distant books, hired out for

labor by the day, and pursued a variety of enthusiasms, including vegetarianism and use of the new crackers sponsored by Dr. Sylvester Graham. Presently, Emerson would put up the money for him to go for a sojourn in England.

At the moment, in lieu of Brook Farm and the scheme Emerson alluded to in his journal with the descriptive words "Mr. Alcott, Liberty, Equality & a common table," the Concord philosopher extended a much plainer invitation to Henry Thoreau to move into the Emerson household for a year and "to have his board, etc., for whatever labour he chooses to do."

To his brother William, Emerson wrote that Henry was a "scholar & poet & as full of buds of promise as a young apple tree" and said moreover that "he is thus far a great benefactor and physician to me, for he is an indefatigable and very skilful laborer." To Carlyle in England went a message essentially the same: "One reader and friend of yours dwells now in my house, Henry Thoreau, a poet whom you may one day be proud of— a noble, manly youth, full of melodies and inventions. We work together day by day in my garden, and I grow well and strong."

Here was a more modest and compact colony of social and physical reform, perhaps somewhat economic too, on the home grounds of Concord philosophy itself. Henry planted and transplanted trees, grafted fruit trees, fixed fences and locks, looked after the children, exercised his natural skill as tinker and mender and handy man of the household. His was no room over the kitchen; he slept at the head of the stairs.

Emerson used again the catch-phrase of the transcendentalists—"plain living" and with it, in connection with Henry, "high thinking"; the house had a "friendly and sturdy inmate." In one of his most quoted references to Henry, Emerson wrote, "I told H. T. that his freedom is in the form, but he does not disclose new matter. I am familiar with all his thoughts; they are mine, quite originally dressed. But if the question be what new ideas he has thrown into circulation, he has not yet told

what that is which he was created to say." This was aside from
the grafting of the apple trees, in respect to which Emerson had
no ideas at all; and in any case it was too early by far to judge
of Henry's originality, which, later, Emerson was to defend
valiantly.

Henry rowed his philosopher-patron on the Concord, the
old Musketaquid, at night, and Emerson wrote in his journal,
"Through one field only we went to the boat and then left all
time, all science, all history, behind us, and entered into Nature with one stroke of a paddle." It made a difference who
was plying the paddle. "I said to him what I often feel. I only
know three persons who seem to me fully to see this law of
reciprocity or compensation—himself, Alcott, and myself: and
'tis odd that we should all be neighbors. . . ."

Henry's satisfactions were different from Emerson's; as he
entered upon his term as handy man and junior assistant philosopher he was not, at any rate, concerned about his future
in worldly considerations.

"My life will wait for nobody," he had written, "but is being
matured still irresistibly while I go about the streets and chaffer
with this man and that to secure it a living. It will cut its own
channel, like the mountain stream. . . . So flows a man's life,
and will reach the sea water, if not by an earthly channel, yet
in dew and rain, overleaping all barriers, with rainbows to announce its victory. It can wind as cunningly and unerringly
as water that seeks its level; and shall I complain if the gods
make it meander? This staying to buy me a farm is as if the Mississippi should stop to chaffer with a clamshell.

"What have I to do with plows? I cut another furrow than
you see. Where the off ox treads, there it is not, it is farther off;
where the nigh ox walks, it will not be, it is nigher still. If corn
fails, my crop fails not. . . ."

A few days before, Henry had earned seventy-five cents
by heaving manure out of a pen, thinking great thoughts and

thereby making all the neater bargain of it. Now he wrote in his journal, "April 26. Monday. At R. W. E.'s." Another few days and he noted, "Life in gardens and parlors is unpalatable to me. It wants rudeness and necessity to give it relish. I would at least strike my spade into the earth with as good will as the woodpecker his bill into a tree."

Of course there was much more at Emerson's than a parlor and a garden. There was a young woman named Mary Russell who came to teach the Emerson children. Not knowing about Ellen Sewall, the man who later became Mary Russell's husband thought that Mary was the "Maiden in the East" of a poem by Henry Thoreau. However Henry may have been interested in this girl, another meant infinitely more to him, for there also was Lidian with her failing health, her gift for amusement, an increasing remoteness from her husband, and some disillusionment with the general run of transcendentalists, whom she could presently refer to as a menagerie. Not that there was anything between Lidian and Henry in the earthly meaning, but in the unspoken dedication of Henry's nature there came to be, day by day and week by week, an incalculable everything.

The house and its surroundings, despite some vexations and inadequacies, were also suited to reading and thought. Henry conceived an interest in the writings of the Hindus that was to take his mind and inclination far. "I cannot read a sentence in the book of the Hindoos without being elevated as upon the table-land of the Ghauts. . . ." The height of the Ghats, as now spelled, would have been about that of Mount Monadnock, a favorite and appropriate altitude for Henry, from which he could see afar.

He had one chair in his room, and received his visitors standing, which seemed a good idea. He noted also, "It is vain to try to write unless you feel strong in the knees."

August had come with its tantalizing fullness. "I sailed on

the North River last night with my flute, and my music was a tinkling stream which meandered with the river...." And also: "I sit here in the barn this flowing afternoon weather, while the school bell is ringing in the village, and find that all the things immediate to be done are very trivial. I could postpone them to hear this locust sing.... Cannot man do something to comfort the gods, and not let the world prove such a piddling concern?"

He sat in a boat on Walden pond in the late twilight, playing his flute and watching the perch and the traveling shape of the moon across the pond bottom.

Unavoidably he chafed at the restrictions he had accepted through his acceptance of Emerson's offer and his life in Emerson's house. He took pains to free himself as much as possible, at least in his own mind.

"There is but one obligation," he wrote, "and that is the obligation to obey the highest dictate. None can lay me under another which will supersede this. The gods have given me these years without any incumbrance; society has no mortgage on them. If any man assist me in the way of the world, let him derive satisfaction from the deed itself, for I think I never shall have dissolved my prior obligations to God. Kindness repaid is thereby annulled. I would let his deed lie as fair and generous as it was intended....

"Of those noble deeds which have me for their object I am only the most fortunate spectator, and would rather be the abettor of their nobleness than stay their tide with the obstructions of impatient gratitude.... If any have been kind to me, what more do they want? I cannot make them richer than they are.... My obligations will be my lightest load, for that gratitude which is of kindred stuff in me, expanding every pore, will easily sustain the pressure. We walk the freest through the air we breathe."

He was impatient: "It does seem as if mine were a peculiarly wild nature, which so yearns toward all wildness. I know of no redeeming qualities in me but a sincere love for some things, and when I am reproved I have to fall back upon this ground. ... My love is invulnerable." On the day before Christmas at Emerson's: "I want to go soon and live away by the pond, where I shall hear only the wind whispering among the reeds. It will be success if I shall have left myself behind. But my friends ask what I will do when I get there. Will it not be employment enough to watch the seasons?"

The next day his mood continued. "I don't want to feel as if my life were a sojourn any longer. . . . It is time now that I begin to live."

So he felt, but there was wood to be chopped, and other winter chores at the philosopher's house.

7. *New Arrivals at Concord*

Most of the transcendentalists came and went. Henry had tried to find a house which Margaret Fuller could afford to occupy, and she thought of establishing a school at Concord, but nothing of this project materialized. Henry's aunts would have rented their house to Miss Fuller, but his mother said it was damp. Even a transcendentalist knew better than to occupy a house that bore the repute of dampness. For a time, Margaret had helped Alcott with his Temple School in Boston, after Elizabeth Peabody left, but she was not satisfied with Alcott's rate of pay, which was nothing.

So she continued to be a visitor at Concord but nothing more, gaining a certain reputation there. One night she took camphor by mistake for her headache medicine and a messenger was sent to arouse Dr. Bartlett. "How much camphor could one take without harm?" the doctor was asked. "Who has taken it?" he countered, and Margaret's name was provided. "A bushel!" said Dr. Bartlett sharply.

Margaret's younger sister, Ellen, the pretty one, married
William Ellery Channing—usually known as Ellery to distinguish him from an eminent ministerial uncle—and in this year
of 1841 the Channings, attracted by Emerson, took up house-
keeping in a Concord cottage close by. Ellery's sentiments toward the town were not much like Henry Thoreau's. He wrote
to Emerson: "I regret you should have chosen for your place
of residence a village so near the city of Boston; in so flat a
scenery, in so cold a climate, with so wretched a soil; where
there are bigots in religion, and fantasts of national opinion.
I regret it but I cannot help it."

The arrival of Ellery Channing was a significant event for
Thoreau, though this could not have been apparent at first; the
two were temperamentally ready for close understanding and
companionship—indeed, Channing had already lived alone in a
log hut in the wilds of Illinois. He was a poet, more so in dreams
and temperament than in achievement, but still a poet. One year
younger than Henry, he had not applied himself to finish at
Harvard but had followed an erratic course. He loved nature,
disliked dullness, and was capable of much good wit and only
a modicum of sustained application. In the course of his Concord years he nourished a distaste for Henry's mother and even
asked Henry to ask Mrs. Thoreau not to appear when he called
at the Thoreau house. Once when she came to the door Channing turned his back and she turned her back and there they
stood. History does not say how long this continued or what
happened, but it may be that Henry broke it up.

Ellen was unlike her sister Margaret. She did not bat her eyes
when in earnest conversation, she was tractable, and she could
put up with a good deal from her husband that must have
seemed sheer nonsense. At Concord she opened a school for
younger children to which the Emersons sent their eldest
daughter, also named Ellen—at Lidian's insistence—after
Waldo's first wife.

Everyone who thought he had a new idea brought it to Emerson for inspection and appraisal. It was pretty much that way with those who had poems, too, and Ellery was ready to unroll his genius at the great man's hearthside and display his samples. Emerson proved encouraging, as almost always to young writing men, and Ellery was by way of being one of his discoveries. The Concord philosopher and the young poet took long walks through the countryside, as Ellery and Henry Thoreau would do later.

Ellery's peculiarities were quickly talked about in Concord, as Henry's had been for a long time. He grew a noble example of weed along with his own corn because it had got so fine a start and seemed to him to have a right to live. Alcott would have done the same thing if he had thought of it first, and, as it turned out, he did make ventures along this line later.

A sojourner of another sort, likewise congenial to Henry, was Lucy Brown, Lidian's sister, she of the poem and sprig of violets, who came for visits in the Emerson household while Henry was living there. These two were on certain terms of understanding which was simple enough in general but, considering Henry's capacity for unexpressed ties of friendship, became not simple at all.

In January 1842 little Waldo, first child of the Emersons and wholly their pride and adoration, died "as the mist rises from the brook, which the sun will soon dart his rays through. Do not the flowers die every autumn? He had not even taken root here." These words were in a letter Henry wrote to Lucy Brown at Plymouth, and he had another death to speak of as well, for John, the object of his admiration and brotherly devotion, died of tetanus that February.

Though John's health had been uncertain, the accident that caused his death was cruel and sudden. Early accounts said he nicked a finger of his left hand while stropping a razor. Joseph Hosmer said he caught his hand on a rusty nail. In any case, he developed the symptoms of lockjaw, Dr. Bartlett was called, and, as John lay dying of the violence of the disease, Henry experienced the same rigidities and paroxysms. So close were the brothers that in this final crisis one could not suffer separately. In his delirium John talked of something he had written that he wanted Henry to read.

To Lucy Brown, Henry wrote, as the year had just turned into March, "Only Nature has a right to grieve perpetually, for she only is innocent. Soon the ice will melt, and the blackbirds sing along the river which he frequented as pleasantly as ever. The same everlasting serenity will appear in this face of God, and we will not be sorrowful if he is not." So Henry wrote, but he grieved long in his heart, and many years later when he was speaking to a friend of John's death he became so agitated that he went to the door for air.

Henry's letters to Lucy Brown were not love letters, yet they held tenderness and a special candor that took for granted a more than ordinary relationship between these two. "I grow savager and savager every day, as if fed on raw meat, and my tameness is only the repose of untamableness. I dream of looking abroad summer and winter, with free gaze, from some mountain-side, while my eyes revolve in an Egyptian slime of health—I to be nature looking into nature with such easy sympathy as the blue-eyed grass in the meadow looks in the face of the sky. . . .

"But I forget that you think more of this human nature than of this nature I praise. Why won't you believe mine is more human than any single man or woman can be? . . . I was going to be soberer, I assure you, but now have only room to add, that if the fates allot you a serene hour, don't fail to communicate some of its serenity to your friends. . . ." But then he added, "No, no. Improve so rare a gift for yourself, and send me of your leisure."

In another letter he referred to their conversations at Concord. "Pray let me know what you are thinking about any day—what most nearly concerns you. Last winter, you know, you did more than your share of the talking, and I did not complain for want of an opportunity. Imagine your stove-door out of order, at least, and then while I am fixing it you will think of enough things to say.

"What makes the value of your life at present? What dreams have you, and what realizations? You know there is a high table-land which not even the east wind reaches. Now can't we walk and chat upon its plane still, as if there were no lower latitudes? Surely our two destinies are topics interesting and grand enough for any occasion."

He called himself a savage and felt so in Concord and in Emerson's house, where he fixed stove doors and lugged out the ashes, but he showed a gentler heart than any savage; and when he assumed that he and Lucy Brown, excluding all others, could share confidences of their secret lives and hopes, he made her more than most people would consider a mere friend in the world's formal meaning.

There was Lucy, but after the two deaths—Waldo's and John's—he grew close in sympathy with her sister Lidian. The routine of the family and of the household which Lidian had long ago described was altered to include him. He played his familiar part in the morning and through the day and when evening fell. He was trusted, he was loyal, he was understanding. And he was also strange, for he was no one else but himself.

That summer Nathaniel Hawthorne, who had just married Elizabeth Peabody's younger and rather frail sister, Sophia, brought his wife to live in the Old Manse where the late Dr. Ezra Ripley had so long made his earthly home. Elizabeth Peabody, Alcott's assistant at his Temple School, had gone on to succeed with her teaching much more than he, though not in a business way, and had now opened a bookshop in Boston, where Margaret Fuller was holding conversations and making a literary center. The middle Peabody sister, Mary, was shortly to marry Horace Mann, secretary of the new state board of education, who was to leave an enduring mark on the public schools.

As for Hawthorne, he had written much but was still short of the fame that would come with his longer masterpieces. A moody personality with deep and shadowy recesses, he contributed an entirely new vein to the already variegated assortment known to Concord. He had reached Concord by way of Brook Farm, bringing his blue smock with him, and was not quite sure why he had been recruited there. Brook Farm was a prescription one might take for almost any ill—it could be a simple return to nature, a defiance of industrialism, or an adventure in creative intellectuality; it could be anything.

"The real ME was never an associate of the community," he wrote. "There has been a spectral Appearance there, sounding the horn at daybreak, milking the cows, and hoeing potatoes, and raking hay, toiling in the sun, and doing me the honor to assume my name. But this spectre was not myself. Nevertheless, it is somewhat remarkable that my hands have, during the past summer, grown very brown and rough, insomuch that people persist in believing that I, after all, was the aforesaid spectral horn-sounder, cow-milker, potato-hoer, and hay-raker."

One of Hawthorne's distinctions, of a sort, was that Emerson did not like his writing, though trying to be kindly toward it. The Concord sage remarked once that Hawthorne and Alcott together would make a man, and since he had always admired and praised Alcott, this assigned to Hawthorne the function of some slight and perhaps stiffening alloy. Just the same, Hawthorne's arrival at Concord was anticipated with the same pleasure that accompanied all increases in the number and specific gravity of the colony of fine spirits and notable

minds, and Emerson assigned Henry Thoreau the task of planting a garden in advance of Hawthorne's occupancy of the Old
Manse.

Once installed there, Hawthorne prepared his paper and
pens in the study where Emerson had written *Nature*. Henry
Thoreau soon made a call, and Hawthorne wrote in his notebook: "He is ugly as sin, long-nosed, queer-mouthed, and with
uncouth and somewhat rustic, although courteous manners,
corresponding well with such an exterior. But his ugliness is
of an honest and agreeable fashion, and becomes him much
better than beauty."

Hawthorne said that the Concord River was no favorite of
his, but he was glad to have any river at all at the bottom of his
orchard. His admiration of the scenery roundabout, and of the
town itself, was conventional and usually measured. When
Ellery Channing took him to Henry's favorite pool in Gowing's
Swamp, where few outsiders and no infidels were taken, Hawthorne's unprepared temperament rebelled. "Let's get out of
this dreadful hole!" he said.

Yet Hawthorne was favorably impressed for the most
part with the phases of the outdoors brought to his attention
through Henry Thoreau, whom he found "a keen and delicate
observer of nature—a genuine observer—which, I suspect, is
almost as rare a character as even an original poet; and Nature,
in return for his love, seems to adopt him as her especial child,
and shows him secrets which few others are allowed to witness. He is familiar with beast, fish, fowl, and reptile, and has
strange stories to tell of adventures and friendly passages with
these lower brethren of mortality."

Henry had just written a paper on natural history for *The
Dial* which Hawthorne found rambling but worth while. It
showed that Henry had "more than a tincture of literature—a
deep and true taste for poetry," and to Hawthorne here was "a
healthy and wholesome man to know."

After having Henry to dinner at the Old Manse one early September day, Hawthorne walked with him to the river bank and they went in Henry's boat up-river, which "soon became more beautiful than any picture, with its dark and quiet sheet of water, half shaded, half sunny, between high and wooded banks." The words were Hawthorne's. Before the trip was ended, he had agreed to buy the *Musketaquid* for seven dollars and wished that he might also acquire the aquatic skill of Henry himself.

The next day Henry delivered the boat and provided a lesson in its management. Again Hawthorne recorded his impressions. "Mr. Thoreau had assured me that it was only necessary to will the boat to go in any particular direction, and she would immediately take that course, as if imbued with the spirit of the steersman. It may be so with him, but it is certainly not so with me. The boat seemed to be bewitched, and turned its head to every point of the compass except the right one. He then took the paddle himself, and, though I could observe nothing peculiar in his management of it, the *Musketaquid* immediately became as docile as a trained steed."

Hawthorne changed the craft's name to *Pond Lily*, learned to navigate her himself after a fashion, and was soon uttering Thoreau-like sentiments: "O that I could run wild! that is, that I could put myself into a true relation with Nature, and be on friendly terms with all congenial elements."

There were many who uttered such longings, and still are, but Henry Thoreau knew what he meant and did not stop there. He was concerned not only with nature but with living as a whole, from first to last. That he was still falling short of real fulfillment troubled him. It was true that he could live healthily only the life assigned to him by God. "My life, my life! why will you linger? Are the years short and the months of no account? How often has long delay quenched my aspirations! Can God afford that I should forget him? Is he so in-

different to my career? Can heaven be postponed with no more
ado?"

There were times when Henry expressed misgivings because
of his apparent failure to meet the standards of the ambitious,
toiling world; almost defensively he maintained that his loiter-
ing was not without reason. "I would fain communicate the
wealth of my life to men, would really give them what is most
precious in my gift. . . ."

To communicate meant to speak, to write—especially to
write, for that was what he intended, prepared for, practiced.

8. *Sam Staples and Others*

In July, Henry went for a holiday walk and climb to the top
of Wachusett, Concord's nearest mountain, slightly higher
than 2,000 feet, which he termed the observatory of Massachusetts. Dick Fuller went with him, and Emerson wrote to
Margaret: "This morning your brother Richard whose face is
a refreshment, set out with Henry Thoreau on the road to
Wachusett. I am sorry that you & the world after you, do not
like my brave Henry any better. I do not like his piece very
well, but I admire this perennial threatening attitude, just as
we like to go under an overhanging precipice."

On Wachusett, Henry and Dick read Vergil and Wordsworth in their tent and noted with satisfaction the amplitude
and roominess of nature and the blue seas of the air. Most important, however, was Henry's account of the expedition,
which he wrote and had accepted by the Boston *Miscellany*,
not knowing then that the prospect of any payment was
dubious.

When cold weather came and the river froze, Henry went
skating with Emerson and Hawthorne, or they with him.
Emerson wrote later that Thoreau "figured dithyrambic dances
and Bacchic leaps on the ice. Hawthorne, wrapped in his cloak,

moved like a self-impelled Greek statue and I closed the line, just charging head foremost, half lying on the air."

Early in 1843 Emerson went off lecturing on the cultural rebirth of New England, a subject that seemed to attract listeners and on which he, partly as one of the parents and partly as an officiating physician at the rebirth, was qualified to speak. But he called this sort of thing "peddling" and took to it out of necessity because the dividends from his investments had been cut. In Baltimore, Philadelphia, and Brooklyn he peddled, leaving Henry Thoreau as guardian and companion in his house at Concord.

Henry's letters to the absent Emerson disclosed more than he usually felt like saying in the casual discourse of everyday. As he reported on people and events in Concord, he reported also on his own thoughts. In January he wrote: ". . . Elizabeth Hoar still flits about these clearings, and I meet her here and there, and in all houses but her own, but as if I were not the less of her family for all that. I had made a slight acquaintance also with one Mrs. Lidian Emerson, who almost persuades me to be a Christian, but I fear I as often lapse into heathenism."

Among those Henry saw from day to day was also, of course, Hawthorne. Hawthorne invited him to the Old Manse to meet an editor named O'Donnell who ran the *Democratic Review*, a puny-looking man, but still an editor. "We had nothing to say to one another," Henry reported to Emerson, "and therefore we said a great deal. . . . After tea I carried him and Hawthorne to the Lyceum." Here Hawthorne was recognizing Henry's literary aims and trying to help them along.

Then Henry wrote to Emerson about Alcott and Alcott's English friend Lane, who had the money to establish another ideal colony, an Alcottian improvement over Brook Farm. The venture was pending for the spring just ahead, Alcott having brought Lane back with him from the trip to England that

Emerson had generously financed; but at the moment the question was whether Alcott should go to jail for nonpayment of his poll tax.

He thought he should go to jail, by way of protest against an unjust government. Lane thought so too, and planned to be a protester himself with a similar gesture when circumstances permitted. But Squire Hoar thought differently and had his way because he put up the money for Alcott's tax, acting on his own responsibility. Governments would suffer more for their sins if it were not for men like Squire Hoar, and so would idealists like Bronson Alcott.

"I suppose they have told you," Henry Thoreau wrote to Emerson, "how near Mr. Alcott went to jail, but I can add a good anecdote to the rest. When Staples came to collect Mrs. Ward's taxes, my sister Helen asked him what he thought Mr. Alcott meant—what his idea was—and he answered, 'I vum, I believe it was nothing but principle, for I never heerd a man talk honester.'

"There was a lecture on Peace by a Mr. Spear (ought he not to be beaten into a ploughshare?), the same evening, and, as the gentlemen, Lane and Alcott, dined at our house while the matter was in suspense, that is, while the constable was waiting for his receipt from the jailer—we there settled it that we, Lane and myself, perhaps, should agitate the State while Winkelried lay in durance. But when, over the audience, I saw our hero's head moving in the free air of the Universalist Church, my fire all went out, and the State was safe as far as I was concerned."

Winkelried, whose name and mantle Henry thus bestowed on Alcott, was a Swiss hero of warfare against the Austrians in 1386 when, according to the legend, he gathered all the enemy spears within reach on his own breast and, falling dead, left a breach through which the Swiss rushed to victory. But posterity, or some of it, raised doubts at the tales of Winkelried's exploit with something of the spirit adopted by Henry in making Winkelried an Alcottian character and vice versa.

The tax incident carried a larger significance because it stood as a sort of preliminary for Henry's own defiance of the same tax collector later on. Alcott, after this one episode, was out of the lists for good, some of his respectable relatives promptly arranging to remit directly any of his obligations to the state that he might default on. Vainly he was to plead after this for the privilege of nonpayment of taxes.

Likewise significant here was the part played by Sam Staples, not native-born to Concord but a man on the make in business and public life there. Who had performed Sam's wedding ceremony a few years ago but Emerson, and who had officiated as witness on that occasion but Alcott! In his time Sam Staples was to be auctioneer, real-estate dealer, constable, jailer, deputy sheriff, farmer of sorts, representative in the General Court, and man of property. Incidentally, he was also to carry the rod for Henry Thoreau on certain surveying trips.

Who was the more important man in Concord—Sam Staples or Emerson? Posterity would give one answer, but the ordinary people of Concord might have given another. The really important personage at the time, of course, was Squire Hoar—no room for argument there.

Sam Staples himself remarked, "I suppose there's a great many things that Mr. Emerson knows that I couldn't understand, but I *know* that there's a damn sight of things that I know that he don't know anything about." Such a note of pride and confidence goes into the thinking of the common people always, especially when encouraged by those who can make capital of it.

While Emerson was away lecturing, Alcott held "conversations" in his house, and of course Henry Thoreau was present. Lidian wrote to her husband about one of these occasions on which "Love of Nature" was a topic. Henry, of course, spoke for the love of nature, supported by Elizabeth Hoar and Lidian, though Lidian admitted a lack of experience in the larger outdoors. Mr. Lane, Alcott's Englishman, on the other hand, asserted that love of nature was "the most subtle and dangerous of sins, a refined idolatry . . . because the gross sinner would be alarmed by the depth of his degradation, and come up from it in terror, but the unhappy idolaters of nature were deceived by the refined quality of their sin and would be the last to enter the kingdom."

Henry said, in effect, that Alcott and Lane did not know what they were talking about, and their ignorance of nature was so complete that they could hardly have any worth-while opinion on the matter. Mr. Alcott conceded his own shortcomings in respect to nature but asserted that he and Lane were beyond material things, filled to the ears with spiritual love and perception, whereas Henry was bogged down in Concord's swamps.

To Lidian the scene was comic. She wrote to Emerson, "Henry was brave and noble. Well as I have always liked him, he still grows upon me."

Emerson was back in Concord by March, in time to meet a crisis in the affairs of *The Dial*, now reduced in circulation to 220 subscribers in spite of Margaret Fuller's consecrated efforts of editorship. She had made so great a commitment of faith, time, and energy to the magazine that Emerson determined to keep it going for one more year at least. He called on Henry for proofreading and other duties, even to the soliciting of subscriptions.

Of far greater importance, however, representing a new forward mark in the world of letters for Henry Thoreau, was the fact that he was entrusted with the editing of the April issue. Not only this, but now came the chance for firsthand acquaintanceship with publishing circles in New York.

Emerson, it is supposed, had concluded that Henry should go onward and upward. On Emerson's motion, then, brother William who lived on Staten Island, wrote to propose that young Thoreau join his household as tutor. The correspondence was conducted on the Concord side by Emerson himself, who wrote that Henry was interested in becoming an active influence for a boy "not yet subdued by schoolmasters" and would go to the woods with his pupil as well as instruct him in grammar and geography. William's offer included board and lodging, a room by himself, and a hundred dollars for the year. Emerson, turning bargainer, wrote that Henry felt he ought to make some money beyond his expenses; more likely, Emerson felt so. He wrote that Henry's health was not up to manual labor.

The matter of a separate room was vital. Young Thoreau must be autocrat of a chamber, even one six by six, where he would study, dream, write, and declaim alone. "Henry has always had it & always must. He can very well sleep all year without fire in his apartment."

The arrangements were made, and at the beginning of April Henry wrote to Dick Fuller, "I expect to leave Concord, which is my Rome, and its people, who are my Romans, in May and go to New York."

Hawthorne was witness to the preparations: ". . . I was interrupted by a visit from Mr. Thoreau, who came to return a book, and to announce his purpose of going to reside on Staten Island. . . . We had some conversation upon this subject, and upon the spiritual advantages of change of place, and upon the Dial, and upon Mr. Alcott, and other kindred or concatenated subjects. I am glad, on Mr. Thoreau's account, that he is going away, as he is out of health, and may be benefited by his removal; but, on my account, I should like to have him remain here, he being one of the few persons, I think, with whom to hold intercourse is like hearing the wind among the boughs of a forest-tree; and with all this wild freedom, there is high and classic cultivation in him too. . . ."

Henry left at the Old Manse his music box, the gift of Dick Fuller, of which he was fond, and in a day or two Hawthorne was noting, "Many times I wound and re-wound Mr. Thoreau's little musical-box; but certainly its peculiar sweetness had evaporated, and I am pretty sure that I should throw it out of the window were I doomed to hear it long and often. It has not an infinite soul."

The owner of the music box had supposed differently, but he lived at a more deliberate pace and was slow to exhaust the possibilities of experienced things.

Emerson recorded in his journal these words: "And now goes our brave youth into the new home, the new connexion, the new city." The shift of direction was an extreme one for Henry, yet the lodge on the southern slope of some hill, of which he had dreamed, lay still within the shadow of a larger vision. Henry had realized that a man in this life had not everything to do, but something. William Emerson was warned that the new tutor might pester him with "some accidental crochets and perhaps a village exaggeration of the value of facts."

4

"I DO NOT LIKE THEIR CITIES"

❦

1. *Hunger of the Heart*

HENRY THOREAU reached New York on a vessel that "curtseyed up to a wharf just the other side of their Castle Garden," and the first demand the city made of him was whether he wanted a cab. He did not, but he was soon aware of other demands that the city could not supply on any terms.

He settled into the household of the William Emersons, explored Staten Island, found its highest hills, walked its beaches, talked with its salty, home-abiding fishermen. During the early part of his stay he was troubled by a cold which seemed to develop into bronchitis. He wrote to his mother that he had not taken cold entirely from imprudence but more likely from the process of acclimatization. After a while he was better again.

Here was no Concord, though he responded to much that was new and stimulating, especially the sea, least of all in any affirmative way to the great city so close at hand. He found it "rather derogatory that your dwelling place should be only a neighborhood" to such a hive—"to live on an inclined plane.

I do not like their cities and forts, with their morning and evening guns, and sails flapping in one's eye. I want a whole continent to breathe in, and a good deal of solitude and silence, such as Wall Street cannot buy—nor Broadway with its wooden pavement. I must live along the beach, on the southern shore, which looks directly out to sea, and see what the great parade of water means, that dashes and roars, and has not yet wet me, as long as I have lived."

Elizabeth Hoar had given him an inkstand as a farewell present, and he used it in writing his letters home. Her note with the gift illumines the relationship between these two Concord-born, Elizabeth some three years older than himself, both dwellers in the twin spheres of the town, sharing one community with the old Squire, Sam Staples, Dr. Bartlett and the rest, and another with Emerson, Alcott, Hawthorne, Channing. Alcott said that Henry was the Concord aborigine, therefore Elizabeth was also, since she was the same as he in this respect.

She had written: "Dear Henry—The rain prevented me from seeing you the night before I came away, to leave with you a parting assurance of good will and good hope. We have become better acquainted within the past two years than in our whole life as schoolmates and neighbors before; and I am unwilling to let you go away without telling you that I, among your other friends, shall miss you much, and follow you with remembrance and all best wishes and confidence. Will you take this little inkstand and try if it will carry ink safely from Concord to Staten Island? and the pen, which, if you can write with steel, may be made many times the interpreter of friendly thoughts to those whom you leave beyond the reach of your voice."

With a Greek phrase she bade him farewell and signed herself, "Truly your friend, E. Hoar."

Whatever pen Henry wrote with now was fluid with much

homesickness and heart hunger. He showed no antagonism, no
cross-grain. In later years, on some far different occasion, he
could wonder what demon possessed him that he behaved so
well, but now his tenderness was free and unfeigned. To Lidian
he wrote in more than friendship.

"My Dear Friend—I believe a good many conversations with
you were left in an unfinished state, and now indeed I don't
know where to take them up. But I will resume some of the un-
finished silence. I shall not hesitate to know you. I think of you
as some elder sister of mine, whom I could not have avoided—
a sort of lunar influence—only of such age as the moon, whose
time is measured by her light. You must know that you repre-
sent to me woman, for I have not traveled very far or wide—
and what if I had? . . . I thank you for your influence for two
years. I was fortunate to be subjected to it, and am now to
remember it. . . . Your moonlight, as I have told you, though
it is a reflection of the sun, allows of bats and owls and other
twilight birds to flit therein. But I am very glad that you can
elevate your life with a doubt, for I am sure that it is nothing
but an insatiable faith after all that deepens and darkens its
current. And your doubt and my confidence are only a difference of expression. . . ."

This reached Lidian in Concord as a proper, suitable letter,
one that she could—and did—show her husband, yet she must
have known how truly Henry wrote with mind and heart alike.
The phrases of the heart were such as any woman might prize
coming from any man who loved her much. All the more
should Lidian prize them who had from her husband literary
letters that were of the mind only.

In June Henry wrote to her again, and now Lidian was "My
Very Dear Friend."

"I have only read a page of your letter, and have come out
to the top of the hill at sunset, where I can see the ocean, to
prepare to read the rest. It is fitter that it should hear it than

the walls of my chamber. The very crickets here seem to chirp around me as they did not before. I feel as if it were a great daring to go on and read the rest, and then to live accordingly. There are more than thirty vessels in sight going to sea. I am almost afraid to look at your letter. I see that it will make my life very steep, but it may lead to fairer prospects than this.

"You seem to speak out of a very clear and high heaven, where any one may be who stands so high. Your voice seems not a voice, but comes as much from the blue heavens as from the paper. . . ."

So the words came as he sat, deeply moved, on the hilltop overlooking the ocean beyond and something of an ocean within himself as well. Back in Concord Lidian mentioned to Mrs. Thoreau that she had received two or three letters from Henry. Eagerly and with characteristic family possessiveness, Henry's mother wished to see what he had written. Lidian, according to her husband, was almost ashamed to show the letters because "Henry had exalted her by very undeserved praise"—a proper explanation though hardly a complete one— and Mrs. Thoreau replied, "Oh, yes, Henry is very tolerant."

Apart from this strain of rare and singing music for Lidian, Henry had more forthright feelings and observations to write about. "Am I not made of Concord dust?" he asked rhetorically. "I cannot realize that it is the roar of the sea I hear now, and not the wind in Walden woods."

"In New York," he reported to Emerson, "everything disappoints me but the crowd; rather, I was disappointed with the rest before I came. . . ." And in another letter: "I don't like the city better, the more I see it, but worse. I am ashamed of my eyes that behold it. It is a thousand times meaner than I could have imagined. It will be something to hate—that's the advantage it will be to me. . . . When will the world learn that a million men are of no importance compared with *one* man?"

Here was a stumper for old Concord, which would gladly

have become a great city if it could—another of Henry Thoreau's queer sayings, a turning of ordinary things backside to. Any storekeeper, any hewer of wood or digger of earth knew that a million of anything must be worth more than one; mortal accounts, whether kept on a slate or in a neatly ruled book, or in the head, proved their view to an unmistakable end. But Henry was thinking of immortal accounts, and not thinking in a dry rut; he was seeing, feeling, rebelling against the suffocation of himself, of the one man. As he was one man, so was any other of the million, one only, one always, not to be multiplied, lumped, or included.

Men were not made for wholesale lots. The dignity and spirit of man could not be diminished by putting him in a herd; the herd still remained less, the man remained more. So at the age of twenty-six Henry held to this life's truth and stated the challenge of it in his letter to Emerson; and as long as he lived he saw the right and condition of man no differently.

Yet, having no eyes for the churches of New York and most else that the city bragged about, he saw the crowd with respect. "The crowd is something new and to be attended to. It is worth a thousand Trinity Churches and Exchanges while it is looking at them, and will run over them and trample them under foot one day."

In the way of sight-seeing in New York, Henry visited that astonishing vessel, the *Great Western*, the Croton waterworks, and the picture gallery of the National Academy of Design. For reading and not for sight-seeing he found his way to the Society Library and Mercantile Library and was allowed to borrow hard-to-take-out books.

He wrote to his father and mother that New York was large enough already "and they intend it shall be larger still. Fifteenth Street, where some of my new acquaintances live, is two or three miles from the Battery, where the boat touches—clear brick and stone, and no 'give' to the foot; and they have laid

out, though not built, up to the 149th street above. I had rather
see a brick for a specimen, for my part, such as they exhibited
in old times."

He would have preferred to be in Walden woods with his
mother, but not, preferably, with the new railroad touching
the pond. "I think of you all very often. . . . This life we live
is a strange dream, and I don't believe at all any account men
give of it. Methinks I should be content to sit at the back-door
in Concord, under the poplar tree, henceforth forever."

He imagined the household of his parents on a Sunday evening and so made it possible to posterity to look over his shoulder long afterward: his mother would be "poring over some
select book, almost transcendental, perchance, or else 'Burgh's
Dignity,' or Massilon, or the 'Christian Examiner.' Father has
just taken one more look at the garden, and is now absorbed in
Chaptelle, or reading the newspaper quite abstractedly, only
looking up occasionally over his spectacles to see how the rest
are engaged, and not to miss any newer news that may not be
in the paper. Helen has slipped in for the fourth time to learn
the very latest item. Sophia, I suppose, is at Bangor; but Aunt
Louisa, without doubt, is just flitting away to some good meeting, to save the credit of you all."

When they wrote him that Daniel Webster had been in Concord, Henry replied: ". . . I suppose the town shook, every step
he took. But I trust there were some Concordians who were not
tumbled down by the jar, but represented still the upright
town. Where was George Minott? he would not have gone far
to see him. Uncle Charles should have been there—he might as
well have been catching cat naps in Concord as anywhere.

"And then, what a whetter-up of his memory this event
would have been! You'd have had all the classmates again in
alphabetical order reversed—'and Seth Hunt and Bob Smith—
and he was a student of my father's—and where's Put now? and
I wonder—you—if Henry's been to see George Jones yet! A

little account with Stow—Balcom—Bigelow, poor miserable
t-o-a-d—(sound asleep). I vow, you—what noise was that?—
saving grace—and few there be—That's clear as preaching—
Easter Brooks—morally depraved—How charming is divine
philosophy—some wise and some otherwise—Heighho! (sound
asleep again) Webster's a smart fellow—bears his age well—
how old should you think he was? you—does he look as if he
were ten years younger than I?' "

So ran Henry's imagined discourse and napping of his Uncle
Charles, a bit more jumbled now than it must have seemed then,
but still an eloquent sample of how things went when Uncle
Charles was around.

To his sister Helen, Henry sent a poem he had written some
time before about John, the lost brother, but had not shown to
the family. Two of the stanzas were:

> Brother, where dost thou dwell?
>   What sun shines for thee now?
> Dost thou indeed fare well
>   As we wished here below? ...
>
> Dost thou still haunt the brink
>   Of yonder river's tide?
> And may I ever think
>   That thou art by my side?

2. *Literary Quest*

Little as Henry liked New York, the great city, he found it
the hunting ground for a hopeful writer that he had imagined
and that Emerson had said it would be. He made the rounds
of all the bookstores and publishers and "discussed their affairs
with them." At Little & Brown's he saw a customer buy a copy
of Ellery Channing's poems.

He conversed with the Harpers, "to see if they might not
find me useful to them; but they say they are making $50,000

annually, and their motto is to let well alone. I find that I talk with these poor men as if I were over head and ears in business, and a few thousands were no consideration with me. I almost reproach myself for bothering them so to no purpose; but it is a very valuable experience, and the best introduction I could have had."

Henry was, to be sure, in the right place to meet publishers and to discuss books, but his difficulty was that it turned out to be all hunting and next to no quarry bagged at the end of a day. He sold a piece or two to the *Democratic Review*, whose editor, O'Donnell, he had met at Hawthorne's in Concord. When his sister Helen reproached him for not sending her a copy of the *Review* containing his essay, he replied that he did not have one to send, nor was it worth fifty cents to buy.

"Literature comes to a poor market here," Henry wrote to Emerson in September, "and even the little that I write is more than will sell. I have tried 'The Dem. Review,' 'The New Mirror,' and 'Brother Jonathan.' The last two, as well as 'New World,' are overwhelmed with contributions which cost nothing and are worth no more. . . ."

And to his mother: "As for El Dorado, that is far off yet. My bait will not tempt the rats—they are too well fed. . . . They say there is a 'Lady's Companion' that pays—but I could not write anything companionable."

During the summer on Staten Island, Henry had finished writing a paper in which he described a winter walk at Concord, and this he submitted to Emerson for *The Dial*. After misgivings and revision, to which Henry assented, the piece went along to the printer. But Emerson charged Henry with the fault of mannerism for calling "a cold place sultry, a solitude public, a wilderness *domestic* (a favorite word), and in the woods to insult over cities, armies, etc."

It was useless to try to cure Henry of such methods of expression, and Emerson was still dwelling on the subject, sadly, in a funeral oration after Henry was dead. Some problems had to be solved in a writer's own way. Henry knew that you could go only halfway into an experience and then you were coming out on the farther side—the same thing happened when you went into the woods. There was always something deeper and more significant than an initial experience, a greater and richer intensity perhaps, or a change in the orientation of the observer.

Emerson might at least have smelled Henry's meaning, or heard it sigh past his ears like a breath of wind, or seen it in the transparency of sunlight at certain times on breathless, indulgent days in Concord.

Despite his criticism, Emerson liked some things about "A Winter Walk," especially the sketch of a pickerel fisherman who stood "his lines set in some retired cove, like a Finlander, with his arms thrust into the pouches of his dreadnought; with dull, snowy, fishy thoughts, himself a finless fish, separated a few inches from his race; dumb, erect, and made to be enveloped in clouds and snows, like the pines on the shore."

Publication of this essay would be progress, but Henry had not yet been paid by the Boston *Miscellany* for "A Walk to Wachusett" and was asking Emerson to help get his money.

Always, of course, amid literary questing and all else that filled his days, Henry was remembering Concord.

"I am pleased to think of Channing as an inhabitant of the gray town. Seven cities contended for Homer dead. Tell him to remain at least long enough to establish Concord's right and interest in him. I was beginning to know the man. . . . And Hawthorne, too, I remember as one with whom I sauntered in old heroic times, along the banks of the Scamander, amid the ruins of chariots and heroes. Tell him not to desert, even after the tenth year. Others may say, 'Are there not the cities of Asia?' But where are they? Staying at home is the heavenly way."

At about this time Hawthorne, in Concord, was taking a solitary walk to Walden Pond, admiring the scenery and getting lost, so that when he started home he was really heading toward Boston instead. At length a signboard corrected his geography, he accepted a lift, and was set down in Concord village by a friendly farmer.

3. *Greeley and the Great Ones*

At appropriate times, Henry presented various letters of introduction given to him by Emerson. Thus he met Henry James the elder, father of the future philosopher and the future novelist, and felt that James humanized the city for him. Their first interview lengthened into three hours of solid talk, much of it about Carlyle and transcendentalism. James asked the young man from Concord to make free use of his house.

Ellery Channing, who met James a year later, described him in a letter to Henry as "a little fat, rosy Swedenborgian amateur, with the look of a broker, and the brains and heart of a Pascal." Pascal had been known as an exalter of mysticism. In any case, Henry James was a theologian having trouble with his thoughts and looking to Emerson to help straighten them out. Years afterward, in Concord, he and Henry exchanged compliments of a different kind.

Now, in New York, Henry Thoreau's real and lasting prize was friendship with Horace Greeley, just turned thirty-two, and riding into influence and position with the *Tribune*, which he had been editing with increasing success for two years. Henry described Greeley as "a hearty New Hampshire boy." How countrified must any man have been in order to earn this comment from the youth of the Concord woods?

"Now be neighborly," Greeley said, and meant it.

He was much occupied at the time with the Sylvania Association, an ideal community projected in Pennsylvania, and a similar association planned for New Jersey. Both were the outgrowth of Fourierism, one of the schools of a more general socialism.

Charles Fourier had adduced in his native France the notion of "attractive industry," basis of a sort of social organization in which men would perform the work they liked. Fourier's society was intended to be largely agricultural, arranged systematically in social units known as phalanxes, each accommodating 1,620 persons who would divide the necessary or suitable work according to their inclinations.

Fourierism had affected Brook Farm and likewise the current venture of Bronson Alcott and his English friend Lane. While Henry Thoreau was in New York, these two were off to a place they had bought near Harvard, Massachusetts, christened Fruitlands. From Alcott's point of view, farm animals were entitled to the fruits of their labor just as humans were, and at Fruitlands, his ideal community, a good deal of labor ordinarily performed by animals was therefore done by the members of the colony. Perhaps the fact that Alcott did not like or trust farm animals had something to do with this; he liked only vegetables, and liked vegetables with deep and warm affection, appreciating their fine qualities. So long as summer lasted, affairs at Fruitlands flourished.

Another of the Fourierists was Albert Brisbane, father of a widely known Hearst newspaper columnist and editor of the future, and Greeley had turned over to him a column in the *Tribune*. But Henry Thoreau did not like Brisbane much; the man looked as if he had lived in a cellar.

On the steps of the Society library, Henry met Ellery Channing's cousin, Reverend W. H. Channing, and described him as "a concave man"—"you see by his attitude and the lines of his face that he is retreating from himself and yourself with sad doubts."

Much more impressive was a different sort of preacher, Lucretia Mott, of Nantucket background, crusader against slavery, exponent of women's rights. The Quaker meeting in Hester Street picked up slowly through a long period of silence and brooding of the Spirit. At last Lucretia Mott "rose, took off her bonnet, and began to utter very deliberately what the Spirit suggested. Her self-possession was something to see, if all else failed; but it did not. Her subject was, 'The Abuse of the Bible,' and thence she straightway digressed to slavery and the degradation of woman. It was a good speech—transcendentalism in its mildest form. She sat down at length, and, after a long and decorous silence, in which some seemed to be really digesting her words, the elders shook hands, and the meeting dispersed."

One interesting personage, an old friend now, came for a visit with the William Emersons—Margaret Fuller, batting her eyes and full of high discourse. She and Henry drove out to one of the Staten Island forts, and she was so absorbed that she forgot to pay the driver; she sent the money to Henry later. It was likely she felt more warmly toward Henry than Emerson had thought.

With such impressions and indeterminate results, Henry's New York adventure wore on and reached its end. He was surely the gainer though there was no El Dorado—as, indeed, he had really known all along. Among the various opportunities, great and small, that the city offered, he had grasped one by purchasing a pair of pants, ready-made, for $2.25, and was now glad to wear them back to Concord, where he would be making pencils in his father's shop.

5

LIVING IS SO DEAR

৺ঌ ৡঌ

1. *Concord in the Sun*

HERE WAS Concord again, working the round of seasons in field or shop, idling in the post office while waiting for the mail, talking politics, walking out to church or to the lyceum, treasuring its currency of gossip. Concord had missed Henry Thoreau truly enough in one sense; yet it had been complete without him, and nobody had to move over to make more room when he arrived again from New York.

Lidian of the smooth-brushed hair and contemplative eyes, Lidian who was real enough as a mother but shadowy as a wife, and withal a perennial invalid, was far advanced in pregnancy. Her husband was occupied with his usual round of walking, correspondence, writing of essays, and readying a new volume for publication. He had bought apples from Hawthorne and paid Channing to chop wood, but neither of these maladjusted souls was doing well in worldly terms. Hawthorne found difficulty in meeting the rent for the Old Manse, did not meet it in fact, and Channing, who wanted to practice poetry as some men practiced law, making it a pure and sufficiently gainful profession, brimmed with discontent.

Bronson Alcott was still at Fruitlands, as yet unnipped by

the approaching inevitable frost. He and Channing, if things had been arranged a little differently, might have made good characters for Dickens, a degree or two removed from life. The fore part of Alcott's head was bald, the after part draped with straggling locks, his eyebrows furzing, lips and cheeks both full. His schoolmasterish face expressed zeal and mellowish idealism, but its look was not wind-swept and keen like Emerson's. As for Channing, he presented a countenance from which the hair would recede more and more, eyebrows poised upward, eyes lighted with bland, upward expectation also, as if to see what was not there for most other people. Channing, though, possessed humor; he was an incubator of wit. Both he and Alcott had the most beneficent blemishes to their characters.

Margaret Fuller, as intense as ever, perhaps more intense, alive with ideas, had watched *The Dial* die, but its ending by now had passed into acceptance and resignation. Emerson helped her find a publisher for a fresh manuscript, *Summer on the Lakes in 1843,* that would presently attract Horace Greeley's attention.

Henry Thoreau, home again, resumed an old life in the household of his parents amid the same stir of relatives and boarders so familiar to him in other times. But the household was about to be removed physically from the center of town to a site beyond the railroad track in a district known as Texas, perhaps because of its apparent remoteness in Concord's terms of compact geography and compact viewpoint. Henry was soon engaged in digging the cellar and stoning the foundation walls for the new house.

Some say it was Henry who designed the Texas house and made of it a plain, ungracious box, with pencil shed attached. His theory of architecture was different, at any rate, for once he argued with Emerson that architectural beauty should grow from within outward, "out of the character and necessities of the indweller and builder, without even a thought for mere ornament, but an unconscious nobleness and truthfulness of character and life. . . ." This should have produced a comely homestead; but Henry did better when he planted syringas—the old-fashioned bridal wreaths, grapevines, and apple trees.

Besides pencil-making and house-building, he found time for his old walks and projects of observation and contemplation. That summer he was to set out with Ellery Channing for an expedition to the Hoosacs and the Catskills, but a briefer journey in early April proved more eventful.

2. *That Fire at Fair Haven*

With Edward Hoar, Elizabeth's younger brother who was then a student at Harvard, Henry set out by boat to visit the headwaters of the Concord River—an enterprise that would require camping at night and catching fish for provender.

"At the shoemaker's near the river, we obtained a match, which we had forgotten. . . ."

That match was important. Notwithstanding the season, the river happened to be low, since rain had fallen only lightly, and the voyagers readily caught a mess of fish before they were out of town. Then they stopped on the shore of Fair Haven to cook their dinner.

As Henry recorded long afterward, "The earth was uncommonly dry, and our fire, kindled far from the woods in a sunny recess in the hillside on the east of the pond, suddenly caught the dry grass of the previous year which grew about the stump on which it was kindled."

Henry was a discreet and experienced outdoorsman, but now he found himself in the plight of many a novice. He and Edward fought the spreading fire quickly with hands and feet, then with boards from their boat, but almost at the beginning it was clear that a conflagration was in the making; no matter what efforts they might exert, the event was beyond them.

"Well, where will this end?" asked Edward, no doubt panting.

Well Meadow Brook would be a barrier on one side, Henry realized, but he saw nothing to check the fire on the other. "It will go to town," he said.

Edward took the boat back down the river and Henry ran through the woods to give the alarm to owners of the land and in the town. The flames crackled, leaped wildly, kept spreading fanwise into the woods. Making all the haste he could, Henry came up with a farmer who asked where the smoke was rising from. When he was told, he remarked,"Well, it's none of my stuff," and drove on with a gesture of indifference he regretted later when the fire caught the wood he had cut and corded that winter.

Henry ran two miles without pausing save momentarily, and found the owner of the burning woodland in a field. The owner and two or three other men who joined him hurried back with Henry to look the situation over. There was no comfort in it. The only thing to do was to turn out the men of the town for a major effort; but Henry, who was spent with running, remained at the scene.

"What could I do alone against a front of flame half a mile wide?" Until now he had been a guilty person, overwhelmed with shame, regret, and apprehension. He walked slowly to Fair Haven Cliff, climbed to the highest rock, and sat down to watch the fire he had set loose in his beloved countryside. Flames licked upward now a mile from where they had started. The sound of the bell came faintly from Concord, and Henry knew the town was turning out. Taking council with himself, he decided that this fire might have been set by lightning, and the chance that, instead, he and Edward Hoar had caused it was just that—a chance and not a matter of moral responsibility.

Having come to this conclusion, as he wrote in his journal later, he looked on the rest of the fire as a glorious spectacle.

"It burned over a hundred acres or more and destroyed much young wood. When I returned home late in the day, with others of my townsmen, I could not help noticing that the crowd who were so ready to condemn the individual who had kindled the fire did not sympathize with the owners of the wood, but were in fact highly elate and as it were thankful for the opportunity which had afforded them so much sport; and it was only half a dozen owners, so called, though not all of them, who looked sour or grieved, and I felt I had a deeper interest in the woods, knew them better and should feel their loss more, than any or all of them. The farmer whom I had first conducted to the woods was obliged to ask me the shortest way back, through his own lot."

This was in the spring of 1844. Not until 1850 did Henry record his account of the fire in his journal. It could not have been an easy subject to come to. At last he wrote: "It has never troubled me from that day to this more than if the lightning had done it. The trivial fishing was all that disturbed me and disturbs me still."

So he wrote, and in a sense he wrote truly, for he had been guiltless of any intent or even of carelessness as men and boys outdoors are usually careless. But there remained the loss of the woods, and that he did mind deeply, even though in 1844 the railroad began running past Walden Pond, and the locomotive's sparks were to burn over nearly all the same ground and more too.

Some thought that but for his companion, the son of Squire Hoar, Henry would have been prosecuted for setting the fire; yet it was never the custom in New England towns to take men or boys to court for setting such fires out of doors. Talk, yes; action, no. But much of Concord imposed its own penalty of resentment against Henry through long years.

The fire, of course, was only an aside, an excursion in the irony of chance and the times. Pencil-making occupied a good deal of Henry's earnest attention, and this went well. For the production of pencils, graphite had been mixed with spermaceti or bayberry wax, which produced an indifferent result as compared with foreign pencils. The Thoreaus began to use clay, as was done abroad, and Henry has been credited generally with the skill and initiative which brought so much success that experts in Boston said his pencils were equal to any made in London.

When Concord friends congratulated him on having opened a new way to fortune, Henry stated bluntly that he intended to make no more pencils. "Why should I? I would not do again what I have done once."

He made his meaning clear, and it was a good meaning. But he did turn out many more pencils. To his ingenuity also is attributed much of the Thoreau success in developing a new process for refining graphite. A narrow, churnlike chamber was provided for grinding the graphite, and a box above was fitted with a sort of shelf on which the finest, smoothest dust was caught. This remained a secret process and worked to the advantage of the family business, not alone so far as pencils were concerned but especially for the supplying of graphite—plumbago, as it was called—for the new process of electrotyping that came in during the late Forties and increased rapidly in importance.

As he was handy man in the household, so he might have been a native genius in certain kinds of industry that demanded the same resourcefulness. Emerson was impressed with many of his practical skills: he could pace sixteen rods as accurately as another man could measure that distance; he could gauge heights, weights, sizes with a quick glance. He knew that sound acorns would sink in water just as he knew that the blossom of the skunk cabbage usually opens toward the south—but the fact that some information had useful applications seldom led him to prize it more than other information having none.

3. *A Bell Is Rung, a Voice Raised*

In July 1844 Emerson's second son was born, an event that gave him much happiness; but unceasingly the problems of the greater world pressed for his attention. As to slavery, an issue of issues, his attitude had been less than forthright. Once he remarked to Elizabeth Hoar that he disliked dogmatism in reform as much as in conservatism. He particularly admired her father's support of the existing social order—yet the old squire had enough of the firebrand in him when he was roused.

Emerson would not be a man "to prescribe laws for nations and humanity before we have said our own prayers or yet heard the benediction which love and peace sing in our bosom"; yet his conscience was drawn inexorably to "that hapless class who see the faults and sins of our social order, and who pray and strive incessantly to right the wrong."

For such people as dwelt in Concord to keep slaves would be intolerably evil, Emerson believed, but for a Southern planter slaveholding might "indicate only a degree of self-indulgence which we may parallel readily enough nearer home." When a Northerner attacked the Southerner, was he not demanding of his neighbor a superiority to conditions that he did not demand of himself?

This sounded well, but it left out of consideration the point of view of the slave who was concerned not with any kind of self-indulgence but with the right of a man to be free. For a while Emerson seemed to attach some responsibility, even some sin, to the slave himself for his condition. But now, in this humming, drowsy summer, Mrs. Mary Merrick Brooks, president of the Anti-Slavery Society of Concord, asked Emerson to deliver an address on the occasion of the anniversary of West Indian emancipation. Though until now he had kept aloof from agitating abolitionists and politicians of reform, he was moved to comply.

None of the Concord ministers, however, would open their churches for the purpose, and the selectmen withheld permission for use of the town hall. Respectability mumbled. We don't want a lot of agitating and trouble around here, people said. Freedom once had been quite the thing in Concord, but times had changed.

In this emergency, a man without timidity and whose belief in liberty was without qualification stepped forward. He was, of course, Henry Thoreau. He cared nothing for what was on paper unless it was ratified by nature, and he was ready for any dogmatism that he believed a just one. Henry, acting as chore man and something more, arranged for the use of the old courthouse and himself pulled the rope and rang the bell to attract an audience.

Henry and Emerson and the peal of the bell were in tune, their vibrations ringing out truly on the breezes of Concord town. As for the address of the day, Emerson said exactly what the cautious, pusillanimous, and conservative had most feared; his commitment, at least the essence of it, was unreserved: "The civility of no world can be perfect while another race is degraded; . . . the might and right are here: . . . here is man: and if you have man, black or white is an insignificance."

The heavens did not fall.

Emerson had alluded to the encroachments of the South in searching and making seizures on New England ships, a practice that infuriated many Northerners more than the matter of slavery itself. When November came, Squire Hoar, newly resigned from the school committee, decided to go south to winter in a gentler climate, and took his daughter Elizabeth with him. Disembarking at Charleston, he was announced as official delegate from the Commonwealth of Massachusetts to confer with the government of South Carolina over the question of slaves, or those presumed to be slaves, being taken from Massachusetts ships.

This was enough for Charleston. Squire Hoar was advised to look after his own safety and his daughter's. He declined the suggestion, even though it was repeated and emphasized in various ways; only in the face of imminent violence did he consent to withdraw. So, as the year ended, he and Elizabeth were at home again in the same old climate, but with a tale that added a good deal of heat of its own. For the present there was a pause, but the chain of circumstances would soon go on again —and on.

In Concord then the usual change-abouts of the transcendentalists were taking place. Ellery Channing was off to join his sister-in-law, Margaret Fuller, on the editorial staff of Greeley's New York *Tribune*. Alcott arrived back from winter-blasted Fruitlands, his material fortunes as bleak as the frosted hills. And Emerson's new essays, published that October, were running their course through the cultural arteries of the Western world.

Henry Thoreau, to be sure, was in residence and was unlikely to call any other place than Concord his home ever again, but he felt far from settled. How long ago was it that he had written, "I want to go soon and live away by the pond"? The old dream pressed close. It was his great desire. "I will build my lodge on the southern slope of some hill, and take there the life the gods send me."

4. *To the Pond*

It was in the early spring of 1845 that Henry Thoreau began to build a hut in the woods beside Walden Pond for the purpose of going to live there alone. This was to be the great exploit of his life, though in some ordinary conversations it was nothing at all, even, if you liked to say so, a piece of shiftlessness. He was almost twenty-eight and already in default under most of the New England laws of thrift and consecrated toil.

Why did he want to go to the woods, as he called it? The trouble was that the answers were too many and too easy for Concord and for a good deal of posterity; after hearing them all, some minds still asked vainly for an explanation in words directed to their own practical understanding.

Walden had been in Henry Thoreau's blood since early childhood—"that woodland vision for a long time made the drapery of my dreams"—but did that account for the actions of a man approaching twenty-eight?

He had spoken of his desire, written of it in his journal, but that he should want to go was an explanation that did not explain. A letter of Ellery Channing's, though it was to be widely quoted down the years, remained cryptic to many and many a reader. Channing wrote from New York in March 1845: "My dear Thoreau—The handwriting of your letter is so miserable that I am not sure I have made it out. If I have, it seems to me you are the same old sixpence you used to be, rather rusty, but a genuine piece. I see nothing for you in this earth but that field which I once christened 'Briars'; go out upon that, build yourself a hut, and there begin the grand process of devouring yourself alive. I see no alternative, no other hope for you."

Ellery Channing himself, and Stearns Wheeler, Henry's Harvard classmate, had both tried the life of lonely huts, though briefly and as hardly more than boys. These were precedents, surely, but the real procession of precedents was of a grander sort and extended so far back that it was lost to sight in the mists of history. Some men in all ages and all regions had sought a hermitage in which to reflect and commune with nature.

Would this answer the questions as to Henry's reasons and intentions? Of course not. See him there, in his plain clothes, on his way to make pencils, or to shake down a fire, or carry out a hod of ashes.

Some said then and later that his real reason for going to the woods was to escape from too much family and too many boarders. That was an explanation that would certainly hold water. Perhaps, though, he merely wanted to write a book. He had more than one book to write.

Perhaps there was a reason that would not be spoken of publicly. Those who suspected this felt they had corroboration later when they read Henry's words: "I have thought that Walden Pond would be a good place for business, not solely on account of the railroad and the ice trade; it offers advantages which it may not be good policy to divulge; it is a good post and a good foundation." What did this mean if not that Henry was engaged in forwarding runaway slaves?

Inevitably Walden must be compared with Brook Farm and Fruitlands; they were surely part of the context of Henry's project, even though his procedure seemed to caricature all that the Brook Farmers and Alcottians had been so serious about. These others had solemn rules; Henry had none. He was colony enough all by himself, and what he meant to establish was more elusive than a finished blueprint for a new social order. He was concerned not with men but with man, and even his friends, most of them, did not discover just what he did at Walden that might prove something.

Sanborn—who knew Henry only later, and became one of his biographers—thought that he was registering a protest and that it was as ineffectual as any others of the time. A protest, perhaps, ineffectual, perhaps. Yet one could not be too sure. Better check over the things Henry might be protesting against, and make sure no seams had opened, and no insecurity developed around the foundations.

Henry believed that it was much easier for great expeditions to explore the Atlantic and Pacific than for one man to explore his private sea. He wrote in his journal and again in *Walden* that it was not worth while "to go round the world to count the cats in Zanzibar." Well, then, was he merging his private

sea with Walden Pond, and both with some symbol of the Atlantic and the Pacific and all the other oceans? If so, what did
this *mean* exactly? What could Henry Thoreau accomplish at
Walden that was more important, for instance, than counting
the cats in Zanzibar?

When all was said and done, though to be said over again to-
morrow, and again next month and next year, there was one
acceptable certainty: if opportunity could be counted as part
of his reason, Henry had found this opening neatly just at the
right time. Once again Emerson, philosopher of destinies, un-
latched a gate and held it open.

For Emerson had bought a tract of Walden field and woods.
His purchase came about by chance. Walking in the vicinity
of the pond, as he liked to do, he happened on two or three
men who were talking land, and one of them asked him to
make an offer for a field near the shore. Emerson had enjoyed
almost daily occupancy of these precincts for many years, as
he reflected, and it seemed only proper to back his interest with
money. So he bid for the field and bought it, eleven acres at
$8.10 an acre.

"The next day," as he wrote to his brother William, "I carried some of my well-beloved gossips to the place, and they deciding that the field was not good for anything if Heartwell
Bigelow should cut down his pine-grove, I bought, for $125
more, his pretty wood-lot of fourteen acres, more or less, on
the shore of Walden, and can raise my own blackberries."

Although Emerson referred to his investment as an absurdity,
he was obviously much pleased with himself about it; so, of
course, was Henry Thoreau. Henry later called himself a
squatter, meaning that he paid no rent, at least in money, but
he chose the site for his Walden hut with the owner's blessing
and free consent.

Emerson had, at considerable cost, sent Alcott to England
and was to send Channing to Italy, missions that produced no

world-shaking result. The expense of dispatching Henry Thoreau to Walden Pond was nothing at all out of pocket, and the harvest of this project proved historic and inestimable.

5. *The Hut*

"Near the end of March 1845 I borrowed an axe and went down to the woods by Walden Pond, nearest to where I intended to build my house, and began to cut down some tall arrowy white pines, still in their youth, for timber. . . ."

So runs the account in the book *Walden*, with simplicity and accuracy, adding no exaggeration to the facts. Some said the borrowed ax was Alcott's, but Channing wrote later that it was his.

"I hewed the main timbers six inches square, most of the studs on two sides only, and the rafters and floor timbers on one side, leaving the rest of the bark on. . . . Each stick was carefully mortised or tenoned by its stump, with borrowed tools."

The last of the winter ice remained in the pond when Henry began work. Many an early spring he was to write about in his journal, but this was one of the most memorable of all. He saw the gleam of the wet landscape and was on hand for the arrival and first singing of the birds. He watched a snake glide into the water and lie on the bottom, and with the coming of April he heard a goose cackling over the pond as if lost in the mist. He ate lunches of bread and butter flavored with pitch left on his hands by the morning labor, and when he was through for the day he walked homeward along the railroad track.

By the middle of April he had his house ready for raising and needed boards for roof and siding. Foreseeing the necessity, he had bought a shanty from James Collins, an Irishman who had worked on the new railroad—an exceptionally fine shanty, he called it. Henry knocked the boards apart, removed the nails, and carried his roof and siding by means of a cart and small loads to the site beside the pond.

He dug his cellar in two hours and did not trouble to stone the walls, leaving it as a sort of burrow. Then, "at length, at the beginning of May, with the help of some of my acquaintances, rather to improve so good an occasion for neighborliness than from necessity, I set up the frame of my house. No man was ever more honored in the character of his raisers than I."

Those who assisted were Alcott; George William Curtis of Harvard and Brook Farm, a future editor; and Edmund Hosmer, authentic Concordian and friend of Henry's, who could run a farm and at the same time mingle with the transcendentalists without mixing his seedings or harvests.

The hut was ten feet wide by fifteen feet long, with a large window at the side, a door at one end, and a brick fireplace at the other. Henry had brought stones from the pond and laid a foundation for his chimney, but waited until autumn to build it; the plastering was not done until fall, either. More urgent at the moment was the spring planting, and even before the house was finished Henry had put in about two and a half acres of beans.

For furniture he owned a bed, a table, a desk, three chairs, a looking glass three inches in diameter, a pair of tongs and andirons, a kettle, a skillet and a frying pan, a dipper, a wash bowl, two knives and forks, three plates, one cup, one spoon, a jug for oil, a jug for molasses, and a japanned lamp. The list is in *Walden*. A copy of Homer's *Iliad* he kept on his table all that first summer, but the outdoors claimed almost all his time and energy.

He wanted no more possessions. "Thank God, I can sit and I can stand without the aid of a furniture warehouse." When a woman offered him a mat he declined it, for "I had no room to spare within the house, nor time to spare within or without, to shake it." He preferred to wipe his feet on the sod before the hut door.

At last he wrote in his journal the words of an old dream fulfilled: "July 5. Saturday. Walden. Yesterday I came here to live. My house makes me think of some mountain houses I have seen, which seemed to have a fresher auroral atmosphere about them, as I fancy of the halls of Olympus."

The next day he wrote of his reason for coming to the pond —words that were to be amplified in *Walden* later, but the gist of it was here already: "I wish to meet the facts of life—the vital facts, which are the phenomena or actuality the gods meant to show us—face to face, and so I came down here. Life! Who knows what it is, what it does? If I am not quite right here, I am less wrong than before; and now let us see what they will have. . . ."

6. *To Live Sturdily*

"Still we live meanly like ants," Henry wrote in *Walden*. ". . . our life is frittered away by detail . . . simplicity, simplicity, simplicity! I say, let your affairs be as two or three, and not a hundred or a thousand; instead of a million, count half-a-dozen, and keep your accounts on your thumb nail. In the midst of this chopping sea of civilised life, such are the clouds and storms and quicksands and thousand-and-one items to be allowed for, that a man has to live, if he would not founder and go to the bottom and not make his port at all, by dead reckoning, and he must be a great calculator indeed who succeeds. Simplify, simplify."

Many readers made heavy work of this when they read it and thought about it, for surely there must be something deeper and cunningly elusive here, something requiring a good deal of learned interpretation. How difficult to understand that when Henry said "Simplify" he meant "Simplify."

Not that this was the whole story. "Let us spend one day as deliberately as Nature, and not be thrown off the track by every nutshell and mosquito's wing that falls on the rails. . . . If the engine whistles, let it whistle till it is hoarse for its pains. If the bell rings, why should we run?"

Let us, Henry suggested, settle ourselves "and work and wedge our feet downward through the mud and slush of opinion, and prejudice, and tradition, and delusion and appearance, that alluvion that covers the globe, through Paris and London, through New York and Boston and Concord, through church and state, through poetry, philosophy and religion, till we come to a hard bottom and rocks in place, which we can call *reality*. . . ."

Here was the elixir of Henry's exaggeration, certainly, and for that reason perhaps the more open to suspicion. What did he mean? Well, certainly he was not expecting to reach and define some universal, immovable reality for everyone, as some of the philosophers of all ages had done. He was expecting to find only something for himself, analogous to a goal all men might reach, and to demonstrate how this might be accomplished—not something rare and remote, but something alive and common, intelligible through experience, perception, thought.

Thus he recounted the substance of his afternoons away in the meadows occupied "in the well-nigh hopeless attempt to set the river on fire or be set on fire by it, with such tinder as I had, with such flint as I was. Trying at least to make it flow with milk and honey, as I had heard of, or liquid gold. . . ."

Concord men and boys enjoyed fishing in the river, and most of the townspeople liked an occasional summer picnic when the weather was right, but few of them had any tinder of the sort Henry meant, and little of that flint within themselves. How, then, could they attempt to kindle his kind of fire either at home or under the sky?

"So many autumn days spent outside the town, trying to hear what was in the wind, to hear it, and carry it express. . . ."

No time, then, for the things that New England thought important, even the expected cultural and intellectual voluntaries. Once, when he was living at home, Henry's Aunt Maria asked him to read the life of Dr. Chalmers, something he had no place for in the occupation of his hours, and later, on a Sunday, he heard her through the partition, shouting to Aunt Jane, who was deaf, "Think of it! He stood half an hour today to hear the frogs croak, and he wouldn't read the life of Dr. Chalmers!"

No matter what his aunts thought, or Concord, or whatever part of the outside world might learn of his venture, Henry settled in at his woodland retreat to please himself. Beside Walden he was at home as he had never been so far in all his years.

"It struck me again tonight, as if I had not seen it almost daily for twenty years—Why, here is Walden, the same woodland lake that I discovered so many years ago; where a forest was cut down last winter another is springing up by its shore as lustily as ever; the same thought is welling up to its surface that was then; it is the same liquid happiness to itself and its Maker, ay, and it *may* be to me. It is the work of a brave man surely, in whom there was no guile! He rounded this water with his hand, deepened and clarified it with his thought, and in his will bequeathed it to Concord. I see by its face that it is visited by the same reflection; and I can almost say, Walden, is it you?"

He swam in the pond in the early morning before breakfast, then, barefooted, hoed his beans—hoed them when the dew was still on the leaves, though farmers advised against it and said beans must be hoed only when the plants were dry. At noon he knocked off and usually bathed in the pond again, "swimming across one of its coves for a stint, and washed the dust of labor from my person, or smoothed out the last wrinkle which study had made, and for the afternoon was absolutely free."

His bean field that first season was too large to be hoed all at one period of labor, and woodchucks ate many of the plants so long as they remained tender. Henry was not dissatisfied on either score; he gave his beans no manure and hoed them unusually well as far as he went, enjoying his daily acquaintance with the weeds and the sound of a brown thrasher overhead.

"In my front yard grew the strawberry, blackberry, and life-everlasting, johnswort and goldenrod, shrub oaks and sand-cherry, blueberry and ground-nut—The sumach grew luxuriantly through the embankment which I had made. . . ."

On warm evenings he drifted in his boat on the pond, playing his flute. Or he walked along the shore and heard "the bull-frogs thump to usher in the night, and the note of the whippoorwill. . . . Sympathy with the fluttering alder and poplar leaves almost takes away my breath; yet, like the lake, my serenity is rippled, but not ruffled."

Sometimes he ranged the woods "like a half-starved hound, with a strange abandonment," loving the wild not less than the good. In the fall he went after wild grapes and chestnuts, and in winter he sought out the northeast slope of the pond where reflected sunlight from pitch pines and stony bank made a sort of fireside—leftover embers of summer, as he suggested.

Domestically, Henry experimented with the making of hoe-cakes and bread, and cooked such weeds as purslane, which he found a satisfactory meal. He found he could make a very good molasses from pumpkins or beets, but sweetening came yet more easily from the sap of the maples. He decided not to bother about salt, and would therefore drink less water.

His housework came under the heading of pastime. "When my floor was dirty, I rose early, and, setting all my furniture out of doors on the grass, bed and bedstead making one budget, dashed water on the floor, and sprinkled white sand from the pond on it, and then with a broom scrubbed it clean and white; and by the time the villagers had broken their fast the morning sun had dried my house sufficiently to allow me to move in again, and my meditations were almost uninterrupted. It was pleasant to see my whole household effects on the grass. . . . It was worth the while to see the sun shine on these things, and hear the free wind blow on them. . . ."

That first summer Henry had little time for reading. During the planting season he liked to eat his lunch beside a spring where, "in a very secluded and shaded spot, there was yet a clean firm sward to sit on. . . . Thither too the woodcock led her brood, to probe the mud for worms, flying but a foot above them down the bank, while they ran in a troop beneath; but at last, spying me, she would leave her young and circle round and round me, nearer and nearer till within four or five feet, pretending broken wings and legs, to attract my attention, and get off her young, who would already have taken up their march, with faint wiry peep, single file through the swamp, as she directed. Or I heard the peep of the young when I could not see the parent bird. There too the turtle-doves sat over the spring, or fluttered from bough to bough of the soft white-pines over my head; or the red squirrel, coursing down the nearest bough, was particularly familiar and inquisitive. You only need sit still long enough in some attractive spot in the woods that all its inhabitants may exhibit themselves to you by turns." Besides welcoming the companionship of the out-doors at these secluded luncheon periods, Henry would read a few pages, perhaps of the *Iliad*.

Every day or two he walked to the village, usually along the tracks of the newly opened railroad. The crews on the freight trains knew him well and waved to him. Concord was not pleased later on when it learned that the town seemed to him like a colony of muskrats. As he observed the life of these small creatures in the river meadows, so he was interested in the village of busy men under the elms and buttonwoods "as curious to me as if they had been prairie dogs, each sitting at the mouth of its burrow, or running over to a neighbor's to gossip."

Even at Walden he was sometimes aware of the town from afar, as when during a holiday celebration the sound was like a swarming of bees, or when bands were playing it seemed as if the village were a vast bellows. Yet even on Concord's greatest days, the sky over Henry's Walden clearing wore "only the same everlasting great look that it wears daily."

When on his trips into town he had stayed late, he found it pleasant "to launch myself into the night, especially if it was dark and tempestuous, and set sail from some bright village parlour or lecture room, with a bag of rye or Indian meal upon my shoulder, for my snug harbour in the woods, having made all tight without and withdrawn under hatches with a merry crew of thoughts. . . . It is darker in the woods, even in common nights, than most suppose. I frequently had to look up at the opening between trees above the path in order to learn my route. . . ." Or he steered by the relationship of trees or felt the faint path with his feet.

"Sometimes, after coming home thus late in a dark and muggy night, when my feet felt the path which my eyes could not see, dreaming and absent-minded all the way, until I was aroused by having to raise my hand to lift the latch, I have not been able to recall a single step of my walk, and I have thought that perhaps my body would find its way home if its master should forsake it, as the hand finds its way to the mouth without assistance."

But in winter when the snows were deep, his path became a "meandering dotted line," showing how he took exactly the same number of steps, and of the same length, coming and going, "stepping deliberately and with the precision of a pair of dividers in my own deep tracks—to such routine the winter reduces us—yet often they were filled with the heaven's own blue."

Those free afternoons of Henry's were adventurous and well used. "Shall I go down this long hill in the rain to fish in the pond? I ask myself. And I say to myself: Yes, roam far, grasp life and conquer it, learn much and live. Your fetters are knocked off; you are really free. Stay till late in the night; be unwise and daring."

That early first summer he wrote in his journal: "I am glad to remember tonight, as I sit by my door, that I too am at least a remote descendant of that heroic race of men of whom there is tradition. I too sit here on the shore of my Ithaca, a fellow-wanderer and survivor of Ulysses. How symbolical, significant of what I know not what, the pitch-pine stands here before my door!"

He liked the rainy days, fancied a special friendliness in the sounds made by the drops on his roof. "The rain which is now watering my beans and keeping me in the house waters me too. I needed it so much. And what if most are not hoed! Those who send the rain, whom I chiefly respect, will pardon me.

"Sometimes," he went on, "when I compare myself with other men, methinks I am favored by the gods. They seem to whisper to me beyond my deserts, and that I do have a solid warrant and surety at their hands, which my fellows do not. I do not flatter myself, but if it were possible they flatter me...."

There were mornings when Henry could not afford to sacrifice the bloom of the present moment and sat in the sunny doorway of his hut until noon, "rapt in a reverie, amidst the pines and hickories and sumachs, in undisturbed solitude and stillness, while the birds sang around or flitted noiseless through the house. . . . I grew in those seasons like corn in the night, and they were far better than any work of the hands could have been."

Could this be the heroic life of a fellow wanderer of Ulysses? An everyday world would not be brought even to consider the point. Henry's projects included walks to the Cliffs, to Annursnack "to telegraph any new arrival, to see if Wachusett, Wataic, or Monadnock had got any nearer. Climbing trees for the same purpose." Or, by way of more specific research, to find the bottom of Walden Pond and what inlet or outlet it might have.

All his enterprises of one kind or another, mystic or symbolic or practical, great or small, he himself could summarize briefly: "In any weather, at any hour of the day or night, I have been anxious to improve the nick of time, and notch it on my stick, too; to stand on the meeting of two eternities, the past and future, which is precisely the present moment; to toe that line."

In the fall he plastered his house and built the chimney in his own fashion, and when the ponds were frozen in winter he walked across them for new views of the landscape, skated and slid on Walden, listened to the hoot owl at night, or to the foxes under the moon, after their quarry. "I also heard the whooping of the ice in the pond, my great bed-fellow in that part of Concord, as if it were restless in its bed and would fain turn over."

No weather, he wrote later, interfered with his walks abroad and he often walked eight or ten miles through the deepest snow "to keep an appointment with a beech-tree or yellow-birch, or an old acquaintance among the pines."

The strong main themes of his Walden life were celebrated in such words as those quoted, whether one could understand them or not, but Concord continued to know him in other and more familiar roles and relationships. Often while he was living at the pond he was sought out to perform some sort of work around town—building fences, painting, gardening, carpentering, and once the bricking up of a fireplace. Those who could not recognize the naturalist or philosopher never lost sight of the handy man in Henry and thus found it less needful to look a hairbreadth farther.

For one period Henry was employed by Emerson, who had bought a lot neighboring his own premises and was putting a thousand dollars into a house for Lidian's sister, Lucy Brown. Now Henry Thoreau, who had first been brought to Emerson's discriminating notice by Lucy and had thrown his verses in at her window, helped to build the new house that was to bring the sisters into congenial and settled proximity.

Henry was no stranger about the center of the town, or in the household of the Thoreaus, where he ate supper or dinner often. How, then, was it possible for observers in general to know what he was really up to, or what, if anything, was being proved by his manner of life?

7. *Friends and Acquaintances*

Henry did not altogether discourage visitors to his Walden hut; a good many he welcomed. The leaner itinerants of society were those who interested him most, but he liked children and berry pickers, and took the Alcott girls and other children of Concord for boat trips on the pond.

Another visitor and friend was "a true Homeric boor, one of those Paphlagonian men . . . Alek Therien, he called himself, a Canadian now, a woodchopper, a post-maker. . . . And he too has heard of Homer, and if it were not for books would not know what to do rainy days."

Paphlagonia was an ancient country of Asia Minor, on the Black Sea coast, mountainous, and noted for timber. Henry talked often with Therien and found the discourse worth while. "Asked Therien this afternoon if he had got a new idea this summer. 'Good Lord,' says he, 'a man that has to work as I do, if he does not forget the ideas he has had, will do well. . . .' " Into the pages of *Walden* this exchange went later, and it was suitable that Therien, who could hole fifty posts in a day, should find his deathless place there.

Likewise in *Walden* emerged portraits of John Field, an Irishman who lived in a hut a mile from the road, and of Hugh

Quoil, Irish too, who had been a soldier at Waterloo. The great wave of migration from Ireland, mass flight from an incalculable tragedy of famine, lay still ahead, but men like John Field had come to perform such rough labor as the building of railroads. Henry took shelter in Field's pitiful dwelling during a hard rain, tried to share an easy and plain philosophy with this man, told him how he himself did not use tea, coffee, or butter, or milk, or fresh meat, "and so did not have to work to get them; again, as I did not work hard, I did not have to eat hard, and it cost me but a trifle for my food."

John Field found this philosophy more difficult than a strange new tongue, as difficult in fact as most of Concord found it, and was not to be saved from his human fate of toiling on at an overwhelming disadvantage. Even when he went fishing he used the wrong bait for the ponds of New England.

As for Hugh Quoil, Henry spoke to him but once. Quoil's hut was half a mile away through the woods and he lived "from hand—sometimes to mouth—though it was commonly a glass of rum that the hand carried. . . . What life he got—or what means of death—he got by ditching. . . ."

This was "a man of manners and gentlemanlike, as one who had seen the world, and was capable of more civil speech than you could well attend to. At a distance he had seemingly a ruddy face as of biting January, but nearer at hand it was bright carmine. It would have burnt your finger to touch his cheek. He wore a straight-bodied snuff-colored coat which had long been familiar to him, and carried a turf-knife in his hand—instead of a sword. He had fought on the English side before, but he fought on the Napoleon side now. Napoleon went to St. Helena; Hugh Quoil came to Walden Pond. . . ."

This was a sort of character George Borrow, a student of byways and casuals of life then living in England, might have met and held converse with on Mousehold Heath or elsewhere. Henry Thoreau was to become known for his companionship

with birds, trees, muskrats, and so on, but he was not backward
in observing mankind. He was grieved that Hugh Quoil died
before this acquaintanceship of the woods could ripen.

Henry was drawn to such Concord men as Edmund Hosmer and George Minott. He thought they should be asked to
lecture at the lyceum instead of some of the dull-important
figures who were brought from away and paid for coming, or
some of the dull-unimportant ones, either. Henry would pre-
fer to hear either of these two refuse to lecture than to hear
someone else go the whole distance.

Edmund Hosmer had been included in conversations at the
Emerson house and represented not only the New England
lineage of devoted labor and shrewd thrift on the soil but also
the point of view of men who identify the things they do with
their hands with the thoughts their minds entertain. There
could be no lapses in the lives of such thinkers and doers, since
for them everything was brought into one harmony or at least
into one system. Hosmer was, therefore, a sort of philosopher
of plain things. He had never been idle in a long life and did
not desire to be, but he had got to the place where he wanted
rest.

George Minott, it seemed to Henry, most nearly realized
the poetry of a farmer's life. He did nothing with haste and
drudgery, but as if he loved it, and knew by instinct when to
plant and when to harvest. The cycle of seasons and of years
too was in his blood. No garden in Concord was kept so beauti-
fully clean as his—but, like Henry, he loved to walk in a swamp
in windy weather and hear the wind groan in the pines. Henry
wrote of him with warm respect and affection always. "With
never-failing rheumatism and trembling hands, he seems yet
to enjoy perennial health. Though he never reads a book—
since he finished the 'Naval Monument'—he speaks the best of
English."

There was also old Mr. Joseph Hosmer, who told of seeing

a squirrel gnaw the bark of a maple one spring day and suck the juice—told of other things he had observed, also. He knew from a life's observations the differences in oak wood, many rare items of this kind.

For Henry Thoreau, a walk that included a few words with one of these usually offered an extra reward, a modest bounty over and above what could be supplied by the countryside. There were, of course, unexpected and occasional encounters too, as when five railroad laborers stopped at the Walden hut and displayed a rude wisdom much to Henry's liking. "And one of them, a handsome younger man, a sailor-like, Greek-like man, says: 'Sir, I like your notions. I think I shall live so myself. . . .' " It appeared, then, that these callers had found rude wisdom in Henry. But one visitor said he would live as Henry was living—if he could afford it. The qualification appealed to Henry's humor.

Channing and Alcott were among those Henry celebrated in *Walden* as winter visitors, who shared some of those long, dark, mellow evenings in the hut beside the pond. Henry alluded to Alcott's hospitable intellect; did this mean the man was easily imposed upon, and easily imposed upon himself? This was the case; but Alcott was also, to Henry, the sanest man with the fewest crochets—"a blue-robed man, whose fittest roof is the over-arching sky which reflects his serenity." These two had each "some shingles of thought, well dried" and so "sat and whittled them" in the winter hut.

Alcott, on his side, held an opinion of Henry that was high and understanding: "Thoreau's is a walking muse, winged at the anklets, and rhyming her steps," his special task that of "delineating these yet unspoiled American things, and of inspiring us with a sense of their homelier beauties—opening to us the riches of a nation scarcely yet discovered by her own population."

Ellery Channing was the poet who came from farthest to the

Walden lodge—"nothing can deter a poet, for he is actuated by pure love.... We made that small house ring with boisterous mirth, making amends then to Walden vale for the long silences. Broadway was still and deserted in comparison."

Channing returned from his New York sojourn, defeated in practical respects but still a poet, while Henry was at Walden, and he was to describe the hut both as a wooden inkstand for Henry's convenience in writing and as a sort of sentry box. "By standing on a chair you could reach into the garret, and a corn broom fathomed the depth of the cellar. It had no lock to the door, no curtain to the window, and belonged to nature nearly as much as to man."

This last was always a special point with Henry himself, who had observed that he could retire indoors without losing the freshness of the air, for the hut simply enclosed air that was as fresh as that of the pondside itself. And so Henry and Channing understood each other well.

Emerson too looked in at the Walden hermitage to see how Henry was getting on, and he too was understanding, though history had cast him in the role of patron that prevented him from being, as these others were, friends only.

"All honest pilgrims, who came out to the woods for freedom's sake, and really left the village behind, I was ready to greet with," Henry wrote later. And there was "one real runaway slave, among the rest, whom I helped to forward toward the north star." It is likely that Alcott was also concerned with the succoring and forwarding of this runaway.

At Walden, as everywhere, Henry was to write, "I sometimes expect the Visitor who never comes. The Vishnu Purana says, 'The householder is to remain at eventide in his court-yard as long as it takes to milk a cow, or longer if he pleases, to await the arrival of a guest.' I often performed this duty of hospitality, waited long enough to milk a whole herd of cows, but did not see the man approaching from the town."

8. *Stone Walls*

It was only paper politics that failed to engage Henry's attention or interest. With the ideas and causes that wrung men's consciences, forced from them their best energies or their worst, and, most of all, touched the liberties and rights of humanity, he was deeply involved, early and late. His refusal to pay his church tax had been an overt political act that, from his standpoint, seemed more effective than casting a ballot on election day, which he did not trouble to do.

When he rang the bell for Emerson's anti-slavery address, the waves of sound did not seem to die away entirely. He continued to hear them in the long, high vaults of a certain special awareness that links some men in all generations to the causes and crusades of the spirit. The election of James K. Polk to the Presidency was an event far off from Walden Pond, yet because it meant an unchecked drive for the annexation of Texas and the extension of slavery the shadow of it was plainly visible on Henry Thoreau's horizon.

On a July afternoon Henry walked to town in his usual way, the particular errand being to get a mended shoe from the cobbler, and unexpectedly met the policies of imperialism and oppression in the person of Sam Staples. Sam would have disclaimed any such relationship, for as far as he knew he was only the constable acting as agent for tax collector and selectmen of Concord.

Henry had not paid his poll tax for several years, and with each abstention his reasons became stronger and clearer. He did not want to trace the course of his dollar "till it buys a man, or a musket to shoot one with." He paid his highway taxes readily enough and wished to be understood as meeting the obligation of a sustaining member of the community, but the poll tax would serve as complete symbol, significance established without reference to the amount of money involved.

Up to now nothing had been done about Henry's default, but political tensions were drawing tighter. This was one reason why Sam Staples was directed to put Henry under arrest until he paid; the example must be set. It is not unlikely, too, that Concord intended a rebuke to a flagrantly nonconforming son. As for Sam Staples himself, he was willing to go all the way to ease Henry's path, even to advancing the money, if Henry said he was hard up, though Sam would not have done it for old man Alcott.

Henry, even though he was mad as a hornet at the time of his arrest, according to Sam, did not say he was hard up. With him as with Alcott on that earlier occasion, it was nothing but principle.

So Sam took Henry into custody and the jail door closed, leaving the prisoner's thoughts—as he pointed out later—as free as always to pass and repass and to set up a habitation wherever a mind or a conscience wished to entertain them. There is a story that goes on and on, and probably always will, to the effect that Emerson visited the jail and inquired, "Henry, why are you here?" Henry is supposed to have replied, "Waldo, why are you not here?" The only trouble is that there was no such exchange. Emerson did not visit the jail, and anyway he knew perfectly well why Henry was there, as soon as the news spread through Concord—knew and disapproved.

Emerson believed in man and the individual conscience, but he thought the dissenting citizen ought to go along with the majority. Henry did not. Emerson wrote in his journal: "My friend Mr. Thoreau has gone to jail rather than pay his tax. On him they could not calculate." Others protested and attempted to influence the course of the state, but, once defeated, they obeyed orders. Henry did not mean that the state should calculate on him in this sense. Alcott, of course, did approve his attitude.

After Sam Staples had his boots off and was settled for the

night, a woman with a shawl over her head came and paid the amount of Henry's tax to Sam's daughter, Ellen. Sam believed at the time that this female figure was Elizabeth Hoar, but the conclusion of history is that she was Henry's Aunt Maria, set on by his mother. At any rate, Sam waited until morning when it was convenient for him to set Henry free.

Once out of jail "I proceeded to finish my errand, and, having put on my mended shoe, joined a huckleberry party, who were impatient to put themselves under my conduct; and in half an hour—for the horse was soon tackled—was in the midst of a huckleberry field, on one of our highest hills, two miles off, and then the State was nowhere to be seen."

Though he may have been as mad as the devil at the particular interruption of his plans by Sam Staples that July day, what Henry set down later in his famous essay, finally entitled "Civil Disobedience," was certainly as true, or even truer—the facts having been wrung out and made taut and bright like new wash on the line, flapping in the breeze as gloriously as banners, homely, useful, forever challenging.

"I have paid no poll tax for six years," Henry wrote. "I was put into jail once on this account, for one night; and, as I stood considering the walls of solid stone, two or three feet thick, the door of wood and iron, a foot thick, and the iron grating which strained the light, I could not help being struck with the foolishness of that institution which treated me as if I were mere flesh and blood and bones, to be locked up. I wondered that it should have been concluded at length that this was the best use it could put me to, and had never thought to avail itself of my services in some way. I saw that, if there was a wall of stone between me and my townsmen, there was a still more difficult one to climb or break through before they could get to be as free as I was.

"I did not for a moment feel confined, and the walls seemed a great waste of stone and mortar. . . . I could not but smile to see how industriously they locked the door on my meditations, which followed them out again without let or hindrance, and *they* were really all that was dangerous."

Henry shared a cell with a man who was accused of burning a barn.

"He occupied one window, and I the other; and I saw that if one stayed there long, his principal business would be to look out the window. . . . I pumped my fellow-prisoner as dry as I could, for fear I should never see him again; but at length he showed me which was my bed, and left me to blow out the lamp.

"It was like traveling into a far country, such as I had never expected to behold, to lie there for one night. It seemed to me that I never had heard the town-clock strike before, nor the evening sounds of the village; for we slept with the windows open, which were inside the grating. It was to see my native village in the light of the Middle Ages, and our Concord was turned into a Rhine stream, and visions of knights and castles passed before me. They were the voices of old burghers that I heard in the streets. . . .

"In the morning, our breakfasts were put through the hole in the door, in small oblong-square tin pans, made to fit, and holding a pint of chocolate, with brown bread, and an iron spoon. When they called for the vessels again, I was green enough to return what bread I had left; but my comrade seized it, and said that I should lay that up for lunch or dinner. . . ."

After he had been released, Henry did not perceive any great changes in the Concord common "and yet a change had to my eyes come over the scene—the town, and State, and country—the greater than any that mere time could effect. I saw yet more distinctly the State in which I lived. I saw to what extent the people among whom I lived could be trusted as good neighbors and friends; that their friendship was for summer weather only; that they did not greatly propose to do

right; that they were a distinct race from me by their prejudices
and superstitions, as the Chinamen and Malays are; that in their
sacrifices to humanity, they ran no risks, not even to their
property. . . . This may be to judge my neighbors harshly; for
I believe that many of them are not aware that they have such
an institution as the jail in their village."

Emerson thought that Henry had not reached the evil so
nearly as other possible methods would do, but no one much
remembers what those other methods may have been.

9. *Book*

In his hut at Walden Henry wrote an essay on Carlyle that
was published later, and journal entries and other passages that
were later woven into his book named after the pond, but his
major writing occupation was with *A Week on the Concord
and Merrimack Rivers*, usually and more conveniently referred
to as the *Week*. The basis of the book was, of course, the river
journey he had taken with his brother John long ago, but with
the flow of that narrative ran many another stream, eddy, and
reflection. Henry made his manuscript swallow ninety-four
poetical quotations from such sources as Pindar, Homer,
Donne, Tennyson, Chaucer, Spenser, and Emerson, as well as
much that he himself had written for *The Dial* or for other
purposes.

He invoked the "vast and cosmogonal philosophy" of the
Bhagavad-Gita, a great poetic expression of Hinduism, which
Emerson had been reading a little while before. But Emerson's
enthusiasm for these Indian writings was not Henry's introduction to Indian philosophy; he had made his first step earlier,
and on the river journey itself he and John had eaten rice somewhat in emulation of the wisdom of the East.

In the *Week* Henry suggested that the sacred writings of
the Chinese, Hindus, Persians, Hebrews, and others should be

printed together as the Scripture of mankind. Naturally this was to offend many readers who wanted a scripture of their own but none of mankind.

It was natural that Henry should put into his book also some reflections based on his arrest and night in jail. He wrote: "When I have not paid the tax which the State demanded for that protection which I did not want, itself has robbed me; when I have asserted the liberty it is presumed to declare, itself has imprisoned me. Poor creature! if it knows no better I will not blame it. If it cannot live but by those means, I can. I do not wish, it happens, to be associated with Massachusetts either in holding slaves or in conquering Mexico. I am a little better than herself in these respects."

He struck out in sentences bold and rhythmic like the tall, swaying limbs of great trees: "If, for instance, a man asserts the value of individual liberty over the merely political commonweal, his neighbor still tolerates him, that he who is living near him even sustains him, but never the State. Its officer, as a living man, may have virtues and a thought in his brain, but as the tool of an institution, a jailer or a constable it may be, he is not a whit superior to his prison key or his staff. Herein is the tragedy: that men doing outrage to their proper natures, even those called wise and good, lend themselves to perform the office of inferior and brutal ones. Hence come war and slavery in; and what else may not come in by this opening?"

"All men are partially buried in the grave of custom, and of some we see only the crown of the head above the ground."

"I must conclude that Conscience, if that be the name of it, was not given us for no purpose or for a hindrance. However flattering order and expediency may look, it is but the repose of a lethargy, and we will choose rather to be awake, though it be stormy, and maintain ourselves on this earth, and in this life, as we may, without signing our death-warrant. Let us see if we cannot stay here, where He has put us, on his own con-

ditions. Does not his law reach as far as his light? The ex-
pedients of the nations clash with one another, only the absolutely right is expedient for all."

Henry quoted passages from the *Antigone* of Sophocles,
expressed his feeling toward the New Testament—"all mortals
are convicted by its conscience"—and offered philosophical
guideposts from the Bhagavad-Gita, which had moved him
deeply in every way.

Then, alone in the hut at Walden, he struck out for himself: "What, after all, does the practicality of life amount to?
The things immediate to be done are very trivial. I could postpone them all to hear this locust sing. The most glorious fact
in my experience is not anything that I have done or may hope
to do, but a transient thought, or vision, or dream which I have
had. I would give all the wealth of the world, and all the deeds
of all the heroes, for one true vision. But how can I communicate with the gods, who am a pencil-maker on earth, and not
be insane?"

Then, after a page or two, back to the river journey with
John, dropping their melon rinds in the Merrimack, rowing
upstream in solitude, listening to a kingfisher "sounding his
rattle along the fluvial street."

Emerson sat with Henry on the bank of the Concord under
the branches of an oak tree and heard him read his manuscript
aloud. This book was, Emerson thought, "pastoral as Isaak
Walton, spicy as flagroot." Alcott went to the Walden hut on
a winter night and Henry read the manuscript to him too, and
afterward Alcott "came home at midnight through the snowy
woodpaths, and slept with the pleasing dream that presently
the press would give me two books to be proud of—Emerson's
'Poems' and Thoreau's 'Week.' "

Oh, but there was a catch. The press, that combination of
time-hallowed craft and mechanics, capable of translating the
written word into the currency of print, was to be engaged

only if the cordon of men who controlled it, the publishers, could be stormed or breached. Emerson would gladly help, but even he lacked a final say in this all-important matter.

10. *Out of the Woods*

Late in the summer of 1846, the second of his life at Walden, Henry made a journey to Maine, where, in company with a cousin who lived there, he did some exploring of the upper reaches of the Penobscot River and climbed to the top of Ka-tahdin (Ktaadn was the form of the name he used), mile-high summit which is Maine's loftiest. He added to his river lore and mountain lore: "the tops of mountains are among the un-finished parts of the globe, whither it is a slight insult to the gods to climb and pry into their secrets, and try their effect on our humanity. Only daring and insolent men, perchance, go there."

He was fascinated by the Indian, paddling upstream in a bark canoe sewed with spruce root. "He is but dim and misty to me, obscured by the aeons that lie between the bark canoe and the batteau. . . . He glides up the Millionocket and is lost to my sight, as a more distant and misty cloud is lost in space. So he goes about his destiny, the red face of man."

Henry was gone from Walden only a fortnight, though his mind and experience of the trip encompassed a wide span of time. A little while more at the hut and then, on September 6, 1847, he left it for good, after two years and two months as a resident, mixed with much coming and going. His firm declara-tion was that he left the woods for as good a reason as he went there. No one could quarrel with that, though a great deal seemed to remain unexplained.

In his journal more than four years later, as if turning for a long retrospect, he wrote: "But why I changed? why I left the woods? I do not think that I can tell. I have often wished myself back. I do not know any better how I ever came to go there. Perhaps it is none of my business, even if it is yours." Many passages in his journal, like this, he meant to address one day to the public. "Perhaps I wanted a change. There was a little stagnation, it may be. About 6 o'clock in the afternoon the world's axle creaked as if it needed greasing, as if the oxen labored with the wain and could hardly get their load over the ridge of the day."

He added: "Perhaps if I lived there much longer, I might live there forever. One would think twice before he accepted heaven on such terms. A ticket to Heaven must include tickets to Limbo, Purgatory, and Hell. Your ticket to the boxes admits you to the pit also. And if you take a cabin passage, you can smoke, at least forward of the engine—you have the liberty of the whole boat. But no, I do not wish for a ticket to the boxes, or to take a cabin passage. I will rather go before the mast and on the deck of the world. . . ."

So on with the succession of metaphors, and some of these same words turned up in *Walden*, until he said more plainly still, "Perhaps it seemed to me that I had several more lives to live."

11. *Once More at Emerson's*

The wider prospect held many an ill, as in Mexico, where the forces of imperialism and slavery were pressing an evil war—if Concord was right about it—but in the town itself affairs proceeded without much change.

Emerson had given up the use of fireplaces and had installed airtight stoves. He and Lidian, having witnessed or experienced most other forms in which domestic life could be ordered, had finally tried the experiment of living as boarders in their own home. A Mrs. Marston Goodwin, with her four children, had moved in as landlady with permission to take other boarders,

an arrangement that lasted until September 1847, the month in
which Henry emerged from the woods and in which Emerson
was planning another journey overseas.

That year Hawthorne's *Mosses from an Old Manse* was
published. That year Emerson had raised money for Ellery
Channing to go to Europe to improve his poetry—and Ellery,
who had planned a year in Italy, was back in Concord within
four months. And that year Margaret Fuller, who had gone
abroad on the invitation of Marcus Spring, New York merchant and philanthropist who had been a backer of Brook
Farm, and of course Mrs. Spring, met the Marquis Ossoli, an
adherent of Young Italy, in Rome. Margaret was widening
her horizons.

Since Emerson was Europe-bound to deliver lectures, he
needed someone to look after the home premises, and Lidian
suggested Henry for that responsibility. The arrangement was
so apt that it might have been foreordained. To Boston went
Lidian, the Alcotts, and Henry himself to see Emerson off on
the packet ship *Washington Irving* in a stateroom resembling
a carpeted dark closet, and when the little group returned to
Concord, Henry was once more handy man, protector, and
good genius of the Emerson household.

"I have banked up the young trees against the winter and
the mice," Henry wrote to the absent patron that November,
"and I will look out, in my careless way, to see when a pale is
loose or a nail drops out of place. The broad gaps, at least, I
will occupy. I heartily wish I could be of good service to this
household. But I, who have only used these ten digits so long
to solve the problem of a living, how can I? The world is a
cow that is hard to milk—life does not come so easy—and oh,
how thinly it is watered ere we get it!"

He went on: "Lidian and I make very good housekeepers.
She is a very dear sister to me. Ellen and Edith and Eddy and

Aunty Brown keep up the tragedy and comedy and tragi-
comedy of life as usual."

Eddy, Henry reported, had asked seriously, "Mr. Thoreau,
will you be my father?" So Henry became "occasionally Mr.
Rough-and-tumble with him that I may not miss *him*, and lest
he should miss *you* too much. So you must come back soon,
or you will be superseded."

The fond, gay references to the Emerson children were
followed later in this same letter by an astonishing paragraph:
"I have had a tragic correspondence, for the most part all on
one side, with Miss ——. She did really wish to—I hesitate to
write—marry me."

Bluntly the fact was set down, and Henry indicated that
he had returned a distinct and perhaps explosive "No" to the
woman in question. But who was she? If one could help history
out with romantic suggestions and literary turns, it would be
tempting to suggest Margaret Fuller, as one biographer has,
but with candid admission of no real evidence. Was not Margaret already in love with Italy—or in Italy?

The candidate near at hand would have to be Sophia Foord,
a woman fifteen years older than Henry who was then living
in the Emerson household where Henry's presence could con-
ceivably have touched off a proposal note. But would he have
referred in such case to correspondence—too broad a word to
apply to the narrow circumstances? The mystery remains. The
incident, reported in this letter, seemed to stand quite by itself
and no sequel ever turned up.

With Alcott, Henry was building a summer house on the
Emerson property. Originally this project had been for a lodge
to stand on an eminence near Walden Pond, suited for purposes
of study and writing, and commanding a view of Concord's
favorite mountains, Wachusett and Monadnock, but now it
was shrinking into an Alcottian pagoda in the household gar-

den. Alcott insisted on extemporizing as he went along, shunning straight lines. Henry would have preferred solid, thought-out, straight-line construction. Alcott was offended because Henry laughed at the performance, though all Concord was laughing too and without any prompting. After a while Henry withdrew and Alcott went on alone in his crazy, inspired fashion.

During her husband's absence Lidian was ill repeatedly, the children had their illnesses, and there was not money enough to meet household bills. Yet from Emerson came his characteristic letters, hoping that Henry would order a large planting of melons, suggesting a grand scheme to bring Margaret Fuller back to Concord to the Emerson house, saying all sorts of things but never the dear, immediate word a wife needed to hear. Lidian wrote to inform him of some of the facts and he responded generously, abandoning the scheme for Margaret Fuller, agreeing that from Lidian's standpoint it must have looked calamitous, apologizing about the money.

Emerson thought he had left all affairs in order, and of course he accepted the fact of Lidian's invalidism as beyond change, so that she could be ill as uneventfully and normally if he was in England hobnobbing with Tennyson and seeing Macready on the stage as King Lear as she could if he remained in Concord.

While Henry's return engagement at the Emerson house was continuing, the manuscript of the *Week* went the rounds of the publishers. Wiley & Putnam, Munroe, Harpers, and Crosby & Nichols all rejected it, but Wiley & Putnam were willing to bring it out at Henry's expense.

"If I liked the book well enough," he wrote to Emerson, "I should not delay; but for the present I am indifferent. I believe this is the course you advised—to let it lie."

But Emerson urged that the book be brought out without any further delay, for it would surely find readers. Henry's essay on Carlyle, written at Walden, had been sold to *Graham's Magazine* through the mediation of Horace Greeley, and it appeared in the March and April issues in 1847, but no payment was forthcoming until Greeley succeeded in collecting seventy-five dollars in May 1848. Of this, twenty-five dollars went for expenses, and Henry received fifty.

Meantime, in his room at the head of the stairs in Emerson's house, Henry was writing of his trip to Maine, making a lecture of it for delivery before the lyceum. Already he had twice delivered before the lyceum a lecture called "History of Myself," and he now worked on a lecture on Friendship which would become part of the *Week*, and still another on "The Rights and Duties of the Individual in Relation to Government" which would become the celebrated "Civil Disobedience."

Henry took long walks with Ellery Channing, with whom he came closer and closer in companionship. Channing and Alcott did not always get along so well; their spirits clashed if the exposure was too much prolonged. Alcott was reading Plato, Montaigne, Ben Jonson, Beaumont and Fletcher, Sir Thomas Browne, so Henry reported to the absent Emerson, and was "rallying for another foray with his pen, in his latter years, not discouraged by the past, into that crowd of unexpressed ideas of his, that undisciplined Parthian army. . . ."

And Lidian, poor Lidian, was shut away from true companionship by her illnesses. In February 1848 Henry wrote to Emerson: "Lidian is too unwell to write to you; so I must tell you what I can about the children and herself. I am afraid she has not told you how unwell she is—or today perhaps we may say has been. She has been confined to her chamber four or five weeks, and three or four weeks, at least, to her bed with the jaundice. The doctor, who comes once a day, does not let her read (nor can she now) nor hear much reading. She has written her letters to you, till recently, sitting up in bed, but

he said he would not come again if she did so. She has Abby
and Almira to take care of her, and Mrs. Brown to read to her;
and I also, occasionally, have something to read or to say. . . .
She wishes me to say that she has written two long and full
letters to you about the household economies, etc., which she
hopes have not been delayed. . . ."

She wrote of the household economies, but the true message
was not contained therein and could be liberated only by a
word from him. A month later he was writing to her from
London: "Dear Lidian . . . Ah, you still ask me for that unwritten letter, always due, it seems, always unwritten from
year to year by me to you, dear Lidian: I fear, too, more widely
true than you mean—always due and unwritten by me to
every sister and brother of the human race." But Lidian was
not interested in the human race in this matter, but only in the
letter that never came.

That July, however, Emerson was home again, and Henry
Thoreau went once more to his father's house and could call
himself a pencil-maker.

6

A DISTINCT FRUIT AND KERNEL

❦ ❦

1. *Certain Wild Flavors*

"I T IS FIVE YEARS that I have been maintaining myself entirely by manual labor—not getting a cent from any other quarter or employment," Henry wrote to Horace Greeley in May 1848. He had just received from Greeley the sum of fifty dollars for his essay on Carlyle.

Henry's letter continued: "Now this toil has occupied so few days—perhaps a single month, spring and fall each—that I must have had more leisure than any of my brethren for study and literature. I have done rude work of all kinds. From July, 1845, to September, 1847, I lived by myself in the forest, in a fairly good cabin, plastered and warmly covered, which I built myself. There I earned all I needed and kept to my own affairs. During that time my weekly outlay was but seven-and-twenty cents; and I had an abundance of all sorts. Unless the human race perspire more than I do, there is no occasion to live by the sweat of their brow...."

The scholar, Henry contended on the basis of his own experience, should not starve or go mad in a garret but should turn the tables on a conventional and acquisitive society by earning his necessary dollars—the fewest he could do with—as any able-bodied man could earn them always. The labor of the body never lacked a market, some sort of market, and if it proved a cheap one, this should not trouble a scholar with a scholar's wisdom to limit his material requirements.

But Henry himself was not exactly a scholar. No man had ever lived just the sort of life he now saw opening ahead like a path twisting through the trees. His months at Walden had been a sort of trial run, perhaps a rough forecast of what he might do when he came to apply over the long term some principles of living he had been exemplifying and writing about. Exactly what would materialize from the forecast depended a good deal on time and circumstance.

The Thoreau roof was over Henry's head, though not usually for many hours of any day. His family had changed little, merely growing older in years and ways, ripening in a New England pattern that naturally meant a good deal of suffering under the Lord. John Thoreau, head of the house, was a victim of spells of faintness that no one could account for. His wife, Cynthia, Henry's mother, slipped into nervousness and undefined ailing, though she went on sturdily enough.

Helen, Henry's older sister, was really ill with the family affliction, consumption. Sophia had sick headaches and other complaints that worried her mother. If you looked at the Thoreaus they might seem like dry and worn oak leaves, but if you looked again they might seem sunny and mellow like August. The elements could hardly be separated, for this was the nature of New England family life: it ailed, endured, maintained vitality.

A fresh concern was the book Henry was now writing or had, indeed, mostly written in an early draft, already named *Walden* though Alcott had suggested the title *Sylvania*. As the Thoreau family had watched over Henry so long, followed

his letters and lectures, even his journal, ready to take pride
in his accomplishments, now it examined the manuscript of
Walden.

Aunt Maria said he was putting in things that never ought to
be there, and some parts sounded like blasphemy. Sophia
agreed about the blasphemy, to Henry's surprise, for he had
thought Sophia would understand his book and she did not.
She read some of it aloud to the doomed Helen.

In any case, no one thought Henry could be persuaded to
leave anything out. But the family need not have been concerned too much over *Walden*, for the *Week* was not published
yet, though it soon would be. Encouraged by Emerson's advice and by certain modest sums in hand, Henry had con-
tracted to have it brought out, at his risk, by James Munroe &
Co. of Boston and Cambridge.

Here was the book Emerson and Alcott had believed so
original, so American, and likely to attract readers. They were
wrong only as to the reading public of their own day; its appearance did not set the Charles River on fire, or the Concord
either, but posterity was to rise to a sustained appreciation. Unfortunately Henry could not wait that long, and his obligation
to his publisher demanded immediate sales.

The *Week* embodied a good deal that he believed in. He
thought, and wrote, that "a writer, a man writing, is the scribe
of all nature; he is the corn and the grass and the atmosphere
writing." Good writing should be "a distinct fruit and kernel
itself." In particular as to the *Week*, it seemed to him in retrospect that "it had little of the atmosphere of the house about
it, but might wholly have been written, as in fact it was to a
considerable extent, out-of-doors." He had wanted it to be an
unroofed book, but the reviewers were put off by all the
poetic quotations, so many of them from the classics, and by the
passages that, even if not roofed or enclosed, could be dragged
into a study for dissection.

George Ripley, once of Brook Farm, now writing a new sort of literary criticism for Greeley's *Tribune*, gave the *Week* much space and sympathetic treatment but boggled at Henry's pantheistic turn. Ripley was not ready for any Scripture of Mankind, either. His strictures outweighed his favorable comments.

Emerson had declined a chance to write a review of the *Week* because he was "of the same clan and parish" as Henry and thought the book should be given to a good foreigner. Theodore Parker, with whom Emerson exchanged letters on the subject, thought the *Week* contained "a good deal of sauciness and a good deal of affectation," this latter arising from a tendency he detected of Thoreau trying to be like Emerson.

James Russell Lowell, who, as a college senior, had also put Thoreau down as an imitator of Emerson, now wrote about the *Week* for the *Massachusetts Quarterly Review* and liked the river journey but not the digressions. Snags, he called them. "We were invited to a river party—not to be preached at."

The general public did not seem to care either way. Nobody much bought the book or paid any attention to it—which also meant that no notice was taken of the advertisement the *Week* contained of another book by the same author, to be called *Walden, or Life in the Woods*. "Will soon be published," the advertisement said, but this optimism had assumed a favorable reception for the *Week* itself.

Henry made no fuss about the slow silence into which his first book and hazard of fortune began to settle and did not even make any comments in his journal until long afterward. There was plenty for him to do, plenty to press on his time and attention.

That same year Elizabeth Peabody, long ago Alcott's assistant in his Boston school, now a bookstore lady of Boston and something of a publisher at times, brought out the first and, as it proved, the only issue of *Aesthetic Papers*, a sort of reprise of the old *Dial* days, and she included Henry's lecture on "The Rights and Duties of the Individual in Relation to Government," using a shorter title, "Resistance to Civil Government." Though the circulation of *Aesthetic Papers* was small, it launched "Civil Disobedience," as the *Week* was launched, upon a long journey toward far horizons.

"Under a government which imprisons any unjustly, the true place for a just man is also a prison."

"I know this well, that if one thousand, if one hundred, if ten men whom I could name—if ten *honest* men only—ay, if *one* HONEST man, in this State of Massachusetts, *ceasing to hold slaves*, were actually to withdraw from this copartnership, and be locked up in the county jail therefore, it would be the end of slavery in America. For it matters not how small the beginning may seem to be: what is once well done is done forever."

Concord heard these words, a few persons here and there read them, but history learned them by heart.

No sign of appreciable income from Henry's writings was materializing then, but some of his spoken words carried a certain earning power. Elizabeth Peabody's brother-in-law, Nathaniel Hawthorne, with whom Henry had sauntered "in old heroic times, along the banks of the Scamander," had moved out of the Old Manse while Henry was at Walden. He had gone to Salem, where he had an appointment in the customs house, good for as long as one set of politicians controlled federal patronage.

It was Hawthorne's friendly duty, and a result of his own suggestion, to invite Henry Thoreau to lecture in Salem for a fee of twenty dollars. Henry's first appearance led to another. In April 1849 he lectured in Worcester, where also he had a friend in literate circles, Harrison Gray Otis Blake, now a retired Unitarian divine.

Blake had been a little ahead of Thoreau at Harvard and

had become a member of the class in divinity school before
which Emerson had delivered his address that set the old fogies
heaping figurative sandbags to protect the bastions of their
faith. One of Blake's classmates had been Ebenezer Rockwood
Hoar, Squire Hoar's oldest son, two years junior to Elizabeth.
It was natural that Blake should have visited Concord, should
have met Emerson, and that he should have formed some slight
acquaintance with Thoreau.

Now, in 1848, his interest was suddenly awakened by a re-
reading of something Thoreau had written in the old *Dial*.
Blake entered on a correspondence with Henry that was soon
thriving, and Henry thus found a friend to whom he could talk
more freely and pleasurably than he could, for instance, with
Emerson. This new relationship was all downhill and easy-
going; that with Emerson went on uneven ground.

"At present I am subsisting on certain wild flavors which
nature wafts to me, which unaccountably sustain me," Henry
wrote to his Worcester friend, "and make my apparently
poor life rich. Within a year my walks have extended themselves, and almost every afternoon (I read, or write, or make
pencils in the forenoon and by the last means get a living for
my body) I visit some new hill, or pond, or wood, many miles
distant. . . ."

"Certain wild flavors"—these represented the new turn in
Henry's life, a natural essence, tempting in all directions and
in no certain one, offering their own reward, impressed with a
sort of general scheme but with no particular pattern or practical requirement. What might have happened if the *Week*
had brought Henry a prompt and, for him, ample financial return no one could say, except that then *Walden* would have
been published sooner. But as it was, Henry had a kind of un-
official degree in letters and the slow-gathering seeds of future
reputation, though this merit was acknowledged mostly by his
family and the Emersonians and not by all of the latter.

He could not turn back, or would not; the question was, how should he go on? Why, surely, through the use of his legs, afoot, walking—to Walden, Flag Hill, the Cliffs, Second Division Brook, and Ministerial Swamp, to Burnt Plain, and all such places. As for that necessary minimum income, he began to practice more frequently the profession of surveyor that went so well for a man devoted to outdoor life.

2. *Huge and Real, Cape Cod*

This was Channing's portrait of Thoreau: "In height he was about the average; in his build spare, with limbs that were rather longer than usual, or of which he made a longer use. His features were marked; the nose aquiline or very Roman, like one of the portraits of Caesar (more like a beak, as was said); large overhanging brows above the deepest-set blue eyes that could be seen—blue in certain lights and in others gray; the forehead not unusually broad or high, full of concentrated energy and purpose; the mouth with prominent lips, pursed up with meaning and thought when silent, and giving out when open a stream of the most varied and unusual and instructive sayings. His whole figure had an active earnestness, as if he had no moment to waste; the clenched hand betokened purpose. In walking he made a short cut if he could, and when sitting in the shade or by the well-side, seemed merely the clearer to look forward into the next piece of activity. The intensity of the mind, like Dante's, conveyed the breathing of aloofness—his eyes bent on the ground, his long swinging gait, his hands perhaps clasped behind him, or held closely at his side—the fingers made into a fist."

Channing was best able to describe him well, for not only was he a friend and the most frequent walking companion but he was skilled in observation and words, though not much of a poet.

Besides taking their walks and river trips in and around Concord, Henry and Channing went traveling, made real expeditions. That fall of 1849, California was drawing the gold-hungry. "The whole enterprise of this nation, which is not an upward but a westward one, toward Oregon, California, Japan, etc., is totally devoid of interest to me," Henry wrote, "whether performed on foot or by Pacific railroad. It is not illustrated by a thought; it is not warmed by a sentiment; there is nothing in it which one would lay down his life for, nor even his gloves. . . . It is perfectly heathenish—a filibustering toward heaven by the great western route. . . ."

So while many a man who thought differently, or thought not at all, was off for the golden West, Henry and Channing set out for Cape Cod—"the bare and bended arm of Massachusetts," Henry called it, in a phrase that has since become as basic as the backbone of a codfish. The two companions proceeded to Boston, found that the Provincetown steamer had been delayed in arriving by storm, and decided to move on to Cohasset, where the brig *St. John* of Galway had been tragically wrecked in a mighty gale. There they saw the bodies of poor drowned refugees from green, stricken Ireland, and a litter of rags and wreckage on the sands.

A single body would have affected him more, Henry wrote later. "It is the individual and private that demands our sympathy. A man can attend but one funeral in the course of his life, can behold but one corpse."

From Cohasset, Henry and Channing took the cars through Bridgewater to Sandwich, where the railroad ended, and then went on by stage through Barnstable, Yarmouth, Dennis, and Brewster to Orleans, where they struck off afoot through Eastham and reached the outer beach at Nauset. This was where Henry had most wanted to be.

"I was glad to have got out of the towns, where I am wont to feel unspeakably mean and disgraced—to have left behind for a season the bar-rooms of Massachusetts. . . . My spirits rose in proportion to the outward dreariness. The towns need to be ventilated. . . ."

All the Cape was ventilated by bleak wind and much driving mist and rain which made the umbrellas, part of the customary walking equipment of these two, a doubtful advantage. But Henry rejoiced in the desolation of sand and sea, the unremitting tumble and roar of the breakers, for all this was what he had come to experience, and simply added up on a grand scale to one more proof of the boundless significance of nature.

The walkers entered no more towns until they reached Provincetown, but they kept abreast of Cape Cod history by reading it under their umbrellas, as well as by observing pebbles and seaweed, beach grass and bayberry. They met a beachcomber, first of a number of this characteristic Cape Cod breed, "too grave to laugh, too tough to cry, as indifferent as a clam." He directed them toward an easy way up the bulwark of sand that was flanking their walk, and they mounted the "escarped rampart of a stupendous fortress, whose glacis was the beach, and whose champaign the ocean." For sixteen miles that open way led.

"I was comparatively satisfied. There I had got the Cape under me, as much as if I were riding it barebacked. It was not as on the map or seen from the stage-coach; but there I found it all out of doors, huge and real, Cape Cod!"

Another beachcomber told them that sea clams were good to eat, and Henry built a fire and cooked one, finding it tough but sweet and savory, though later he was made sick by it. At Wellfleet he and Channing were paying guests of an old oysterman, the sort of character that appealed to Henry.

They lodged at the Highland lighthouse and, standing on the narrow Cape, looked at two seas, one on either hand, and felt as if they were aboard a vessel. Between sunrise and sunset they went on to Provincetown, where Henry rejoiced in an autumnal landscape—huckleberry thickets glowing red, pine trees with living green undimmed and accentuated against the white sands, "and the various golden and yellow and fawn-colored tints of the birch and maple and aspen—each making its own figure, and, in the midst, the few yellow sandslides on the sides of the hills looked like the white floor seen through rents in the rug." And Provincetown harbor was crowded with white sails.

Cape Cod entered deeply into Henry's regard; its aspect and philosophy were lean and independent, its outlook shaped by such vastnesses as sea and sky—all so much like his own. He would come back again to these dunes and bluffs. Meantime he felt that at the far extremity of the Cape a man could put all America behind him.

3. *A Great Wave Came*

Henry, as a matter of fact, could stand almost anywhere and put America behind him, all except the not inconsiderable part of America which he, as an inhabitant grown from native elements, embodied within himself. Back in Concord, he moved with the Thoreau family from the "Texas" house to Main Street, on the inner or town side of the railroad, and resumed the novel but equitable division of time between his own devices and the exigencies of society.

His next major excursion away from home was an errand commissioned by Emerson but of quite a different character from the building of fires or the grafting of fruit trees. Buying a ticket with funds Emerson had provided, he got on the cars and was off to search for whatever remained of the effects and relics of Margaret Fuller.

Three years had passed since Margaret had sailed for Europe with the Marcus Springs. Her burning, impassioned destiny had overshot Concord, Boston, and New York, and lay now in the color, antiquity, and flame of Italy. She left the Springs and in 1847 went to Rome to live in a room on the Corso. The love of liberty was astir—all those other loves, too—and in 1848 she bore a child to Angelo Ossoli, an Italian patriot of noble blood who was ten years younger than she; then their marriage was announced.

The Roman revolution led by Mazzini was near its crest, and while Ossoli fought beside the adherents of this cause, Margaret left her infant son Angelino and helped to organize the hospitals. When French troops entered Rome, she and her husband fled to Florence, where, her spirit undimmed, Margaret wrote a history of the revolution and corresponded with Emerson about a publisher. Then, on May 17, 1850, she and Angelo and little Angelino sailed from Leghorn for New York aboard the bark *Elizabeth*, a voyage that ended in disaster.

The captain of the *Elizabeth* died of smallpox, Angelino almost died, and with the sanctuary of Margaret's own America before their eyes the bark was battered and wrecked at Fire Island. Thither Henry Thoreau went on behalf of Margaret's Concord friends. He reached Patchogue, Long Island, aboard an oyster boat, making the passage with a drunken Dutchman who reminded him of Shakespearean characters. Presently he was dating a letter to Emerson at Fire Island beach:

". . . all hands, being mostly in their nightclothes, made haste to the forecastle, the water coming in at once. There they remained; the passengers *in* the forecastle, the crew above it, doing what they could. Every wave lifted the forecastle roof and washed over those within. The first man got ashore at nine; many from nine to noon. At flood tide, about half past three o'clock, when the ship broke up entirely, they came out of the forecastle, and Margaret sat with her back to the foremast, with her hands on her knees, her husband and child already drowned. A great wave came and washed her aft. . . ."

Angelino's body was found, Margaret's and Ossoli's never.

Henry searched for their scattered effects, questioned anyone who might have found the manuscript of Margaret's history of the Roman revolution—the beachcombers were vague—or have seen any of her belongings carried off. Reverend William H. Channing, Ellery's cousin, came out from New York to help.

In his journal Henry recorded some impressions, included later in a letter to Harrison Blake: "I have in my pocket a button which I ripped off the coat of the Marquis of Ossoli on the seashore the other day. Held up, it intercepts the light and casts a shadow—an *actual* button so called, and yet all the life it is connected with is less substantial to me than my faintest dreams. This stream of events we consent to call actual, and that other mightier stream which alone carries us with it—what makes the difference? On the one our bodies float, and we have sympathy with it through them; on the other, our spirits. We are ever dying to one world and being born into another, and possibly no man ever knows whether he is at any time dead in the sense in which he affirms that phenomenon or not. Our thoughts are the epochs of our life; all else is but as a journal of the winds that blew while we were here."

In his narratives published under the title *Cape Cod*, Henry elaborated afterward a fragment of a different sort, defining the solemn quality of his Fire Island experience:

"Once also it was my business to go in search of a human body, mangled by sharks, which had just been cast up, a week after a wreck, having got the direction from a light-house: I should find it a mile or two distant over the sand, a dozen rods from the water, covered with a cloth, by a stick stuck up. I expected that I must look very narrowly to find so small an object, but the sandy beach, half a mile wide, and stretching farther than the eye could reach, was so perfectly smooth and bare, and the mirage toward the sea so magnifying, that when I was half a mile distant the insignificant sliver which marked the spot looked like a bleached spar, and the relics were as con-

spicuous as if they lay in state on that sandy plain, or a generation had labored to pile up their cairn there.

"Close at hand they were simply some bones with a little flesh
adhering to them, in fact, only a slight inequality in the sweep
of the shore. There was nothing at all remarkable about them,
and they were singularly inoffensive both to the sense and the
imagination. But as I stood there they grew more and more
imposing. They were alone with the beach and the sea, whose
hollow roar seemed addressed to them, and I was impressed as
if there was an understanding between them and the ocean
which necessarily left me out, with my snivelling sympathies.
That dead body had taken possession of the shore and reigned
over it as no living one could, in the name of a certain majesty
that belonged to it."

But this was the mortal relic of a sailor; of Margaret the real
memory drifted in the solitary sea air, and in the shadows of
Sleepy Hollow back at Concord, where she had sat on the soft
grass with Emerson long ago. At home again, Henry reported
all the circumstances to the Emersons and to Elizabeth Hoar,
who had admired Margaret Fuller so much in the old days, as
these friends gathered in sadness at the Emerson house. The
voice that had so often challenged, goaded, led, aspired was
silent, and yet it was still heard and would always be.

Horace Greeley and William H. Channing thought Emerson should write a memoir of Margaret and after some misgivings he did so. She had liked his preaching when he was a young
minister and had foreseen a future for him; now he sealed up
and tidied the past for her.

4. *The Nearer Home, the Deeper*

That fall Henry set off with Ellery Channing for a trip to
Canada, taking advantage of a bargain-rate tour. Henry's expenses, as he recorded them, came to $12.75, including the price

of two guidebooks and a map, although he was gone a week and covered eleven hundred miles.

His inexpensive traveling costume included an unlined palm-leaf hat that cost a quarter, and "one of those unspeakably cheap, as well as thin, brown sacks of the Oak Hall pattern which every summer appear all over New England, thick as the leaves upon the trees." Some of his traveling companions, he said, wore such garments to protect their coats, but in his case it looked better than his coat. His shoes he greased, causing distress to any porter along the way who tried to shine them. Henry would never use shoe polish.

When he returned home and sat down to write about the trip, he began, "I fear that I have not got much to say about Canada, not having seen much; what I got by going to Canada was a cold. I left Concord, Massachusetts, Wednesday morning, September 25th, 1850, for Quebec. Fare, seven dollars there and back; distance from Boston, five hundred and ten miles; being obliged to leave Montreal on the return as soon as Friday, October 4th, or within ten days. . . . I wished only to be set down in Canada and take one honest walk there as I might in Concord woods of an afternoon."

This was as saucy an offering to a reader as he had yet made; but really he had seen a great deal in Canada: the Plains of Abraham, the falls of Montmorency, the shrine of Saint Anne. He also saw succory in blossom at the citadel above Quebec. His observations covered a wide range, from the "thorn-bushes, Canada thistles, and ivy on the very summit of Cape Diamond" to the tomb of Simon McTavish on Mount Royal: "He could not have imagined how dead he would be in a few years, and all the more dead and forgotten for being buried under such a mass of gloomy stone, where not even memory could get at him with a crowbar."

Most of the tourists carried valises, but Henry had only a plain parcel. He could not imagine, he said, any reason for showing Canada to a lot of valises when, as likely as not, these people had left nieces at home for lack of an escort.

Henry's excursions were important and characteristic—the Maine woods, Cape Cod, Canada—and they led eventually, though not in his lifetime, to published books, but his wider travels, as he himself declared, were at home. Now he resumed them.

"The further off, the nearer the surface. The nearer home, the deeper. Go in search of the springs of life, and you will get exercise enough. . . . My profession is to be always alert to find God in nature, to know his lurking places, to attend all the oratorios, the operas, in nature."

More practically, as Concord saw it, Henry was a surveyor, and though surveying sometimes ran overlong in his thoughts and interfered with his real business in the woods, to which he resorted after he had sold his forenoons to society, on the whole he had hit on a satisfactory arrangement. He was jealous of his freedom, and noted in his journal that if he should sell his afternoons too, "neglecting my peculiar calling, there would be nothing left worth living for." It did not matter that Concord's face was so often turned the other way, and that only one or two of his fellow townsmen or acquaintances felt the least attracted by nature at large.

The town, at work or gossiping in shop and office, did not understand those special rewards experienced by Henry Thoreau in the lonely countryside. One July day he wrote, "I bathe me in the river. I lie down where it is shallow, amid the weeds over its sandy bottom; but it seems shrunken and parched; I find it difficult to get wet through. . . . I bathe and in a few hours I bathe again, not remembering that I was wetted before. When I come to the river I take off my clothes and carry them over, then bathe and wash off the mud and continue my walk. I would fain take rivers in my walks endwise."

A man who wanted his rivers endwise and had trouble in get-

ting wet through was naturally a puzzle to the ordinary sort
who was willing to take them sidewise and did not notice
whether he was wet through or not. When autumn came,
Henry boiled a quart of acorns for breakfast and found them
bitterish, perhaps because he had cooked them with the shells
and skins. Even so, he thought it likely that one would get used
to the bitter taste. When winter came he skated with free, headlong speed over the river and the frozen Great Meadows.

In his surveying duties Henry officiated at the ancient ritual
of perambulating the town bounds. "As I am partial to across-
lots routes, this appears to be a very proper duty for me to perform, for certainly no route can be well chosen which shall be
more across-lot, since the roads in no case run round the town
but ray out from its center, and my course will lie across each
one. . . . It is a sort of reconnaissance of its frontiers authorized
by the central government of the town, which will bring the
surveyor in contact with whatever wild inhabitant or wilderness its territory embraces."

But the company of the selectmen, who by law and custom
took part in the ritual of perambulation, depressed Henry so
much that he could not entirely shake off the feeling for days.
If these men were "select," it seemed to him, Concord and society owed a poor boast.

Another time, out with the county commissioners for the
survey of a road, Henry followed the example of one of the
commissioners who cut off chunks of early turnip and munched
them raw, thinking of himself from the standpoint of cows or
oxen, and of the habit as one that might be useful.

On the whole, Henry was living the life that Walden represented. He had come out of the woods, but he was pursuing a
further realization of Walden values; this, still, was what the
book was about, too. It was an unpublished book, but his life
was being published day by day, at least to his close acquaint-

ances, and Concord might even have taken notice had there been enough ferment and desire.

Henry walked to Flint's Pond for the sake of the mountain view from the hill overlooking Concord: "It is worth while to see the mountains in the horizon once a day." He made sorties in the moonlight. "It is three thousand years since night has had possession." This antiquity settled about him like a cloak. Again, relishing the prospect over Fair Haven from the Cliffs in the moonlight, he felt that "this light and this hour take the civilization all out of the landscape."

A man should feed his sense with the best that the land affords, he wrote. In the summer he should lay up a stock of experience for winter. Yet, as for weather, all seasons were "pretty much alike to one who is actively at work in the woods. I should say that there were two or three remarkably warm days and as many cold ones in the course of a year, but the rest are all alike in respect to temperature. This is my answer to my acquaintances who ask me if I have not found it cold being out all day." Henry did not always simplify upward; sometimes he simplified downward, if this appeared more convenient.

He walked through Wheeler's cornfield in the October twilight, the darkness of the earth contrasting with the luminous sky, and felt as if he were walking in night up to his chin. In August he bathed at Walden at half past five in the fresh morning of a day following rains. In September he saw the smoke of burning brush above the western horizon and set off for the view from a high hill.

English forests, he wrote, were divided into "walks," and added, "My walk is ten miles from my house every way...."

5. *A Law Under Foot*

The year was 1851, the season spring; a pine warbler had sung and alders hung out reddish-brown catkins. Nut Meadow

Brook burbled freshly, and green was the color of life. Once again Ralph Waldo Emerson's voice was raised in a storm of controversy, espousing a great issue, for the Fugitive Slave Law outraged his heart and conscience alike.

It was a filthy enactment, Emerson wrote in his journal, adding, "I will not obey it, by God."

And he addressed his fellow citizens in Concord on the great iniquity, applying most of his remarks to Massachusetts. Daniel Webster he denounced as the arch betrayer—"all the drops of his blood have eyes that look downward."

What would Henry Thoreau say and do? He had liked to toss out such pot shots as these: "Blessed are the young for they do not read the President's Message" and "Your Congress halls have an ale-house odor—a place for stale jokes and vulgar wit. It compels me to think of my fellow-creatures as apes and baboons." Long ago, at the age of twenty-three, he had cast forward the bent of his life: "How shall I help myself? By withdrawing into the garret and associating with spiders and mice, determining to meet myself face to face sooner or later. Completely silent and attentive I will be this hour and the next and forever. The most positive life that history notices has been a constant retiring out of life, a wiping one's hands of it, seeing how mean it is, and having nothing to do with it."

Through eleven years since then his way had led not to the garret but to Walden and the open country, attentive but not silent, and if he had noted the meanness of life, he had reduced it to small proportions. He had rung bells and spoken out. He had exerted himself to meet face to face all thoughts that marched against freedom.

Now he suggested that the Concord monument should be painted black in mourning for liberty lost in Massachusetts, but the town generally was disapproving. Real respectability does not make itself conspicuous. There is a proper way of going about such matters—so people talked then as now.

One who agreed with Emerson and Thoreau was Ebenezer Rockwood Hoar, eldest of the Squire's sons, who had been a Conscience Whig and a leader of the bolt to the Free Soil party, for which Emerson was presently to go campaigning. He had got himself made a judge, and from the bench he chose to characterize the Fugitive Slave Law in harsh terms: "If I were giving my private opinion I might say that this statute seems to me to evince a more deliberate and settled disregard for the principles of constitutional liberty than any other enactment that has ever come under my notice."

It was clear, or at any rate it seems clear now, that attempts to enforce the Fugitive Slave Law in Boston would have lively consequences. The first test concerned a Negro named Fred Wilkins, who had escaped from slavery in Norfolk and had found a job as a waiter at Boston's Cornhill Coffee House. Wilkins was known in the newspapers and more generally as Shadrach. He was apprehended and taken before a federal commissioner, and young Richard Henry Dana volunteered to act as his counsel.

Dana applied for a writ of habeas corpus, vainly as it turned out, but at least the proceedings were somewhat delayed; and during the delay Wilkins' friends hustled him out of the hearing room and into freedom before the officers and the commissioner realized what was happening. A rescue by force had been effected, or, as the commissioner declared afterward, there had been an act of rebellion.

Wilkins was taken by his friends to Concord, where he was aided by the same Mrs. Mary Merrick Brooks who had persuaded Emerson to speak out in his West Indian Emancipation address. Concord, by virtue of its minority, could still serve as a symbol of liberty, and the Thoreau family belonged in the circle which sheltered and forwarded runaway slaves.

In April 1851 another Negro, Thomas M. Simms, was arrested in Boston, actually as a fugitive slave though technically on a more convenient charge of theft. This time there was no rescue and Simms went back to servitude. Henry Thoreau wrote angrily in his journal, his notes ready, as it turned out, for an address a later occasion would call forth.

A man had been handed into "a slavery as complete as the world ever knew. Of course it makes not the least difference —I wish you to consider this—whether he was Jesus Christ or another—for inasmuch as ye did it unto the least of these his brethren ye did it unto him."

"I wish my townsmen to consider," Henry wrote, "that, whatever the human law may be, neither an individual or a nation can ever deliberately commit the least act of injustice without having to pay the penalty for it. . . . I hear a great deal about trampling this law under foot. Why, one need not go out of his way to do that. This law lies not at the level of the head or the reason. Its natural habitat is the dirt."

These words and others waited a while in the pages of the journal, losing no force, and meantime Henry's surveying and his long walks continued. Moonlight, the liberty of man, mouse-ear in blossom, crowfoot on the Cliffs, saxifrage, the warm-weather sound of the wood peewee—all these overlapped and became indistinguishable in respect to the natural world and the rightness of the human inheritance that ran beyond the limit of streets and fences.

When October came, Henry noted in his journal how he had put a fugitive slave on the cars for Canada. The man's name was Henry Williams and he had escaped from Stafford County, Virginia. Like Fred Wilkins, alias Shadrach, he had worked in the Cornhill Coffee House; it happened that his master was also his father, and through an agent he had attempted through correspondence to buy himself free. The father-master wanted $600, and Williams had been able to raise no more than $500 when word was passed that writs were out in Boston for fugitives of his assumed surname. The police were stirring, including the picturesquely named Auger-Hole Burns. As soon as he could, Williams fled to Concord on foot.

The Thoreaus put him up at their house, in a room used frequently for this purpose, while money was collected for his passage to Canada. Emerson contributed. Then Henry went to the depot at noon to buy a ticket as far as Burlington, but he saw a lounger who looked and behaved so much like a Boston policeman that he made up his mind to wait until late afternoon. From Williams Henry learned some of the lore of escape—the reliance on stars, the directional value of telegraph lines and railroads, the superstition of carrying turf in the hat.

Williams was safely forwarded. By this time the state election was near, and when the day came Emerson polled one vote for representative in the General Court. But Sam Staples was elected by a normal majority.

6. *Friends in the Outdoors*

"There is some advantage in being the humblest, cheapest, least dignified man in the village," Henry wrote in his journal, "so that the very stable boys shall damn you. Methinks I enjoy that advantage to an unusual extent. There is many a coarsely well-meaning fellow, who knows only the skin of me, who addresses me familiarly by my Christian name. I get the whole good of him and lose nothing myself. There is 'Sam,' the jailer —whom I never call Sam, however—who exclaimed last evening, 'Thoreau, are you going up street pretty soon? Well, just take a couple of these handbills along and drop one in at Hoar's piazza and one at Holbrook's and I'll do as much for you another time.' I am not above being used, aye abused, sometimes."

"Humblest, cheapest, least dignified"—here Henry was laying himself out to exaggerate again, or possibly exaggerating without having to lay himself out. At least he made his meaning clear. Under the eyes of Concord he lived as he had chosen to live, and to the town his style was small and mean, and he was a rude, plain, contentious figure. If he lived largely and magnificently beyond the town, who could explain this convincingly in the shops and dwelling houses?

Yet Henry Thoreau was no outcast in any sense. He was not only accepted as a surveyor but respected, although he said himself that plenty of others could ply that profession as well, whereas at lecturing, which brought out the best of him, his talents were not in demand. Surveying earned money but few friends. "All I find is old boundmarks, and the slowness and dullness of farmers reconfirmed. They even complain that I walk too fast for them. Their legs have become stiff from toil."

Many of his customers wanted only such surveying as would profit them, by showing that they owned more land than had been believed, to frustrate some enemy, or to shift a line to their advantage.

Henry drove twelve miles with Squire Hoar to do some surveying for him in Carlisle, and on the long drive neither man had anything special to say. "I treated him simply as if he had bronchitis and could not speak," Henry wrote, "just as I would a sick man, a crazy man, or an idiot. The disease was only an unconquerable stiffness in a well-meaning and sensible man."

The landscape was better company.

As for farmers, they usually attempted to moralize or philosophize in serious conversation and were not themselves. Henry liked the company of sportsmen and loafers better. He dined out sometimes—five times in one single week—and also went out to tea, but society for its own sake meant nothing. Even in the Thoreau home it made him feel confined and wasted, as that summer when the heat of his attic room forced him to sit below with the family each evening for a month on end.

"I feel the necessity of deepening the stream of my life," he wrote. "I must cultivate privacy. It is very dissipating to be

with people too much. . . . I cannot spare my moonlight and
my mountains for the best of man I am likely to get in exchange."

Once Henry recorded in his journal that he had been to a
party. "It is a bad place to go—thirty or forty persons, mostly
young women, in a small room, warm and noisy. Was introduced to two young women. The first one was as lively and
loquacious as a chickadee; had been accustomed to the society
of watering places, and therefore could get no refreshment out
of such a dry fellow as I. The other was said to be pretty-look-
ing, but I rarely look people in their faces, and, moreover, I
could not hear what she said, there was such a clacking—could
only see the motion of her lips when I looked that way."

Henry could think of better places for conversation. "Why,
this afternoon, even, I did better. There was old Mr. Joseph
Hosmer and I ate our luncheon of crackers and cheese together
in the woods. I heard all he said, though it was not much, to be
sure, and he could hear me. And then he talked out of such a
glorious repose, taking a leisurely bite at the cracker and cheese
between his words; and so some of him was communicated to
me, and some of me to him, I trust."

It was likely to be Joseph Hosmer or George Minott who
said something worth preserving, as when Ellery Channing
talked with Mr. Minott about his health and remarked, "I suppose you'd like to die now." "No," said Mr. Minott, "I've
toughed it through the winter, and I want to stay and hear the
bluebirds once more."

A few times, at least, Henry called upon Emerson's aunt,
that durable and outspoken old lady, Mary Moody Emerson,
who did not rattle on like a chickadee but was witty and loquacious all the same. She must have liked Henry, for she did
not suffer fools or strangers tolerantly. He thought she, more
than any other woman he knew, could accompany him far in
the sharing of a poetic experience.

Once when he read from his manuscripts to Miss Emerson, the word "god" occurred in no reverent meaning. "Is that god spelt with a little 'g'?" she inquired, and the lightning lay poised in her darkening cloud. "Fortunately it was," Henry noted later. "So I went on as if nothing had happened."

On the whole, reviewing his list of acquaintances as impartially as possible, and considering each one's excesses and defects of character—"which are the subject of mutual ridicule, astonishment, and pity—and I class myself among them"— Henry inquired of himself, "If this is the sane world, what must a madhouse be?" He observed that it was only with the lubrication of flattery and the looking away from many faults that even the best of his contemporaries were fitted into society.

Ellery Channing, Henry's closest friend, now inhabited a house not far from the Thoreaus, across the way and near the Sudbury River. Henry kept his boat at the foot of Channing's river garden. These two—almost always, though not invariably —could walk together and the conversation would, as Henry believed it must, "vary exactly with the scene and events and contour of the ground." They would be side by side or Indian file in their thoughts as well as geographically.

This was the positive side of it. Once, when Henry was not of a mind for Channing's company on a boating trip, he stated the same thing the other way around: "He thinks I could merely take him into my boat and then not mind him. He does not realize that I should by the same act take him into my mind, where there is no room for him, and my bark would surely founder in such a voyage as I was contemplating. I know very well that I should never reach that expansion of the river I have in my mind, with him aboard with his broad terrene qualities. . . . I could better carry a heaped load of meadow mud and sit on the tholepins. There would be no room for me, and I should reach that expansion of the river nevertheless."

This seemed to make the point, but Henry felt strongly that

day and added, "I could better afford to take him into bed with
me, for then I might, perhaps, abandon him in my dreams. . . ."

Most often Channing's company was to Henry's liking.
This is Emerson's description of Henry on a walk: "Under his
arm he carried an old music-book to press plants; in his pocket,
his diary and pencil, a spy-glass for birds, microscope, jack-
knife and twine. He wore a straw hat, stout shoes, strong gray
trousers, to brave scrub-oaks and smilax, and to climb a tree for
a hawk's or squirrel's nest. He waded into the pool for the
water-plants, and his strong legs were no insignificant part of
his armor."

Channing tried taking along a notebook and writing in it as
Henry did, but the thing did not work; he lacked the facility
of it, or the patience. Then he declared that, after all, he was
interested only in the universal and not in details that were particular and definite. This was quite the opposite of Henry's
curiosity, for Henry wanted not the universal law but to be
allowed to see and experience the particular instance of it.

Henry noted Channing's oddities, most of them not uncon-
genial. He found his companion "as naturally whimsical as a
cow is brindled. He can be incredibly selfish and unexpectedly
generous. He is conceited, and yet there is in him far more than
usual to ground conceit upon." Channing was humorous, too,
and his wit and laughter were important ingredients of this
walking friendship.

During one expedition afoot, Channing "kept up an inces-
sant strain of wit, banter, about my legs, which were so springy
and unweariable, declared I had got my double legs on, that
they were not cork but steel, that I should let myself out to
Van Amburgh, should have them sent to the World's Fair, etc.
etc." This was a line that might have worn thin, but it did well
enough between Concord and Long Pond on a carefree afternoon.

So the two walked in easy friendship. On one July evening

a little past seven they set out across dry hills and pastures to view the moon. Henry picked milkweed blossoms in the twilight, relishing the special evening sweetness. White flowers of Jersey tea flecked the slopes of hills, and so also bloomed the sturdy and astringent yarrow as they crossed the fields. They entered a woodland path, the branches enclosing them above like black clouds, until they came to the aspens at the foot of the Cliffs and out into the young moonlight.

Near Well Meadow Head toward Baker's Farm the path was almost waist high with sweet fern and indigo, all moistened by dew, and a faint mist rose from the pond holes. The companions sat on a fence, went through Baker's wood, then emerged again into open pasture, all taken and possessed by moonlight.

Another time, on an October morning, they set off up the river by boat, the Thoreau Newfoundland pup sole passenger in the stern. Henry made few references to dogs in his journal, but he quoted Channing, who kept a dog for society "to stir up the air of the room when it becomes dead." Opposite Fair Haven the voyagers cut pine boughs and set them up for a sail, discarding this rig when, with the meanderings of the river, it no longer served. That day they rowed about twenty-four miles going and coming, and at last steered by the lights of Concord as they reached home after sundown.

Another day, in April, they set out afoot in driving mist and rain—an easterly storm—and soon saw a flock of geese on the river near some willow trees. Henry and Channing dropped into the wet grass behind an oak and their umbrella to watch. They heard the report of a gun and saw the geese take off, spreading their wings and making a great noise, settling again into the water and swimming toward the shore where the watchers lay. A gunner wearing a greatcoat came running on the farther shore, but saw that the geese were safely beyond range and walked away in the rain.

Henry and Channing remained "close under our umbrella by the tree, ever and anon looking through a peep-hole between the umbrella and the tree at the birds. On they came, sometimes in two, sometimes in three, squads, warily, till we could see the steel-blue and green reflections from their necks. We held the dog close the while—C., lying on his back in the rain, had him in his arms—and thus we gradually edged round on the ground in this cold, wet, windy storm, keeping our feet to the tree, and the great wet calf of a dog with his eyes shut so meekly in our arms. We laughed well at our adventure. They swam fast and warily, seeing our umbrella. Occasionally one expanded a gray wing. They showed white on their breasts. And not till after an hour, sitting cramped and cold and wet on the ground, did we leave them."

Sometimes the companions walked in a gale so strong that an umbrella was useless. Soaked to his skin, Henry noted that "at last the water in my clothes feels warm to me, and I know not but I am dry." He liked the wild tumult of the wind. There was little in nature that he did not like and that Channing could not enjoy with him; and when they paused in their jaunts, they usually had things to say that fitted the place, as in the dry meadow hay of the Baker barn where the mice nested, and Henry wrote, "Oh, what reams of thought one might have here! The crackling of the hay makes silence audible."

William Wheeler put up "a new staring house beyond the Corner Bridge" and, in Henry's phrase, did irreparable damage to a region the two walkers had cherished. Channing suggested that he and Henry send Wheeler a round robin, Henry's name on one side, his on the other, asking that the new house be put out of view and the nuisance abated. Once the walkers were chased by an ox and escaped over a fence. Once they walked as far as the village of Wayland, which appeared to be a sluggish place, and Channing suggested that the two of them could take the town with a couple of oyster knives.

In winter they skated as, in summer, they bathed and boated, but skating was hard work for Channing, who lacked Henry's skill and forward style.

Throughout the days and years of their long friendship Henry remained discriminating in his estimate of Channing, who, he thought, wrote poetry in a "sublimo-slipshod style" and might well have disciplined himself by writing in Latin, an exercise that would have required him to say something always. Channing wanted something for which he would not pay the price and would learn slowly through failure.

But over a lecture of Channing's Henry could enthuse unreservedly, just as, again, he could regret his friend's "boorish" behavior in shutting his gate in the wake of two young men who had—inoffensively, as Henry thought—walked up from the river through Channing's grounds. And it was worth a disapproving note in Henry's journal when Channing jabbed his cat with the poker.

Of a different sort were severer strictures which, but for the context of Henry's life and writing, might strike many modern readers as prudery: "I am made somewhat sad this afternoon by the coarseness and vulgarity of my companion, because he is one with whom I have made myself intimate. He inclines latterly to speak with coarse jesting of facts which should always be treated with delicacy and reverence. I lose my respect for the man who can make the mystery of sex the subject of a coarse jest, yet, when you speak earnestly and seriously on the subject, is silent."

Henry went on: "The subject of sex is one on which I do not wish to meet a man at all unless I can meet him on the most inspiring ground—if his view degrades and does not elevate. . . . A companion can possess no worse quality than vulgarity. If I find that he is not habitually reverent of sex, I, even I, will not associate with him. I will cast the first stone. . . ."

But there was no real break in Henry's relationship with

Channing, and together at Fair Haven they saw Mount Wachusett loom like a right whale over the bow of their boat; in
spring they looked on the "dark blue meadowy revelation"
of the flooding river waters—"these meadows are the most of
ocean that I have fairly learned"; and they watched for the
bluebirds and listened to "the blue curls of their warblings."

7. *To See How the Pine Lives*

In September 1853 Henry started on his second trip to
Maine, proceeding from Boston to Bangor by steamer and, as
usual, observing each incident of the expedition as if it were
the one real event. His principal companion was the cousin
with whom he had made his excursion to Mount Katahdin in
1846. This time the objective was Chesuncook Lake, and an
Indian guide led them.

The errand of Henry's cousin was moose-hunting, but this
was not Henry's. He was soon sickened by the wanton death
of an admirable creature, for, though he might relish a year in
the woods during which he would sustain himself by hunting
and fishing and live like a philosopher, he found "this hunting
of the moose merely for the satisfaction of killing him—not
even for the sake of his hide—without making any extraordinary exertion or running any risk yourself, is too much like
going out by night to some wood-side pasture and shooting
your neighbor's horses. These are God's own horses, poor,
timid creatures, that will run fast enough as soon as they smell
you, though they *are* nine feet high."

He reflected on the baseness and coarseness of the motives
that usually drew men to the wilderness—"for one that comes
with a pencil to sketch or sing, a thousand come with an axe or
rifle." As for his own experience, he felt his nature coarsened
by the moose-hunting expedition.

Life should be lived tenderly, he wrote, and this was close to the considered judgment expressed in *Walden*, the belief that every boy should be for a time both hunter and fisher, passing through a stage of development that was part of the experience of the race, yet "no human being, past the thoughtless age of boyhood, will wantonly murder any creature, which holds its life by the same tenure that he does." If the young man "has the seeds of a better life in him, he distinguishes his proper objects, as a poet or naturalist it may be, and leaves the gun and fish-pole behind."

So in the Maine woods Henry looked eagerly for life—to see how the pine tree lived, not how it died. "A pine cut down, a dead pine, is no more a pine than a dead human carcass is a man. . . . Every creature is better alive than dead, men and moose, and pine-trees, and he who understands it aright will rather preserve life than destroy it."

On this expedition Henry collected many facts, from observations of Indian life and words, to the varying aspects of Maine's geography and countryside, but the thought that filled his mind most completely was of the need for preserving some region of the wilderness for the sake of mankind.

In England, he wrote, when he came to make a narrative of this experience, there used to be forest preserves to hold the king's game, and why should not America have forests "to hold and preserve the king himself also, the lord of creation—not for idle sport or food, but for inspiration and our own true recreation? or shall we, like the villains, grub them all up, poaching on our own national domains?"

Still later he reflected on the maimed and imperfect nature that he knew in and about Concord. It was as if he studied a tribe of Indians that had lost all its warriors, or listened to a concert in which many parts were wanting.

"Primitive Nature is the most interesting to me. I take infinite pains to know all the phenomena of spring, for instance, thinking that I have here the entire poem, and then, to my chagrin, I hear that it is but an imperfect copy that I possess and have read, that my ancestors have torn out many of the first leaves and grandest passages, and mutilated it in many places. I should not like to think that some demigod had come before me and picked out some of the best stars. I wish to know the entire heaven and the entire earth. . . ."

8. *This Is Authorship*

Ever since the *Week* was published, Henry had been engaged more or less in paying the bill. Surveying had brought in part of the money, and making pencils had yielded also, though not through any easy profit. In his journal he recorded that he had been obliged to manufacture "a thousand dollars' worth of pencils and slowly dispose of and finally sacrifice them in order to pay an assumed debt of a hundred dollars." He had picked and shipped cranberries to market, and once, on the way to New York to peddle pencils, he had looked into the possibilities of cranberry speculation.

Would it be possible to buy cranberries cheaply in Boston and sell them dearly in New York? His inquiries, he thought, might have strengthened the market in Boston for a time, but the answer was that prices at New York were not high enough for any such venture.

At last he settled with his publisher—"falsely so called"— and the remaining copies of the *Week*, 706 out of the edition of 1,000, were shipped to him at Concord. He carried the books up two flights of stairs and reflected that he now had a library of nearly nine hundred volumes, more than seven hundred of which he had written himself.

"This is authorship; these are the work of my brain. . . . I can see now what I write for, the result of my labors."

His financial account of the whole transaction was that he had paid out $290 and had received $15, with postage and incidentals not considered in these figures.

This settlement occurred in late November 1853. Meantime there had been other literary adventures though on a smaller scale. Horace Greeley had continued to act as a friendly literary agent, carrying on through the years the relationship established when Henry was a young tutor looking for a writing man's opportunities in New York. Henry had then thought Greeley "a hearty New Hampshire boy"; now the publisher of the *Tribune* was forty-three and a national figure, his newspaper influential and prosperous.

Greeley's whisker-fringed face and broad-brimmed hat were familiar Americanisms of a turbulent public life. As his influence had grown, so had his reputation for eccentricities of character and dress: he was absent-minded, he wrote undecipherable manuscript, wore strapless trousers, walked like a countryman shambling to a village post office. Further than all this, he followed the gleam of Utopian socialism and could be called a green ignoramus or a vigorous idealist, as one desired.

Henry had addressed him as "My Friend Greeley" and in return was addressed as "Friend Thoreau." In 1852 Henry had borrowed seventy-five dollars from his friend and had paid it back in less than a year. This transaction, the only one of its kind in Henry's career, seems to have been part of his long struggle to get his publisher satisfied.

Henry's trip to Canada in 1850 had been turned into a lecture or travel piece by 1852, and Greeley placed it with *Putnam's Monthly*, edited by George William Curtis, whose Utopian socialism ran along Greeley's own line of philosophy. Curtis, then staying at Concord, had been one of the group that helped raise the Walden hut. "A Yankee in Canada" was too long for a single installment, and before a second part could appear Henry had quarreled and broken off with the editor.

To his Worcester friend Blake, Henry wrote: "I do not wonder that you do not like my Canada story. It concerns me little, and probably is not worth the time it took to tell it. Yet I had absolutely no design whatever in my mind, but simply to report what I saw. I have inserted all of myself that was implicated, or made the excursion. It has come to an end, at any rate; they will print no more, but return me my MS when it is but little more than half done, as well as another I had sent them, because the editor requires the liberty to omit heresies without consulting me—a privilege California is not rich enough to bid for."

What George William Curtis had objected to was what he called Henry's "defiant pantheism," and Greeley pointed out that since "A Yankee In Canada" was printed without the author's name, it would be presumed by readers to reflect the magazine's editorial judgment.

"If you had withdrawn your MSS on account of the abominable misprints in the first number, your ground would have been far more tenable," Greeley wrote.

All this while *Walden* had been approaching the far-off divine event of publication, though at times that event must have seemed to Henry as remote as the stars in the summer sky over Concord. At any rate, the book grew and mellowed, for as long as it was not published it was not finished.

The characterization of Alcott—who had been moving away and moving back—as "a blue-robed man" and the reference to "shingles of thought well dried" did not appear in Henry's journal until May 1853, though in the book they were cast back to the years at the pond. As late as February 1854, a few months before *Walden* appeared, Henry was restating the attractions of the Hollowell Farm that had made him wish to buy it, years earlier; somewhat altered, and further explored, these journal entries were to come out in the book.

Henry had liked, he remembered, the Hollowell Farm's

"complete retirement . . . its bounding on the river; the pleasing ruin of the house and barn; the hollow and lichen-covered
apple trees gnawed by rabbits; above all the recollection I had
of it from my earliest voyages up the river, when the house was
concealed behind a dense grove of red maples, which then
stood between it and the river, through which I once heard the
house-dog bark; and in general the slight improvement that
had been made upon it."

These were unique motives for choosing a farm, and Henry
had been "in some haste to buy before the proprietor finished
getting out some rocks, cutting down some hollow apple trees,
and grubbing up some young birches which had sprung up in
the pasture, all which in my eyes very much enhanced its
value."

So *Walden* was still changing as the appointment of publication day grew closer. The book was finally accepted by the
publishing firm of Ticknor & Fields of Boston. Had Emerson
provided a lift up once more? There may have been some word
of his in the background, but Henry seems not to have shown
him the manuscript of *Walden*.

On March 23, 1854, Greeley wrote to "Dear Thoreau" and
said, "I am glad your 'Walden' is coming out. I shall announce
it at once, whether Ticknor does or not. . . . I referred (without naming you) to your 'Walden' experience in my lecture on
'Self-Culture' with which I have had ever so many audiences.
This episode excited much interest, and I have been repeatedly
asked who it is that I refer to."

A few days later Henry was writing in his journal, "Got first
proof of 'Walden.' " This and nothing more about the book,
or his feeling concerning it—no intimation of an author's growing excitement and anticipation.

Then, on August 9, 1854, after a round of surveying in Lincoln, Henry walked out to Conantum, lying west of Fair
Haven, stayed there long, and set down much description and

many thoughts. That had been a hot time and he had been baked out of his attic room into intimacy with the Thoreau family group.

"For the first time for a month, at least, I am reminded that thought is possible. The din of trivialness is silenced. . . . My life had been a River Platte, tinkling over its sands but useless for all great navigation, but now it suddenly became a fathom-less ocean. It shelved off to unimagined depths."

He sat on a rock on a hilltop after the sun had set, listening to crickets, watching the melting light, keeping company with the great adventure of nightfall and more distant adventures still.

"A few fireflies in the meadows. I am uncertain whether that so large and bright and high was a firefly or a shooting star. Shooting stars are but the fireflies of the firmament. The crickets on the causeway make a *steady* creak, on the dry pasture-tops an *interrupted* one. I was compelled to stand to write where a soft, faint light from the western sky came in between two willows."

The next words in the journal conceal the immediacy of their enormous report: "Fields today sends me a specimen copy of my 'Walden.' It is to be published on the 12th inst."

But he had not to wait until the 12th. His journal entry for August 9, Wednesday, consists of these brief words: "To Boston. 'Walden' published. Elder-berries. Waxwork yellowing."

So now there was the long measure of fulfillment, a book born, but its growth and influence still lying ahead. Greeley meant to help all he could, and he had printed in his *Tribune* on July 29 some extended passages likely to attract public interest. Two brief passages had appeared in *Sartain's Union Magazine of Literature and Art*, but these did not count much more than whispers in a fogbound room.

Emerson, on August 28, wrote to Theodore Parker, one of the transcendentalists, "All American kind are delighted with

'Walden' as far as they have dared say. . . . I do not know if the
book has come to you yet—but it is cheerful, sparkling, read-
able, with all kinds of merits, & rising sometimes to very great
heights. We account Henry the undoubted king of all American lions. He is walking up & down Concord, firm-looking, but
in a tremble of great expectations."

Most of the reviews were favorable, but the book itself had
a vitality beyond reviews, an authority of spirit and expression
that was to carry through the years. Although Emerson was
right in general, of course "all American kind" had not read the
book and would not read it for a long time to come; the sale
went slowly, even though the eventual outcome was secure.
There was to be no new edition until a year after Henry had
died.

Channing had disparaged what he had read of the book some
years before its publication, but afterward he wrote that *Walden* increased Henry's repute as a writer—which was surely
true from the outset—even "if some great men thought him
bean-dieted, with an owl for his minister, and who milked creation, not the cow. It is vain for the angels to contend against
stupidity."

But, on the other hand, stupidity had never vanquished the
angels.

9. *The Wealth of His Truth*

In the long run, across the russet autumns of many years,
scholars and critics were to devote incalculable talent to the
task of making Thoreau other than he seemed.

He had taken pains to shun the commonplace idiom, but
there were many who wished to translate him into the familiar
and ordinary and so put a neat fence around him, and perhaps
a heavily respectable monument over his tomb—like that of
Simon McTavish at Montreal—so that true memory could not

get at him even with a crowbar. In his own perspective, Henry had lived all these Concord and Walden years momentously, but the first remark of literary historians was that his life had been uneventful, showing perhaps that they did not appreciate what he had been up to.

He had asserted as boldly and clearly as a forthright man could that he had no ambition, as the word commonly runs, and apologists set out at once to prove that he really was ambitious after all and that the Walden hut occupied only a brief and minor part of his life.

He had gloried in his freedom from the servitude of toil—society could not force him to get a living by the sweat of his brow—but the apologists assured the public that he had, after all, lived industriously, when everything was considered. The truth of his contentions and theirs, of course, depended on the meaning of words used and the understanding of purposes and principles; he was much clearer as to all this than the writers who came after him, but there were more of them and for a while it seemed as if they might have the last word. *Walden* stuck it out, however, and he had the best of them there, in spite of their respectability and scholarship.

Some looked for a guide or model for society and said Thoreau was a fake because he did not supply it. He had exemplified no universal rule of conduct. He had not even advocated organic gardening. When you thought you detected the pattern coming along, he turned and you were tripped by an inconsistency. Yet he had surely made plain beyond doubt that what a man did of his own choice and pleasure, and of a spirit of independence, rejoicing in his freedom as a human being under heaven, could amount to something in a small way, or even in a greater one, if he cultivated himself rather than the conventions of the unhappy social order.

The fact that everyone could not live a Walden life was, after all, no more surprising than that everyone could not prac-

tice the career of slack-wire artist. Thoreau represented a minority, but any man or every man is a minority, and he must
then have written for the world, because the world is made up
of minorities as a wall is built of bricks. Moreover, if other men,
many, many other men, should become interested, for instance,
in a Scripture of Mankind and in implementing it in their real
lives, then the Thoreau sort of people might emerge as a majority and this apparent difficulty would solve itself. There was
a lot of needless fuss over the possibility that conscience might
lead men in different directions, whereas comparatively few
men would trouble to follow conscience at all, in any direction,
or over the first hurdle.

If a reader of *Walden* should not find *all* that a society or
a man in the world needed, it was not surprising; but it was
fairly astonishing on the other side if any reader of *Walden*
could fail to find *something* that struck deeply into his desires
and needs and most candid relationships.

Those who complained that Thoreau was not constructive,
or not constructive enough for their liking, could still not deny
that they and their friends and neighbors were indeed, as he
had said, living lives of quiet desperation. This being so, was it
for him to do something about it, or for them? His first suggestion, if not constructive, was at least practical: they should
stop in their tracks and turn. They should leave off. Further-
more, he had delivered with homely vigor and memorable sentences—lacking all usual long words—the account of what *one
man* had done about it. The truth was that Thoreau's suggestions and implications were inconvenient rather than that they
lacked constructive quality.

Daniel Ricketson, Thoreau's Quaker friend in New Bedford,
asked why he did not teach men in detail how to live a simpler
life, and so on.

"But I say that I have no scheme about it," Thoreau wrote,
"no designs on men at all; and, if I had, my mode would be to

tempt them with the fruit, and not with the manure. To what end do I lead a simple life at all, pray? That I may teach others to simplify their lives?—and so all our lives be *simplified* merely, like an algebraic formula? Or not, rather, that I may make use of the ground I have cleared, to live more worthily and profitably? I would fain lay the most stress forever on that which is the most important—imports the most to me—though it were only (what it is likely to be) a vibration in the air."

And in *Walden* itself Henry had written: "I would not have any one adopt *my* mode of living on any account; for, beside that before he has fairly learned it I may have found out another for myself, I desire that there may be as many different persons in the world as possible; but I would have each one be very careful to find out and pursue his own way, and not his father's or his mother's or his neighbour's instead."

There was a good deal of search to learn where Thoreau had got his ideas—from what philosophers, prophets, and writers— whereas this matter was really incidental, for if he had not got them in one place, he would have got them in another. These were the ideas that fitted his life, that he could entertain and incorporate into his own growth at the same time that he nourished them and caused them to expand and glisten in the sunlight out of doors.

It was true, as scholars found, that such ideas had been common currency among teachers and thinkers in different places and in different times. They were, in essence, part of the Scripture of Mankind that Thoreau referred to, even if he nor anyone had copied them down in order with subject headings and index.

Having settled the origin of the ideas, many scholars neglected to pursue this matter any further but, instead, devoted themselves to learning why Thoreau had been so odd as to express them and give them meaning in the context of Concord and America.

"I learned this, at least, by my experiment," Thoreau wrote—
and though he was speaking only of the interlude at Walden
he might have referred as well to the whole adventure of his
life—"that if one advances confidently in the direction of his
dreams, and endeavors to love the life he has arranged, he will
meet with success unexpected in common hours."

The difficulty here was with the word "success," just as
there were similar difficulties with the word "ambition." Nobody could be sure he wanted that kind of success. The life of
quiet desperation was the safe and popular one, after all. It
contemplated the chances that the world chose to count on,
and even if they were never realized they could still be contemplated.

Countless readers were tempted to close their eyes to all
Thoreau except the things he said that appealed to them. Thus
a respectable and gentle old lady could know him as the lover
of nature who wrote "the bluebird carries the sky on his back,"
and the social revolutionist had use only for his assaults against
tyranny and an existing order, as when he said, "I would remind my countrymen that they are to be men first, and Americans only at a late and convenient hour." But the revolution
that mattered to Thoreau was the revolution within the individual, and even in the anarchistic "Civil Disobedience" he
pleased himself "with imagining a state at last which can afford
to be just to all men, and to treat the individual with respect as
a neighbor; which even would not think it inconsistent with
its own repose if a few were to live aloof from it, not med-
dling with it, nor embraced by it, who fulfilled all the duties
of neighbors and fellow-men."

Taking Thoreau apart was convenient for special comfort
and prejudices, but the knotty, green-leaved fact was that he
had always been and would remain all one. It was Thoreau the
Yankee, the naturalist, the individualist, the radical, the writer—
it was he, indivisible, and none other who walked out into the

great solitary empty room of freedom and was not affrighted
by the shadows and could note as well the flower of the com-
monest weed, the application of a philosopher's thought, and
the right of a man to liberty and conscience.

"Do not waste any reverence on my attitude," Thoreau
wrote to Harrison Blake. "I merely manage to sit up where I
have dropped."

That was the essence of it all, of course. Had his Uncle
Charles needed someone to suggest that he leap over a yoke of
oxen? Thoreau had picked himself up on the path that led to
Walden Pond, and Emerson wisely pointed to this same truth:
"Perhaps he fell into his way of living without forecasting it
much, but approved it with later wisdom."

Generations of critics were to undertake to formulate Thoreau into generalized meanings, and perhaps succeeded in arriving at statements Thoreau might have accepted; but his own
giant-sized observations never meant exactly the same as the
schoolbook rhetoric drawn from them.

Scholars have difficulty in keeping him company, though
they may praise him as Emerson did. He stands back there
alone, ten miles in any direction from a house at Concord, intent on—just what?

"I, too, love Concord best, but I am glad when I discover,
in oceans and wildernesses far away, the material of a million
Concords: indeed, I am lost unless I discover them."

7

AT THE SIGN OF THE
SHRUB OAK

❧ ☙

1. *"I Am a Commoner"*

"WHAT COUSIN of mine is the shrub oak?" Henry wrote.
"Rigid as iron, clean as the atmosphere, hardy as virtue, innocent and sweet as a maiden, is the shrub oak. In proportion as I know and love it, I am natural and sound as a
partridge."

He was thirty-nine then, a graduate and postgraduate of
Walden Pond and of Emerson's household, no longer a handy
man or a young aspirant looking up to the great man of Concord with matter-of-course reverence. The valuation he put
on his own life and its expression had risen.

Long ago he had believed and written that Emerson had
"special talents unequalled. The divine in man has had no
more easy, methodically distinct expression. His personal influence upon young persons greater than any man's. In his
world every man would be a poet, Love would Reign, Beauty
would take place, Man and Nature would harmonize." The
good of this he believed still, but more and more in these years

Emerson was rubbing him the wrong way. He changed, but Emerson did not change much.

"I am a commoner," Henry declared, and that is what he was: a shrub oak, wild-apple commoner, tart, sturdy, ineradicable in his own ground. "To me there is something devilish in manners. I should value E.'s praise more, which is always so discriminating, if there were not some alloy of patronage and hence of flattery about it. . . . They flatter you but themselves more. Praise should be spoken as simply and naturally as a flower emits its fragrance."

Emerson was a democrat but no commoner. He dwelt upon a New England Olympus, and though poet, philosopher, essayist, and a sort of pagan at times, he had never entirely shaken off the habit of the clergyman, which meant that his attitudes would necessarily glow from within—and with authority. He did not mean to be patronizing, but he could not help being centrifugal. His attitude toward Henry Thoreau was free from any claim: he did not consider Henry a dependent; he was aware of no obligation owed to him; he respected Henry's character and mind. But still, here was Emerson, and here was Thoreau!

"Talked, or tried to talk, with R. W. E. Lost my time—nay, almost my identity. He, assuming a false opposition where there was no difference of opinion, talked to the wind—told me what I knew—and I lost my time trying to imagine myself somebody else to oppose him."

Within a few days from the time Henry entered these words in one Concord journal, Emerson was writing an observation from his point of view in a different journal: "Henry is military. He seemed stubborn and implacable; always manly and wise, but rarely sweet. One would say that, as Webster could never speak without an antagonist, Henry does not feel himself except in opposition. He wants a fallacy to expose, a blunder to pillory, requires a little sense of victory, a roll of the drums, to call his powers into full exercise."

Not long before this time, Henry had heard Thomas Wentworth Higginson at the lyceum, and he asked himself why he did not like the lecture better. Well, for one thing, Higginson reminded him of Emerson "and I could not afford to be reminded of Christ himself. . . ."

To this plain-spoken passage in his journal Henry added a note of realization that he was parting company with the best friend he ever had, possibly with better understanding even than before, but no longer with an expectation of agreement. The fact, he thought, was as elemental as geography—two paths diverged. Emerson, on his side, summed up his feeling in words of rare expressiveness: "Always some weary captious paradox to fight you with, and time and temper wasted."

Henry objected to a man who used "made words," and exclaimed in his journal, "O, would you but be simple and downright! Would you but cease your palaver! . . . Repeating himself, shampooing himself! Passing the time of day, as if he were just introduced! . . . Never a natural or simple word or yawn. It produces an appearance of phlegm and stupidity in me the auditor. I am suddenly the closest and most phlegmatic of mortals, and the conversation comes to naught. . . ."

Of course every literary man used "made words" more or less, be they multisyllabled and obtrusive, or split like a rail fence and weathered; that was "style." The real trouble was with Emerson as a Concord Olympian and writer of so many letters. He should at least have been able to ride away from embarrassing situations in a golden chariot, but when it came to a pinch he was earthbound, handicapped with heavenly weapons.

Emerson's authority and mystery in Concord were less because of certain incidents such as that in which he failed to recognize his own calf and drove it out of the yard while some

cattle were passing in the highway. Or that in which a dele-
gation waited on him to learn how he managed to raise such
poor fruit of such excellent varieties. Or that in which he went
to the Adirondacks with a hunting party, and his son Eddy
said he had taken a double-barreled gun, one side for shot, the
other for ball, but Concord wits maintained the gun would
throw shot from one end and ball from another.

It was not only Emerson, of course, who rubbed Henry the
wrong way. Again and again at this period of his life he returned to the same theme in the pages of his journal: "By myself I can live and thrive, but in the society of incompatible
friends I starve. . . . I cannot trust my neighbors whom I know
any more than I can trust the law of gravitation and jump off
the Cliffs. . . . No fields are so barren to me as the men of whom
I expect everything and get nothing."

The native countryside was his habitat; there alone he felt
at home, expanded his senses, entered into understanding.

"Human beings with whom I have no sympathy are far
stranger to me than inanimate matter—rocks or earth. Looking on the last, I feel comparatively as if I were with my
kindred."

Yet still the tie with the Emersons remained. Emerson's
mother had died late in 1853 and it was Henry Thoreau who
took charge of funeral arrangements and went to Littleton to
accompany Robert Bulkeley Emerson to Concord for the cere-
monies. A few years later when this brother of Emerson's,
whom he called "Bulkeley," died, it was again Henry who arranged the funeral and took burdens from the family. And in
1855, a few months after *Walden* came out, Emerson wrote to
his brother William, "Henry Thoreau is feeble and languishes
this season, to our alarm. We have tried to persuade him to
come & spend a week with us for a change." When Emerson
left for a lecture tour in the West, he put some of his affairs in
Henry's hands, to be looked after as of old.

2. *Love by Refusal*

There had been a slow but great change in the relationship between Henry and Lidian. The essence of this transition was that each had become, was still becoming, older. In the year of *Walden*'s publication Henry was thirty-seven and Lidian fifty-two; when they had first met at Concord he had been eighteen and she thirty-three. Arithmetically, the difference separating them was still just nineteen years—but the measurement of years is a delicate, shifting sort of thing, weighted with strange significances, as if all years were not of the same length or substance.

Youth had drained out of their landscape like the white mists from the pond holes around Concord, and so many other elements were inseparable from youth. Constellations had altered above them, or at least they saw the constellations differently and by rays of light that had left the past far behind. In New England more than in other regions the passing of years meant deepened creases in faces and characters, stiffness of joints and opinions, ailments, complaints, hardened attitudes.

Youth, even the comparative youth of Lidian at thirty-three, could evoke and perceive mystery without disappointing it with definitions and words, could suggest and encourage subtleties of understanding; but middle-age was confirmed, specific, and flat. What had been tender and variable now suffered from crystallization.

"Alas! Alas!" wrote Henry in 1851, "when my friend begins to deal in confessions, breaks silence, makes a theme of friendship (which is then something past) and descends to merely human relations! As long as there is a spark of love remaining, cherish that alone. Only *that* can be kindled into a flame. . . . But now that my friend, rashly, thoughtlessly, profanely speaks, *recognizing* the distance between us, that distance seems infinitely increased!"

Certain passages in Henry's journal, following such a direction, did not specify the sex of the friend referred to, but they have the feeling of a woman—of Lidian, then—in the background. Lidian was long past her taste for transcendentalism and was resorting with considered fervor and tenacity to Christianity. She had known for a good while that the only love letters, the only *real* love letters, written by her husband that she would ever read were those addressed to his first wife. Her only design now would be to affect him with her own sense of the right and the real, in matters visible and invisible, to find expression in household affairs such as New England had ever held a minor sort of godliness, and to wear out her invalidism.

If Henry's feeling for Lidian had changed, then, it was time that should be held responsible first and last, though Lidian was a human agent of time. As Henry poured many of his confidences beyond Concord and into the environs of Worcester, where Harrison Blake lived, he now embodied in a letter to Blake his thoughts on Chastity and Sensuality, an essay in brief.

"Let us love by refusing, not accepting one another." Here, quite plainly, lay the philosophy of the East, the renunciation of desire for the sake of a higher and greater elevation of the spirit; but there was no proving that Henry got it from the East, for there were all sorts of ideas lying around Concord. This one fitted the design and temper of Henry's life—to make his demands on the world small. But such a principle he had applied only to material things, and his demands in the higher mode of life had soared without limit.

Mystically, he was here seeking the broader and untrammeled fields beyond the common way—to gain more by refusing than by accepting, to settle for no particular price or on no stated terms, but to remain open to all paradise. He returned likewise to the theme of his silent romance with Ellen Sewall— the love that would become less or might become nothing at all

if it were mutilated by avowals. "Never to profane one another by word or action, even by a thought. Between us, if
necessary, let there be no acquaintance."

This was the theme that ran on and on.

"The intercourse of the sexes, I have dreamed, is incredibly
beautiful," Henry wrote in the essay he sent to Harrison Blake,
"too fair to be remembered. I have had thoughts about it, but
they are among the most fleeting and irrecoverable of my experience. It is strange that men will talk of miracles, revelation,
inspiration, and the like, as things past, while love remains."

Love remains because it is of each new minute, never translated into the recession of things past.

As in the other figures of his life's design, it was likely that
Henry had scarcely entertained any advance intention that his
relationship with women should work out so; yet, perhaps, he
really had done so, at least mystically. At any rate, he had met
each turning in his characteristic way, as if knowing in advance where the right direction lay for him.

If he seemed committed to this mysticism, and to retreat at
the point at which men advanced, he was yet plainer than most
men in his contemplation of sex. He did not find it necessary
to execute evasions around the subject. He was frank and open.

"Nature allows of no universal secrets," he wrote in his journal. "The more carefully a secret is kept on one side of the
globe, the larger the type it is printed in on the other. Nothing
is too pointed, too personal, too immodest for her to blazon.
The relations of sex, transferred to flowers, become the studies
of ladies in the drawing-room. While men wear fig leaves, she
grows the Phallus impudicus and P. caninus and other phallus-
like fungi.

"The rhymes which I used to see on the walls of privies,
scribbled by boys, I have lately seen, word for word, the same.
. . . They are no doubt older than Orpheus. . . . The poetry of
the jakes—it flows as perennially as the gutter."

He picked and took home a rare and remarkable fungus—"in all respects a most disgusting object, yet very suggestive." Soon the deliquescing fungus scented the whole Thoreau house, "so that it could not be endured. I was afraid to sleep in my chamber where it had lain until the room had been well ventilated. It smelled like a dead rat in the ceiling, in all the ceilings of the house. Pray, what was Nature thinking of when she made this? She almost puts herself on a level with those who draw in privies."

Henry sat at Emerson's table and discussed with Louis Agassiz, the naturalist, the copulation of turtles. The natural functions were everyday affairs.

Naturally a man whose relations with women were detached or idyllic in any sense must become the study of an age instructed and made sophisticated in such matters by the discoveries of Freud. A biographer who neglected this study would be harshly arraigned, yet a biographer who applied himself to it diligently would be arraigned too. The lingo is too glib, the source material too deep in the past, too poorly defined. After all, what could be said beyond the obvious, meantime raising doubts whether the obvious in this case was especially significant?

There might be a question whether Henry Thoreau became the man he was because of forces having to do with the libido and so on, or whether his attitude toward sex resulted from the fact that he was the particular rugged individual known as Henry Thoreau. The scholars of psychiatry are said to be openminded, ready to allow and take account of any other drive as important or as powerful as sex if any turns up, though none has turned up yet; but this is a matter of the society that we know, and it has been shown that other societies are different. Henry Thoreau did not live altogether in the society that we know.

No doubt any exploration would be justified if some qualified inquirer wished to undertake it, yet in the end it is certain that the whole of Thoreau as a personality is bound to remain more authoritative and significant than any dissected psychic fractions. He was integrated and sound, his life based on advance and not on retreat; however he was compounded, how much of heredity, how much of Concord and of Emerson, how much of the Bhagavad-Gita and the renunciations of the East, how much of circumstance in his formative period, how much of physical characteristics such as his beaklike nose, how much of a psyche's yearning, he came out completely integrated and honest like the climate.

Anyone who looked behind his contrariness and paradoxes could find no different person than he said he was, than he wanted to be. As for his devotion to nature, it was never a puppy-love affair. He was a mature suitor of the natural world under the sign of the shrub oak.

It does not appear that he concealed any matter concerning himself of which he was aware. He left even the account of a dream or two for future generations.

"I can remember that when I was very young I used to have a dream night after night, over and over again, which might have been named Rough and Smooth. All existence, all satisfaction and dissatisfaction, all event was symbolized in this way. Now I seemed to be lying and tossing, perchance, on a horrible, a fatal rough surface, which must soon, indeed, put an end to my existence, though even in my dream I knew it to be the symbol merely of my misery; and then again, suddenly, I was lying on a delicious smooth surface, as of a summer sea, as of gossamer or down or softest plush, and life was such a luxury to live. My waking experience *always* has been and is such an alternate Rough and Smooth. In other words it is Insanity and Sanity."

Then there was a dream mountain in the easterly part of our town "where no high hill actually is." The dream had returned so often that it seemed to merge with the real. "My way up used to lie through a dark and unfrequented wood at its base— I cannot now tell exactly, it was so long ago, under what circumstances I first ascended, only that I shuddered as I went along (I have an indistinct remembrance of having been out overnight alone)—and then I steadily ascended along a rocky ridge half clad with stunted trees, where wild beasts haunted, till I lost myself quite in the upper air and clouds, seeming to pass an imaginary line which separates a hill, mere earth heaped up, from a mountain, into a superterranean grandeur and sublimity."

There was an awful and thrilling sublimity on that summit. "In dreams I am shown this height from time to time, and I seem to have asked my fellow once to climb there with me, and yet I am constrained to believe that I never actually ascended it. It chances, now I think of it, that it rises in my mind where lies the Burying-Hill. You might go through its gate to enter that dark wood, but that hill and its graves are so concealed and obliterated by the awful mountain that I never thought of them as underlying it. Might not the graveyards of the just always be hills, by which we ascend and overlook the plain."

There was more of this. Thoreau liked mysticism. He had no fear of it, or of sentiment, or of science either. When the Association for the Advancement of Science asked what branch interested him he "was obliged to speak to their condition and describe to them that poor part of me which alone they can understand. The fact is I am a mystic, a transcendentalist, and a natural philosopher to boot." Henry was roused to indignation when a man brought him a two-headed calf, expecting him to be interested in the freak. He was "not interested in mere phenomena, though it were the explosion of a planet, only as it may have lain in the experience of a human being."

Once he wrote, "I witness a beauty in the form of coloring

of the clouds which addresses itself to my imagination, for which you account scientifically to my understanding, but do not so account to my imagination. It is what it suggests and is the symbol of that I care for, and if, by any trick of science, you rob it of its symbolicalness, you do me no service and explain nothing. . . . What sort of science is that which enriches the understanding but robs the imagination?"

And another time: "Even the facts of science may dust the mind by their dryness, unless they are in a sense effaced each morning, or rather rendered fertile by the dews of fresh and living truth."

He performed feats of exact observation, measurement, enumeration, all in matters that caught his interest, not from any devotion to method or general scientific inquiry, and was no happier in the performance of these literal functions than when he noted that the dogwood blossoms were "like a small flock of white birds passing"—no, nor as happy. He liked new and profound experiments but also to see how well he could swim with one hand while he held up all his clothes with the other, and to note how far his eyes could penetrate a blue October haze in Thrush Alley Path, or among the trees in Abel Brooks's deep hollow.

As Channing observed, the poet and naturalist in him were well mixed. The white-throated sparrows sang under his window in the morning "like a clear sweet squeaking wheelbarrow." A poet, but with his own ear for the songs of the world; a naturalist, but nonconforming, personal, unreliable for the purposes of the textbook zealots who came after him.

"The seasons and all their changes are in me. I see not a dead eel or a floating snake, or a gull, but it rounds my life and is like a line or an accent in a poem. Almost I believe the Concord would not rise and overflow its banks again, were I not here. . . ."

This was the Henry Thoreau who wrote his own farewell

to the emotions he had felt toward Lidian Emerson: "The obstacles which the heart meets with are like granite blocks which one alone cannot move. She who was the morning light to me is now neither the morning light nor the evening star. We meet but to find each other further asunder, and the oftener we meet the more rapid our divergence. So a star of the first magnitude pales in the heavens, not from any fault in the observer's eye nor from any fault in itself, perchance, but because its progress in its own system has put a greater distance between."

A year before *Walden* Henry had written, "To be married at least should be the one poetical act of a man's life." He never ceased to be aware of the poetry, but he must have felt always that the realization of poetry, especially for a man such as he, would be a chancy thing.

Now that he was addressing words of admiration to the shrub oak, he seemed to come closer likewise to his sister Sophia and even to the other women of the Thoreau household. Sometimes he took them on excursions, as he had not often done before.

"With Sophia boated to Fair Haven where she made a sketch."

"Yesterday, toward night, gave Sophia and mother a sail as far as the Battle-ground."

"Up Assabet to cress, with Sophia . . ."

One September he collected and brought home twelve varieties of aster and placed them side by side, so that Sophia could help him decide which, as an individual flower, seemed handsomest. She took an active interest in his collecting, made observations herself that he noted in his journal. He called to Sophia so that she could see two enormous pine sticks going by on the railroad, and when she went to Boston on the cars she described to Henry the dewlike frost of an early September chill on the meadows.

Henry even went a-chestnutting (his word) to Smith's wood lot, and carried four ladies, including Aunt Maria.

When Sophia conducted some visitor to Henry's attic room she remarked, with sisterly depreciation, that he considered the dust on his furniture like the bloom on fruits, not to be swept off. He liked the simile and wrote in his journal that the bloom on fruits and stems was the only dust that settled on nature's furniture.

3. *New Friends*

Emerson's Concord had become like an old orchard with some of the trees sagging and others fallen to the ground. Margaret Fuller was dead, and they were writing their reminiscences of her. Hawthorne was a creature of passage. He had lost his Salem customs-house post after the election of a new President, had then lived awhile in Lenox in the western part of the state, and in 1852 had come back to Concord, buying a house called Hillside, where the Alcotts had lived, renaming it Wayside. Emerson, who owned eight acres of the Hillside land, aided in its purchase. But this return by Hawthorne meant little in further friendship with Thoreau.

The Alcotts, as always, were migratory and at present were out of season in Concord. Channing, estranged from his wife, was living alone and inclined to pull up stakes. He described himself as "a poet, or of a poetical temper or mood, with a very limited income, both of brains and moneys" and was finding the world, which included Concord, a sour place.

The aging and thinning of the orchard made it simpler for Henry to perfect new friendships, his own. Harrison Blake in Worcester was firmly established as correspondent and disciple, and now that *Walden* was published others would write to Thoreau and come to see him. Emerson's influence might be in the background too, as with a young Englishman, Thomas

Cholmondeley, who visited Concord in 1854 and was sent by Emerson to board at the Thoreau home, or the friendship might be all Henry's, as in the case of Daniel Ricketson, a Quaker squire of New Bedford.

Cholmondeley was at Concord only a month then, but he joined Henry and Channing in a walk to Mount Wachusett; a little later he took ship for home to help fight the Crimean War, but found time in London to send Henry twenty-four volumes of Indian history and philosophy, and Henry, in telling another friend of the gift, said he was announcing it as he might the birth of a child.

Daniel Ricketson was about three years younger than Henry and had lived a different sort of life. Though a Quaker, and with this simplicity of principle about him, he was born to wealth. As one of his station should be, he was prepared for college—and that college would naturally be Harvard—at the Friends Academy in New Bedford. But he failed his examinations on the first try and ultimately spent only two college years, though later he studied law in the office of a New Bedford attorney and was admitted to the bar.

Gradually he gave up worldly occupation and devoted himself to the cultivation of literature and nature. He liked to correspond with poets and tried his own hand, not successfully, at verse. When *Walden* was published he had just acquired a rural estate beyond the city limits of New Bedford, and while the house was being rebuilt his family stayed in town and he lived in a small structure he had caused to be put up in the grounds for a study and retreat. This he named "The Shanty," and when he wrote to Henry Thoreau he did not omit to mention it, as well as the fact that the observations about nature in *Walden* were delightful to him.

This letter of Ricketson's was discursive and lengthy. He spoke of a leaning toward vegetarianism and the fact that for two years he had lived in capital health on Dr. Sylvester Graham's system; he described his shanty and referred to birds as "feathered tribes." The date was August 12, 1854, and Thoreau did not reply until October 1. Ricketson thought the reply unsatisfactory and that it indicated overcaution, but he himself wrote again, addressing Thoreau as "Dear Mr. Walden."

Henry's letter, which Ricketson had not much liked, said, "Yours is the only word of greeting I am likely to receive from a dweller in the woods like myself—from where the whippoorwill and cuckoo are heard, and there are better than moral clouds drifting, and real breezes blowing."

The lecturing business had picked up a little for Henry, though, as he said, he did his work clean each time and was not likely to be asked a second time to the same place. He consoled himself with the reflection that the demand for lecturers was for average men, and if he should popularize himself he could not avoid cheapening himself too. At any rate he was now invited to lecture at Nantucket and on his way paid a visit to Daniel Ricketson at Brooklawn, on the rim of New Bedford.

Henry had strong stuff in store for the unsuspecting inhabitants of Nantucket, but why not? "Preaching? Lecturing? Who are ye that ask for these things? What do ye want to hear, ye puling infants? A trumpet-sound that would train you up to mankind, or a nurse's lullaby? . . . Why, a free-spoken man, of sound lungs, cannot draw a long breath without causing your rotten institutions to come toppling down by the vacuum he makes. . . . I will not consent to walk with my mouth muzzled, not till I am rabid, until there is danger that I shall bite the unoffending and that my bite will produce hydrophobia."

"Freedom of speech! It hath not entered into your hearts' to conceive what those words mean. It is not leave given me by your sect to say this or that; it is when leave is given to your sect to withdraw. . . . They want me to agree not to breathe too hard in the neighborhood of their paper castles. . . ."

This outburst, and much more, was to come in Henry's journal somewhat later; for the present he set out in the direction of New Bedford and Nantucket with a lecture that would be printed eventually as "Life without Principle."

Ricketson's own account of Thoreau's arrival at Brooklawn on Christmas Day, 1854, is in these words: "I had expected him at noon, but as he did not arrive, I had given him up for the day. In the latter part of the afternoon I was clearing off the snow from my front steps, when, looking up, I saw a man walking up the carriage road, bearing a portmanteau in one hand and an umbrella in the other. He was dressed in a long overcoat of a dark color and wore a dark soft hat. I had no suspicion it was Thoreau, and rather supposed it was a peddler of small wares."

The disappointment that afflicted Henry's host at finding him slight and quaint-looking—to say the least—rather than robust and impressive was dissipated at the dinner table when Henry's conversation proved more than satisfactory. A new friendship was formed, not closely but firmly. The shared interests of the two men included opposition to slavery and active succoring of runaway slaves, shanties, nature in general and ponds in particular, literature, and so on. Ricketson knew how to live graciously and he liked to play the host to literary men. On his side, Henry was as uncritical in his relationship with Ricketson as in that with Blake; neither represented a first-rate mind in the age of Emerson, or in the age of Thoreau. Once when Alcott turned up at Concord all in a dither about his family tree, Henry observed that he would be better employed with the genealogy of mankind; but Henry drove ten miles with Ricketson while the latter explored some item of family descent, and offered no comment whatever.

The appointments of Ricketson's shanty were different from those of the Walden hut: "a wooden lounge made easy by a pillow or two, a little old settle of the last century, a writing desk, bundles of papers thrown over the rafters above, a great variety of walking shoes, coats, etc., and three or four comfortable chairs were among the most prominent objects." Ricketson could scarcely have moved his belongings to the lawn conveniently while he sluiced out his shanty with a few buckets of water.

Henry's most celebrated stay at Brooklawn supplied a famous incident described by Ricketson as follows: "One afternoon when my wife was playing an air upon the piano—'Highland Laddie,' perhaps—Thoreau became very hilarious, sang 'Tom Bowline,' and finally entered upon an improvised dance. Not being able to stand what appeared to me at the time the somewhat ludicrous appearance of our Walden hermit, I retreated to my 'shanty,' a short distance from my house; while my older and more humor-loving friend Alcott remained and saw it through, much to his amusement."

Once, sheltered by Lee's Cliff at Concord in a driving May rain, Henry sang "Tom Bowline" to the elements, and to himself. It was a song he liked, the words ending:

> Yet shall poor Tom find pleasant weather
>   When He who all commands
> Shall give, to call life's crew together,
>   The word to pipe all hands.
> This death, who kings and tars dispatches,
>   In vain Tom's life has doffed;
> For though his body's under hatches,
>   His soul has gone aloft.

When Sophia and Henry's mother heard about his improvised dance at Brooklawn, they were surprised that anyone should have been surprised; Sophia said they had often seen Henry cut up in such a manner. It did not even surprise them that Henry had taken pains to step on Alcott's toes.

As for Ricketson, forgetting his disapproval at the moment, he embalmed the episode in verses later included in a volume, *The Autumn Sheaf*, which he brought out himself in 1869. Some of the concluding stanzas may be worth quoting as a sample of the poetic style of this friend of Thoreau's:

> Like the Fauns and Satyrs too,
>   Nimbly leaping in the grove
> Now unseen, and then in view,
>   As amid the trees they move—
>
> Like the leaves by whirlwind tossed,
>   In some forest's valley wide,
> Scattered by the Autumn frost,
>   Whirling madly side by side—
>
> Thus, and still mysterious more,
>   Our philosopher did prance,
> Skipping on our parlor floor,
>   In his wild improvised dance.

As it turned out, Henry lectured not only at Nantucket but at New Bedford, though Ricketson, not up to snuff, did not attend. Two communities strongly infused with Quaker tradition, both seats of wealth and ease channeled from afar by means of the whaling industry, may have gulped at some of Henry's plain and sun-bright words.

"The ways by which you may get money almost without exception lead downward."

"I wish to suggest that a man may be very industrious and yet not spend his time well."

"If a man walk in the woods for love of them half of each day, he is in danger of being regarded as a loafer; but if he spends his whole day as a speculator, shearing off those woods and making the earth bald before her time, he is esteemed an industrious and enterprising citizen. As if a town had no interest in its forests but to cut them down!"

"To speak impartially, the best men I know are not serene, a world in themselves. For the most part, they dwell in forms, and flatter and study effect only more finely than the rest."

"I hardly know an *intellectual* man, even, who is so broad and truly liberal that you can think aloud in his society. Most with whom you endeavor to talk soon come to a stand against some institution in which they appear to hold stock—that is, some particular, not universal way of viewing things. They continually thrust their own low roof, with its narrow sky-light, between you and the sky, when it is the unobstructed heavens you would view. Get out of the way with your cobwebs, wash your windows, I say!"

". . . we are warped and narrowed by an exclusive devotion to trade and commerce and manufactures and agriculture and the like, which are but means, and not the end."

4. *"To Be Men First"*

That summer during which *Walden* was published, Henry completed the utterance begun at the time of the fugitive-slave cases of Shadrach and of Simms. Now another runaway was taken in Boston and marched off through cleared streets held by the force of arms, to be returned to Southern servitude. This time it was a man named Anthony Burns, who was seized as less than a man, a slave. A bold demonstration was made of the fact that in Boston, although a mob took the side of freedom—and one of the attacking mob was killed—the authority and power of the state was on the side of slavery and the law, not inquiring whether the law was just or infamous.

On the Fourth of July Henry Thoreau unloosed the accumulated force of his personal testimony on the subject. He spoke in Framingham and for once was in demand as a lecturer. An audience waited eagerly, tensely to hear him express what no other could put in words quite so well.

"Again it happens that the Boston Courthouse is full of armed men, holding prisoner and trying a MAN, to find out if he is not really a SLAVE. Does anyone think that justice or God awaits Mr. Loring's decision? For him to sit there deciding still, when this question is already decided from eternity to eternity, and the unlettered slave himself and the multitude around have long heard and assented to the decision, is simply to make himself ridiculous. . . ."

"The law will never make men free; it is men who have got to make the law free."

"I would remind my countrymen that they are to be men first, and Americans only at a late and convenient hour. No matter how valuable law may be to protect your property, even to keep soul and body together, if it do not keep you and humanity together . . ."

Henry blazed at Massachusetts, at the law, at Concord, at the pretenses of government and men. There was no immediate result, except that he had contributed his best genius to the cause of man's inalienable freedom, and that he had been heard far beyond the hall at Framingham.

The anti-slavery cause became a contributing factor in his association with a new member of the group at Concord, Franklin B. Sanborn, who was to be one of the first biographers. Sanborn was a senior at Harvard when *Walden* came out and also, as it happened, editor of the Harvard Magazine, published monthly, which printed a review of the book. Alert to opportunities, as authors have been and are, Thoreau sought the college editor in his dormitory room to say a word of thanks, missed him, and left a presentation copy of the *Week*. Sanborn later addressed a note to Thoreau saying that the review had not been written by him but by a young man named Morton, a pupil of Marston Watson of Plymouth, and that the copy of the *Week* had been passed on to Morton.

In a few weeks, however, Sanborn arrived at Concord to

take over the teaching of a school, at the invitation of Emerson. He began to take his meals at the Thoreau home and became, if not a friend, at least an intimate of Henry Thoreau's. That Sanborn was to become a significant figure in the anti-slavery cause remained for the future to disclose; but here he was in Concord, and soon was living in Channing's house, Channing having gone to work on the New Bedford *Mercury*.

Through Sanborn's eyes one may observe Thoreau as he impressed a Concord newcomer in April 1855: "Tonight we had a call from Mr. Thoreau, who came at eight and stayed till ten. He talked about Latin and Greek—which he thought ought to be studied—and about other things. In his tones and gestures he seemed to me to imitate Emerson, so that it was annoying to listen to him, though he said many good things. He looks like Emerson, too—coarser, but with something of that serenity and sagacity which E. has. Thoreau looks eminently sagacious—like a sort of wise, wild beast. He dresses plainly, wears a beard at his throat, and has a brown complexion."

Henry's beard was new that year. Daniel Ricketson had described him in 1854 without it, and now considered the beard an improvement in Thoreau's "manly expression."

Sanborn's opinion was somewhat modified in another entry in his diary a month or two later. Then he wrote that Henry was "a little under size, with a huge Emersonian nose, bluish gray eyes, brown hair, and a ruddy weather-beaten face, which reminds me of some shrewd and honest animal's—some retired philosophical woodchuck or magnanimous fox. He dresses very plainly, wears his collar turned over like Mr. Emerson, and often an old dress-coat, broad in the skirts, and by no means a fit. He walks about with a brisk, rustic air, and never seems tired."

Sanborn provided glimpses of the Thoreau home and its occupants. Henry's mother, he noted, as others did, was talkative. "Her conversations generally put a stop to other

occupations; and when at her table Henry Thoreau's talk
with others was interrupted by this flow of speech at the other
end of the board, he would pause, and wait with entire and
courteous silence, until the interruption ceased, and then take
up the thread of his own discourse where he had dropped it;
bowing to his mother, but without a word of comment on what
she had said."

Some who read Sanborn's biography of Henry felt drawn
to defend Mrs. Thoreau against such comments; but what
really seemed to trouble them was that Sanborn did not like
her. Of course she was talkative, and so were most lively New
England women. They gossiped, they talked, they had company manners and everyday manners, they made acute and
often telling remarks about townspeople and even about neighbors and friends.

It was Sanborn who told of Mrs. Thoreau's call on Miss
Mary Moody Emerson at a time when this remarkable aunt of
Emerson's was eighty-four as against Mrs. Thoreau's seventy.
Henry's mother wore long bonnet ribbons of a bright color—
perhaps yellow, Sanborn thought. At any rate, as the call
ended, Miss Emerson said, "Perhaps you noticed, Mrs. Thoreau, that I closed my eyes during your call. I did so because I
did not wish to look upon the ribbons you are wearing, so unsuitable for a child of God and a person of your years."

Miss Emerson was always more severe with women than
with men, whom she thought better worth listening to. She
recognized Henry's worth specifically. "It was not the fashion
to be so original when I was young," she told him, but he noted
that she was readier to take his view—to look through his eyes
for a time—than any of the younger people he knew in Concord.

As for Mrs. Thoreau, she was running the house, managing
the meals, keeping abreast of the ailments of her family. There
were the usual major and minor themes, one of the latter illus-

trated by the chance that led Min, the Thoreau cat, to go to
sleep on the bread dough and cause it to rise all around her.
Another, concerning all who dwelt under the Thoreau roof,
was the escape of Father's pig.

Henry came downstairs, full of plans for a trip on the river,
and was confronted with the news that the pig was out. He
"proposed to Father to sell the pig as he was running (somewhere) to a neighbor who had talked of buying him, making a
considerable reduction. But my suggestion was not acted on,
and the responsibilities of the case all devolved upon me, for I
could run faster than Father. Father looked to me, and I ceased
to look to the river."

Henry caught the pig, though not easily and not without
assistance. "So I get home at dark, wet through and supper-
less, covered with mud and wheel-grease, without any rare
flowers."

Again the pig escaped. "Neighbors sympathized as much as
in them lay. It was the town talk; the meetings were held at
Wolcott & Holden's. Every man told of his losses and disap-
pointments in this line. One had heard of his pig last up in
Westford, but never saw him again; another had only caught
his pig by his running against a post so hard as to stun him for
a few moments. It was thought this one must have been born
in the woods, for he would run and leap like a wolf. . . ."

Father's pig was ultimately recovered and put into a new
pen, a very deep one. It might have been made even deeper,
Henry noted, but Father said he did not wish to keep his pig
in a well.

Thus the minor themes, and illustrative of a major one was
the death of Uncle Charles, that rare old character. When
Uncle Charles was seventy-three and well settled away from
wrestling and into catnapping, he and Henry conversed one
evening about various prominent Americans, the discussion
running on the point as to which of these men were geniuses.

At length Henry showed the old man up to bed, "and when I had got to bed myself I heard the chamber door open, after eleven o'clock, and he called out in an earnest, stentorian voice, loud enough to wake the whole house, 'Henry! Was John Quincy Adams a genius?' 'No, I think not,' was my reply. 'Well, I didn't think he was,' answered he."

With that, Uncle Charles composed himself to slumber, and one white March day he dropped off to sleep for good.

"He was born," Henry wrote, "in February, 1780, the winter of the Great Snow, and he died in the winter of another great snow—a life bounded by great snows."

So ran the major theme of life and death, and for Henry in the spring of 1855 came a long illness shadowing him and the house of Thoreau. Long week on long week he had to lie in bed.

"I should feel a little less ashamed if I could give any name to my disorder," he wrote to Blake "—but I cannot, and our doctor cannot help me to it—and I will not take the name of any disease in vain. However, there is one consolation in being sick; and that is the possibility that you may recover to a better state than you were in before."

Henry did recover, though not to a better state, and it was as if the precedent of grave illness had been established and hung over him from then on, as the authorities hang over a practitioner of the law. When summer came on, he was able to be out and to attempt many of his normal activities.

In July he yielded to Ellery Channing's persuasion and went with him to Cape Cod, the second of three visits, looking forward to a restorative week at Truro. The two boarded with the keeper of the Highland Light for a charge of $3.50 a week, and rejoiced in inhabiting for a time the best place in the United States from which to see the ocean. But long after he had returned to Concord, Henry still spoke of his feebleness and of the difficulty of getting strength back into his legs.

5. *The Age of Miracles*

The Concord assessors called in the author of *Walden* and asked for an inventory of his property. Did he own any real estate?

"No," he said.

"Any notes at interest or railroad shares?"

"No."

"Any taxable property?"

None that he knew of. "I own a boat."

One of the assessors wondered hopefully whether the boat might come under the head of a pleasure carriage and so be regarded as taxable, but he had to give up the notion. So the taxing authorities could do nothing with Henry, but still his complaint was the same as always, not that he possessed too little but that he was in danger of possessing too much.

"Within the last five years I have had the command of a little more money than in the previous five years, for I have sold some books and some lectures; yet I have not been a whit better fed or clothed or warmed or sheltered, not a whit richer except that I have been less concerned about my living, but perhaps my life has been the less serious for it, and, to balance it, I feel now that there is a possibility of failure. Who knows but I *may* come upon the town if, as is likely, the public want no more of my books, or lectures (which is already the case)? Before, I was much likelier to take the town on my shoulders. That is, I have lost some of my independence on them, when they say that I have gained an independence. If you wish to give a man a sense of poverty, give him a thousand dollars. The next hundred he gets will not be worth more than ten he used to get. Have pity on him; withhold your gifts."

When Henry found himself possessed of thirty dollars he had forgotten he owned, he acknowledged himself disappointed. He had no wish to lose the money, yet he had been happier before he came upon it.

Not prosperity, not even so meager a portion of it as Henry's words indicated, had anything much to do with his manner of life. The only thing really capable of changing him was ill health. Though the strength in his legs was so slow in returning, he managed to resume many outdoor projects. Again that fall he was on the river collecting driftwood for fuel. He retrieved a floating pine log and cut off two slices to serve as wheels in getting his boat up. He waited for the freeze so that he could survey a swamp that was usually inaccessible because of water. Then, deep in the Concord winter, he saw a flock of redpolls, "crimson aerial creatures."

"My body is all sentient. As I go here or there, I am tickled by this or that I come in contact with, as if I touched the wires of a battery. . . . The age of miracles is each moment thus returned. Now it is wild apples, now river reflections, now a flock of lesser redpolls. In winter, too, resides immortal youth and perennial summer. Its head is not silvered; its cheek is not blanched but has a ruby tinge to it."

A great elm of Concord was cut down, and Henry found himself the chief mourner, perhaps the only one, though he did not commonly attend funerals. "How much of Concord falls with it! A few such elms would alone constitute a township. They might claim to send a representative to the General Court to look after their interests, if a fit one could be found, a native American one in a true and worthy sense, with catholic principles."

Daniel Ricketson suggested another visit to Brooklawn, but Henry wrote, "I should very much enjoy further rambling with you in your vicinity but must postpone it for the present. To tell the truth, I am planning to get seriously to work after these long months of inefficiency and idleness."

"Seriously to work"—such words would have seemed ironic to Concord, where it was known that Henry worked only in relatively little of his time, at surveying, or at the graphite business at home. What did he mean?

A year after this letter to Ricketson, Henry wrote more plainly in his journal: "I see that my neighbors look with compassion on me, that they think it is a mean and unfortunate destiny which makes me to walk in these fields and woods so much and sail on this river alone. But so long as I find here the only real elysium, I cannot hesitate in my choice. My work is writing and I do not hesitate, though I know that no subject is too trivial for me, tried by ordinary standards; for, ye fools, the theme is nothing, the life is everything."

His work was writing, and so it had been all along and was to be in the future.

This was the year in which the Saturday Club was founded, an assemblage of luminaries that included, or was to include presently, Emerson, Agassiz, Judge Rockwood Hoar, James Russell Lowell, John Lothrop Motley, Henry Wadsworth Longfellow, Oliver Wendell Holmes, and others. Henry Thoreau was invited to join these other men of letters and of high attainments, but his taste ran against clubs. He went once to the Parker House, where meetings were held, when none was in session, and found it hard to see through the cigar smoke.

"The only room in Boston which I visit with alacrity," he wrote to Blake, "is the Gentlemen's Room at the Fitchburg Depot, where I wait for the cars, sometimes for two hours, in order to get out of town. It is a paradise to the Parker House, for no smoking is allowed, and there is far more retirement." "The Town and Country Club," Henry christened it, and wanted no other in Boston or anywhere.

In the early summer of 1856 Ricketson went to Concord, meaning to see Thoreau, but Henry was temporarily absent. Through this chance, the New Bedford Quaker made the acquaintance of Henry's father, "a very short old gentleman" and "a pleasant person." The two walked out before breakfast to the cemetery and over the ridge to see Edmund Hosmer, the farmer.

6. *The Great Walt*

Horace Greeley wrote to invite Henry to become tutor for the Greeley children, which would have meant removal from Concord to Chappaqua, New York. While the invitation hung fire, other events were in the making.

Alcott, who had a way of turning up where things were going on—he had been on hand at the attempted rescue of Anthony Burns in Boston—was now at Eagleswood, near Perth Amboy, New Jersey, advising Marcus Spring as to the plan of an educational colony with Utopian overtones such as those of Brook Farm or Fruitlands. Marcus Spring, it may be recalled, was the benevolent merchant who, with his wife, had taken Margaret Fuller abroad and who had subscribed to Brook Farm.

There were surveying and lecturing to be done at Eagleswood and of course Alcott knew the very man for the job. Thoreau accepted both commissions and set out for New Jersey by way of New York City, where he arrived one morning on the steamer *Commonwealth* and went to look up his friend Greeley. Greeley was out, so Henry did some reading at the Astor Library instead. He likewise visited Barnum's Museum and at length, in company with Miss Elizabeth Peabody, who was to join the councils of educational experts, arrived at Eagleswood in the late afternoon of October 25, 1856.

A few days later he wrote to Sophia, disclosing an unconverted attitude toward the Eagleswood colony and making some rather urchin comments. "This is a queer place," he wrote. Saturday evenings were devoted to dances in which the children, their teachers, and the colony's patrons took part. It was thought "something strange" if you did not attend. "They take it for granted that you want society!"

On Sunday, Henry attended some sort of Quaker meeting "where it was expected that the Spirit would move me (I having been previously spoken to about it); and it, or something else, did—an inch or so. I said just enough to set them a little by the ears and make it lively."

Henry was enlisted to help set out an orchard and a vineyard, occupations as much in his line as the setting out of ideas. At the end of his letter to Sophia he wrote, "The hardest thing to find here is solitude—and Concord. . . . I want you to write me immediately (just left off to talk French with the servant man), and let father and mother put in a word. To them and to Aunts, love from Henry."

Though he had not planned to stay so long, Henry was at Eagleswood past the middle of November. Alcott came and went, and together he and Henry spent a day at Horace Greeley's farm at Chappaqua, then went to New York City and to Brooklyn to hear Henry Ward Beecher preach. Alcott was favorably impressed, but Henry said the preaching was pagan.

They went together to call on Walt Whitman, two years younger than Thoreau, who had published at his own expense in 1855, a year after *Walden* appeared, the first *Leaves of Grass*—twelve poems only. Thoreau and Whitman had something in common to begin with: they had both read Emerson's *Nature*, and Emerson had vouched for them before the world.

As to Whitman, the Concord Olympian had found himself more the sponsor of the new poet than he had intended, for his message of congratulation had not only been published in newspapers but printed as a promotional circular. If Emerson had known he was writing an advertising testimonial to Walt he might have expressed himself somewhat more conservatively.

"There are parts of the book where I hold my nose as I read," Emerson admitted later, referring to *Leaves of Grass*; yet his glowing comments—"most extraordinary piece of wit & wisdom," "beginning of a great career," and so on—had traveled too fast to be overtaken even if he had wished. They had traveled too with the reinforcement of Whitman's strength and originality as well as his shrewd use of opportunity.

Both Thoreau and Whitman were commoners, too, and this was a central and basic fact—though Thoreau was far removed from teeming cities and Whitman was far removed, in general, from the shrub oak. Both these men were grown out of the fertility of the American continent. Alcott wrote in his journal, "I hoped to put him (Whitman) into direct communication with Thoreau, and tried my hand a little after we came downstairs and sat in the parlour below; but each seemed planted fast in reserves, surveying the other curiously—like two wild beasts, each wondering what the other would do, whether to snap or run; and it came to no more than cold compliments between them."

They were to have met again later, but Whitman defaulted on an engagement he made to call at the hotel where Alcott and Thoreau were staying. The encounter, nevertheless, was not a failure. Henry wrote to Blake from Eagleswood referring to Whitman as "apparently the greatest democrat the world has ever seen. Kings and aristocracy go by the board at once, as they have long deserved to. A remarkably strong though coarse nature, of a sweet disposition, and much prized by his friends."

As for Whitman's poems, Henry liked them. Whitman gave him a copy of the second edition and it did him more good, he said, than any reading for a long time. "If we are shocked, whose experience is it that we are reminded of?"

Whitman was put off and perhaps a little hurt because Henry said he did not like America. The two men might have had

some trouble getting together on definitions; it was characteristic of Walt that he should "ride up and down Broadway all
day on the omnibus, sitting beside the driver, listening to the
roar of the carts and sometimes gesticulating and declaiming
Homer at the top of his voice," and it was characteristic of
Henry that he should stand at the Concord cliffs alone, declaiming "Tom Bowline" into the rain.

Back at home again, Henry resumed his more important enterprises and added some new ones. His father thought it a
waste of time to tap the maples around Concord and make
sugar of the sap, for could not Henry buy sugar cheaper at
Holden's store? "He said it took me from my studies. I said I
made it my study; I felt as if I had been to a university."

Henry not only tapped maples but birches and boiled down
two quarts of yellow birch sap to two teaspoonfuls of "smart-
tasting syrup." The taste was slightly medicinal, but he thought
it not disagreeable. He tried black birch too and, another
spring, bottled both kinds of sap, "quite aromatic and alike; but
this year, methinks, it has a more *swampy* taste and musty, and
most of the bottles are merely sour."

He tried pennyroyal tea, collected herbs, climbed tall pine
trees to find only squirrels in a nest. He brought home a great
tortoise, added to his collection of pressed plants.

"We must go out and re-ally ourselves to Nature every day.
We must take root, send out some little fibre at least, even every
winter day. I am sensible that I am imbibing health when I open
my mouth to the wind. Staying in the house breeds a kind of
insanity always. Every house is in this sense a hospital. A night
and a forenoon is as much confinement to those wards as I can
stand. . . ."

All this was familiar to Henry's friends, and to them he did
not seem to change a great deal. It was he who was aware of
change, time, and distance, so much so that his awareness demanded expression: "My former friends, I visit you as one

walks amid the columns of a ruined temple. You belong to an era, a civilization and a glory long past. I recognize still your fair proportions, notwithstanding the convulsions which we have felt, and the weeds and jackals that have sprung up around. I come here to be reminded of the past, to read your inscriptions, the hieroglyphics, the sacred writings. We are no longer the representatives of our former selves."

Channing, however, was always Channing. One rainy November afternoon Henry called outside his house. Didn't he want to take a walk? No, the poet had a cold. "But you can take so much the longer walk. Double it."

Henry liked his friend's humor. Channing told how Bigelow, the tavernkeeper, once put up an advertisement in the streets of Concord: "All those who are in favor of the universal salvation of mankind, are requested to meet at the schoolhouse next Saturday evening to choose officers." And, after they had covered much distance together and emerged on the railroad at Walden: "Channing thought it was a suitably long stretch to wind up with, like one of our old Nashoba walks, so long drawn and taxing our legs so, in which it seemed that the nearer you got to home the farther you had to go."

George Minott did not change, either. "Minott adorns whatever part of nature he touches; whichever way he walks he transfigures the earth for me. If a common man speaks of Walden Pond to me, I see only a shallow, dull-colored body of water without reflections or peculiar color, but if Minott speaks of it, I see the green water and reflected hills at once for he *has been* there. I hear the rustle of the leaves from woods which he goes through."

7. *Errands to Mankind*

In March 1857 a plain man with a plain name, John Brown, arrived in Concord to see Frank Sanborn, the schoolteacher abolitionist. John Brown of Ossawatomie, fresh from the bloodshed of Kansas, where civil war was being fought on the slavery issue, was not the white-bearded patriarch of history books but "a tall, spare, farmer-like man, with head disproportionately small," an inflexible mouth, engaging earnestness and candor, and much authority cited from the Old Testament.

Pro-slavery men in Kansas had attacked, burned, and pillaged the town of Lawrence, and Brown and his sons had murdered five pro-slavery men at Pottawatomie in the name of the Lord. But at Concord little was known of the murders, and John Brown had brought with him, to cast on the platform of the town hall at an appropriate moment, the very trace chain that had shackled one of his sons in Kansas. John Brown was lean and plain, an animated, articulated conscience, with no waste anywhere.

Sanborn, by this time, had about given up teaching to make freedom in Kansas his chief business. He had met John Brown first that January and had become utterly convinced by him, scarcely needing the letters Brown brought from a friend of Sanborn's and from Salmon P. Chase, then Governor of Ohio.

Arriving in Concord at midday, Brown was taken by Sanborn to have dinner at the Thoreau house, and he and Henry talked—or, for the most part, John Brown talked and Henry listened to a kind of speech that rang true in his ears. Emerson dropped in while the talk was going on, and both he and Henry were present at the evening meeting in the town hall where John Brown spoke and dropped the trace chain.

On the following night, Brown took up again at Emerson's house the story of his warfare of conscience, and continued the vivid impression he had stamped on a receptive spirit in Concord. If he had been recorded and proclaimed in plain terms a murderer, as historians were to record and proclaim him later, it is not certain that Henry Thoreau's attitude would have been much changed. Deep in the spirit of the freedom-lover, as in the written lore of anarchism, flourished a conviction that there was nothing sacred in the life of an invader—and it was invaders of human freedom that Brown had killed.

All this was an interlude that was to have consequences later. At the time, nothing happened. John Brown went as he had come, not a line or expression to be forgotten.

Then, presently, Thoreau was setting out again for Cape Cod, this time by himself, and walked the whole length of it before he was done. After he returned to Concord he stayed barely a month before he and Edward Hoar were off to Maine. Riding in the cars from Boston to Portland, Henry said, was like sitting in the flue of a chimney that hot July, but at Portland came the relief of the steamer bound for Bangor. Then followed an expedition of 325 miles—an "excursion into the new world which the Indian dwells in, or is. He begins where we leave off."

On this Maine trip Henry was deeply impressed by Joe Polis, the Indian guide, who, with Thoreau and Edward Hoar, completed the small exploration group. Here again were lakes, rapids, camping in the wilderness. In some of the dense fir and spruce woods of Maine, Henry wrote, there was scarcely room for the smoke to go up. "The trees are a standing night, and every fir and spruce which you fell is a plume plucked from night's raven wing." Though Edward Hoar, who was nearsighted, was lost through one anxious night, the travelers returned safely and richer in experience to Concord.

Late that autumn the business of the country dropped into a state of hard times; in the words of *Scribner's Popular History of the United States,* there was "one of those ebb tides of trade for which no man has yet fully accounted, and which have been referred by bold physicists even to changes in the heavenly bodies. . . ." More realistically, the crisis was blamed on California gold, speculation, fabulous railroad expansion, and so on. But Henry Thoreau, in a letter to Blake, remarked that it was not merely the communities of Brook Farm, Fruit-lands, and so on, that had failed, but the community at large had failed too.

If money was hard, this proved that money was not made to eat. "Only think of a man in this new world, in his log cabin, in the midst of a corn and potato patch, with a sheepfold on one side, talking about money being hard!" Henry wrote as if he had been still at the Walden hut.

When the next summer came, Henry made another expedi-tion, this time to Mount Monadnock with Harrison Blake; the two spent two nights on the mountain and did not go into a house.

Henry's narrative of his second expedition into the Maine woods, which he called "Chesuncook," was now appearing in *The Atlantic Monthly* of which James Russell Lowell had be-come the first editor in 1857. There was a long pull from the time Lowell had visited Concord as a Harvard senior under dis-cipline and had first seen Thoreau there.

Henry's tribute to the living pine tree, which has already been quoted, had led to these words: ". . . it is the living spirit of the tree, not its spirit of turpentine, with which I sympathize, and which heals my cuts. It is as immortal as I am, and per-chance will go to as high a heaven, there to tower above me still."

The Atlantic Monthly stayed with Thoreau until this ref-erence to immortality; then the editorial pencil expunged the rest, reflecting the proprieties of the times and perhaps even the views of the Saturday Club, which included a number of *At-lantic* contributors. But Lowell assumed too much when he undertook to censor Thoreau.

"I am not willing to be associated in any way, unnecessarily, with parties who will confess themselves so bigoted & timid as this implies," Henry wrote to Lowell. "I could excuse a man who was afraid of an uplifted fist, but if one habitually manifests fear at the utterance of a sincere thought, I must think that his life is a kind of nightmare continued into broad daylight."

This terminated Henry's relationship with the *Atlantic* for as long as Lowell remained editor.

Henry was hardly back from his Monadnock trip with Blake when Edward Hoar spoke of going to the White Mountains, to which Henry remarked that he would like to go too —if he could afford it. Without much delay Edward proposed that he hire a horse and covered wagon, inviting Henry as companion for the trip; and so it was settled. The manner of travel was hardly satisfactory to Thoreau, however, for the length of journeying between stops, and the places where stops were made, had to be regulated according to the needs and capacities of the horse.

At a small tavern on Mount Washington, according to an account obtained by Sanborn, Thoreau and Hoar sought a guide to a difficult chasm known as Tuckerman's Ravine. The day was foggy, and the landlord replied that his brother was a guide "but if he went today he could never find his way back in this fog." Thoreau thereupon declared his independence of guides and, using a map and a pocket compass, he projected a line to the ravine and followed it successfully, though in the ravine itself Henry fell and sprained his ankle. He had already noted the presence of arnica mollis and soon plucked some with which to treat his injury.

Harrison Blake and three companions joined Henry and Edward Hoar on the mountain, finding them by means of a smoke signal, and all five slept overnight in a tent. Edward Hoar noted that Henry insisted on the carrying of heavy packs "and rather despised persons who complained of the burden."

That was a year of expeditions for Henry, and he might have made one more, a novel and interesting one, had it not been for the illness of his father. Thomas Cholmondeley wrote suddenly

from Montreal and proposed that Henry go with him to the
West Indies; but John Thoreau's death was looming ahead, and
Henry must remain at home.

8. *The Tender Side of Henry*

The story was that Alcott, too humane to kill potato bugs,
dumped his over the fence into the garden of Sam Staples.
Then it came about that Sam was next door neighbor to Emerson, and Henry Thoreau was asked to survey the division line.
When the job was done, Henry met both proprietors at Emerson's house and proceeded to declare, and to prove, that Emerson's fence was several feet out of bounds on the Staples side of
the division line. Moreover, Henry went on, much to Sam's
amazement, Emerson had appropriated this land intentionally
and would have made good the misappropriation if Sam had
not been too sharp to be imposed on.

All these years, said Henry to Emerson, you have been holding up your nose as an upright citizen and an example to every-
body, yet every time you reset your fence you knowingly
shoved it a little farther until you've stolen about enough land
to feed a yearling heifer.

"If Emerson had been ketched picking pockets at town meeting, he couldn't a-looked more stricken," said Sam Staples later.

But Henry's little speech was all in the way of fooling, and
when Emerson saw the joke on himself he took it so. He and
Sam Staples, the line correctly drawn between them, continued
to be neighbors for many years, and when Emerson was an old,
ill man Sam took a bottle of brandy to him.

One other time, surveying for Emerson, Henry had delighted him by showing that he had an extra sixty rods of woodland.

"Going along the Nut Meadow or Jimmy Miles road,"
Henry wrote, "when I see the sulphur lichens on the rails

brightening with the moisture I feel like studying them again as a relisher or tonic, to make life go down and digest well, as we use pepper and vinegar on salads." This was February, and it was in February that John Thoreau died. Another kind of journal entry now.

"I have touched a body which was flexible and warm, yet tenantless—warmed by what fire? I perceive that we partially die ourselves, through sympathy, at the death of each of our friends or near relatives. Each such experience is an assault on our vital force."

To Ricketson Henry wrote, acknowledging a condolence note: "How swiftly at last, but unnoticed, a generation passes away! Three years ago I was called, with my father, to be a witness to the signing of our neighbor, Mr. Frost's, will. Mr. Samuel Hoar, who was there writing it, also signed it. I was lately required to go to Cambridge to testify to the genuineness of the will, being the only one of the four who could be there, and now I am the only one alive."

Henry remained at home, remembering. John Thoreau's last illness had run through two years during which he had gone downtown in pleasant weather, "doing a little business from time to time, hoeing a little in the garden, etc. Father took to his chamber January 13th, and did not come down again. . . . He sat up for a little while on the Sunday four days before he died. Generally he was very silent for months. He was quite conscious to the last, and his death was so easy that we should not have been aware that he was dying, though we were sitting around his bed, if we had not watched closely."

Not only John Thoreau but part of Concord, quite an old and important part, had slipped away irrecoverably.

"As far as I know, Father, when he died, was not only one of the oldest men in the middle of Concord, but the one perhaps best acquainted with the inhabitants, and the local, social, and street history of the town, for the last fifty years. He belonged in a peculiar sense to the village street; loved to sit in the shops or at the postoffice and read the daily papers. I think that he remembered more about the worthies (and un-worthies) of Concord village forty years ago, both from deal-ing as a trader and familiar intercourse with them, than anyone else. Our other neighbors, now living or very recently dead, have either come to the town more recently than he or have lived more aloof from the mass of the inhabitants."

Thus Henry, who did live aloof, made a small, sympathetic portrait of his father, who did not, and showed that he himself was not beyond this sort of understanding.

It was reported that Mrs. Thoreau said she had never until now seen the tender side of Henry, though of course she had seen it and felt it many times, for there was much tenderness in all his life.

8

NOVEMBER

ક્ષે ફેન્ક

1. *Another Walk, Another Row*

"As the afternoons grow shorter," Henry wrote, "and the early evening drives us home to complete our chores, we are reminded of the shortness of life, and become more pensive, at least in the twilight of the year. We are prompted to make haste and finish our work before the night comes. I leaned over a rail in the twilight on the Walden road, waiting for the evening mail to be distributed, when such thoughts visited me."

He did not intend a broader application of these words, and yet there was a Novemberish feeling about his own life, not of decline but of crispness, shortening, the season's change.

"We'll go nutting once more," Henry wrote. "We'll pluck the nut of the world and crack it in the winter evenings. . . . I will take another walk to the Cliff, another row on the river, another skate on the meadow, be out in the first snow, and associate with the winter birds. Here I am at home. In the bare and bleached crust of the earth I recognize my friend."

Yet now that John Thoreau was dead, Henry had to remember, day by day, that he was the responsible member of the firm named on the letterhead, J. Thoreau & Son. The graphite business interested him too little to deserve comment in his journal, but it subtracted time and energy from his life. He was, despite his predilections and life's commitment, a businessman.

A businessman—but still Henry Thoreau, who wrote now, in different words, the same intense convictions as often before: "You must live in the present, launch yourself on every wave, find your eternity in each moment. Fools stand on their island opportunities and look toward another land. There is no other land; there is no other life but this, or the like of this. Where the good husbandman is, there is the good soil."

No change of direction here, no change of principle: "Though you may have sauntered near to heaven's gate, when at length you return toward the village you give up the enterprise a little, and you begin to fall into the old ruts of thought, like a regular roadster. Your thoughts very properly fail to report themselves to headquarters. Your thoughts turn toward night and the evening mail and become begrimed with dust."

A little while before, Henry had talked with a Concord acquaintance named Goodwin and guessed the man's age. "He is hale and stout and looks younger than he is, and I took care to set him high enough. I guessed he was fifty-five, and he said that if he lived two or three months longer he would be fifty-six. He then guessed at my age, thought I was forty. He thought Emerson was a very young-looking man for his age. 'But,' said he, 'he has not been out o' nights as much as you have.' "

Henry was past forty then, and whether his night walks had anything to do with it, the years were crowding. He had written to Blake that he thought and felt too much like a businessman, attending to irksome affairs, and again that he had been confined at home all year but had not grown any rustier than was to be expected.

Now Henry James the elder, whom Thoreau had met in New York so long ago, with mutual liking, came to Concord and participated in an Alcottian conversation at the Emerson house. Aunt Mary Moody Emerson lit into James and, they said, bested him. Thoreau was anti-James also: "He charges society with all the crime committed, and praises the criminal for committing it. But I think that all the remedies he suggests out of his head—for he goes no farther, hearty as he is—would leave us about where we are now."

James said that Thoreau was "the most childlike, unconscious and unblushing egotist it has ever been my fortune to encounter in the ranks of manhood; so that, if he happened to visit you on a Sunday morning, when possibly you were in a devout frame of mind, as like as not you would soon find yourself intoning sub-audible praises to the meticulous skill which had at last succeeded in visibly marrying such sheer and mountainous inward self-esteem with such harmless and beautiful force of outward demeanor."

Henry had certainly annoyed James, but so had Alcott, who, at one meeting, claimed to be one with both Pythagoras and Jesus. Neither they nor he had ever sinned.

"You say you and Jesus are one," James said to Alcott. "Have you ever said, 'I am the resurrection and the life'?"

"Yes, often," returned Alcott.

"Has anyone ever believed you?"

"I won't talk any more with you," said Alcott, and broke off in indignation.

So the force had not gone from the Concord conversations even after all these years. And Henry Thoreau was setting out four hundred white pines in a lot of Emerson's. But his most important and congenial commission was surveying the Concord River, with a study of its depths, currents, and caprices, in the interest of the river-meadow landowners.

2. *Old John Brown*

White-bearded and in his sixtieth year, John Brown came again to Concord, more than ever the materialized conscience,

the lean, valiant instrument of man's freedom, more fact than
cause, but turned into a cause because man's freedom had been
denied.

In the town hall a public meeting was held, with Henry
Thoreau and Frank Sanborn in the audience listening intently.
Then John Brown was gone, supposedly to Kansas, though
Sanborn knew differently, knew the truth that Thoreau and
Emerson and none of the others in Concord had been told.
News came soon of the raid on Harpers Ferry and John
Brown's arrest on October 16, 1859.

"A smart frost this morning. Ground stiffened. Hear of ice
in a tub," wrote Thoreau on October 17. The next day it rained
and was a little warmer. Henry saw half a dozen yellow-spot
turtles, a small thrush, a tree toad on the ground in a sandy
woodpath. Then, on October 19: "When a government puts
forth its strength on the side of injustice, as ours (especially
today) to maintain slavery and kill the liberators of the slave,
what a merely brute, or worse than brute, force it is seen to be!
A demoniacal force!"

The news about John Brown had reached Concord, and now
for days on end Henry Thoreau teemed with the phrases that
sprang to his mind and, when he gathered them together, were
to be uttered with conviction as earnest and blazing as a man's
conviction, an honest man's conviction, could ever be.

Emerson's response was unsettled. Brown was "a true hero,
but he lost his head there"; yet he was no less a hero of romance
"& seems to have made this fatal blunder only to bring out his
virtues. I must hope for his escape up to the last moment." Hawthorne, away from Concord at the time, thought Brown a
bloodstained fanatic. The postmaster, supposing Brown already
hanged, said that he died as fools die, to which Thoreau replied, "He did not live as the fool liveth, and he died as he
lived."

"It galls me to listen to the remarks of craven-hearted neighbors who speak disparagingly of Brown because he resorted to violence, resisted the government, threw his life away!"

So those others blew hot or cold, thought this or that, evaded any hazardous thought, took refuge in platitudes or pious disclaimers, but not Thoreau. On October 30, with John Brown still living, Thoreau held his own meeting in the vestry of the Universalist church and produced hot, impassioned words he had been storing up in his journal. One story is that he had sent a boy to announce this meeting and that the boy came back to say that Mr. Sanborn thought the plan unwise; it would be better to wait.

"Tell Mr. Sanborn that he has misunderstood the announcement, that there is to be a meeting in the vestry, and that Mr. Thoreau will speak." Such is supposed to have been Henry's reply to the cautious.

Emerson, who heard Henry's plea delivered in the church the night of October 30, said that Concord listened respectfully and that many in the audience were more moved than they had believed possible. Henry directed his fire at those who said John Brown threw his life away. Which way had they thrown *their* lives? And this person or that, Yankee-like, asked, "What will he gain by it?"

"Well, no, I don't suppose he could get four-and-sixpence a day for being hung, take it the year round; but then he stands a chance to save a considerable part of his soul—and *such* a soul! —when *you* do not. No doubt you can get more in your market for a quart of milk than for a quart of blood, but that is not the market that heroes carry their blood to."

Henry threw at them such thunders as these:

"It was his peculiar doctrine that a man has a perfect right to interfere by force with the slave-holder, in order to rescue the slave. I agree with him. They who are continually shocked by slavery have some right to be shocked by the violent death of the slave-holder, but no others. Such will be more shocked by his life than by his death."

"I do not wish to kill nor to be killed, but I can foresee circumstances in which both these things would be by me unavoidable."

"This event advertises me that there is such a fact as death—the possibility of a man's dying. It seems as if no man had ever died in America before; for in order to die you must first have lived. I don't believe in the hearses, and palls, and funerals that they have had. There was no death in the case because there had been no life; they merely rotted or sloughed off, pretty much as they had rotted or sloughed along. No temple's veil was rent, only a hole dug somewhere. Let the dead bury their dead. The best of them fairly ran down like a clock. Franklin —Washington—they were let off without dying; they were merely missing one day. I hear a good many pretend that they are going to die; or that they have died, for aught I know. Nonsense! I'll defy them to do it. They haven't got life enough in them. They'll deliquesce like fungi, and keep a hundred eulogists mopping the spot where they left off. Only half a dozen or so have died since the world began. Do you think that you are going to die, sir? No! there's no hope for you. You haven't got your lesson yet. You've got to stay after school."

"You who pretend to care for Christ crucified, consider what you are about to do to him who offered himself to be the saviour of four millions of men."

"I am here to plead his cause with you. I plead not for his life, but for his character—his immortal life; and so it becomes your cause wholly, and is not his in the least. Some eighteen hundred years ago Christ was crucified; this morning, perchance, Captain Brown was hung. These are the two ends of a chain which is not without its links. He is not Old Brown any longer; he is an angel of light."

These were sentences that Thoreau poured forth, angry, hurt, impassioned. History, it is true, was to depict a different John Brown from the hero and martyr Thoreau knew, but history wrote long afterward, when passions had died, a war had been fought, and the slave was free. Thoreau could not speak of history's John Brown but only of the man he had met and seen and heard, in whom he believed, the John Brown who had said, "I pity the poor in bondage that have none to help them; that is why I am here; not to gratify any personal animosity, revenge, or vindictive spirit. It is my sympathy with the oppressed and the wronged, that are as good as you, and as precious in the sight of God."

Thoreau read his address twice more—in Worcester and in Boston, where no publisher could then be found to print it.

More than a year later Thoreau talked with Sam Staples and a man named Walcott, and these two declared that John Brown had done wrong because he had thrown his life away, and that no man had a right to undertake anything which he knew would cost him his life.

"I inquired if Christ did not foresee that he would be crucified if he preached such doctrines as he did, but they both, though as if it was their only escape, asserted they did not believe that he did. Upon which a third party threw in, 'You do not think that he had so much foresight as Brown.' Of course, they as good as said that, if Christ *had* foreseen that he would be crucified, he would have 'backed out.' Such are the principles and logic of the mass of men."

Sanborn, who had known of the Harpers Ferry plan, made a judicious evasion from Concord to Canada and was not present on the day of Brown's execution when memorial services were held in the town hall.

On November 30 Henry wrote, "I am one of a committee of four, viz. Simon Brown (Ex-Lieutenant-Governor), R. W. Emerson, myself, and John Keyes (late High Sheriff), in-

structed by a meeting of citizens to ask liberty of the selectmen
to have the bell of the first parish tolled at the time Captain
Brown is being hung, and while we shall be assembled in the
town house to express our sympathy with him. I applied to the
selectmen yesterday. Their names are George M. Brooks, Barzillai Hudson, and Julius Smith. After various delays they at
length answer me tonight that they are 'uncertain whether
they have any control over the bell, but that, *in any case*, they
will not give their consent to have the bell tolled.' Beside their
private objections, they are influenced by the remarks of a few
individuals. Dr. Bartlett tells me that Rockwood Hoar said he
'hoped no such foolish thing would be done,' and he also named
Stedman Buttrick, John Moore, Cheney (and others added
Nathan Brooks, senior, and Francis Wheeler) as strongly op-
posed to it; said he heard 'five hundred' (!) damn me for it,
and that he had no doubt that if it were done some counter-
demonstration would be made, such as firing minute-guns. The
doctor himself is more excited than anybody, for he has the
minister under his wing. Indeed, a considerable part of Concord are in the condition of Virginia today—afraid of their
own shadows."

Henry Thoreau was not afraid or troubled with indecision,
but the impending death of John Brown made him physically
ill. He walked in E. Hubbard's gray-oak wood, and as he came
home at dusk along the causeway of the railroad he heard a
hylodes peeping.

In the town hall, at the memorial service, Henry's tone was
altered to the level of elegy and eulogy. He read various poetic
selections, then a translation he himself had made from Tacitus,
beginning: "You, Agricola, are fortunate, not only because
your life was glorious, but because your death was timely" and
ending: "For oblivion will overtake many of the ancients, as if
they were inglorious and ignoble: Agricola, described and
transmitted to posterity, will survive."

The next day Sanborn, in Boston, met a young man named F. J. Merriam, who had been with John Brown at Harpers Ferry and had escaped with Owen Brown. Merriam's purpose now was to raise another party against the slaveholders, but, in Sanborn's words, "he was unfit to lead or even to join in such a desperate undertaking, and we insisted he should return in safety to Canada." Merriam agreed to go back by the Fitchburg railroad (a large reward had been offered for his capture) "but in his hotheaded way he took the wrong train which ran no farther than Concord."

Sanborn's sister took the fugitive into her house, and Sanborn arranged with Emerson to have the Emerson horse and covered wagon ready at sunrise—no questions asked. Then Sanborn arranged with Thoreau to take "Mr. Lockwood" to South Acton by this means the next morning.

In the morning "Merriam was so flighty that, though he had agreed to go to Montreal, and knew that his life might depend on getting there early, he declared he must see Mr. Emerson, to lay before him his plan for invading the South, and consult him about some moral questions that troubled his mind." In the course of an erratic conversation, Merriam remarked that he was insane, a fact Henry realized completely. He "hurried the horse towards Acton. Merriam grew more positive and suspicious. 'Perhaps *you* are Mr. Emerson; you look somewhat like him.' " Thoreau said he was not and drove on. Merriam said he was going back to Concord, and jumped out of the wagon.

Sanborn wrote later: "How Thoreau got him in again, he never told me; but I suspected some judicious force, accompanying the grave persuasive speech natural to our friend. At any rate, he took his man to Acton."

Henry's references to the incident in his journal added nothing; but his entries for the day were concluded with this sentence: "When I hear of John Brown and his wife weeping at length, it is as if the rocks sweated."

3. *A Word for Nature*

"I wish to speak a word for Nature, for absolute freedom and wildness, as contrasted with a freedom and culture merely civil," Henry wrote, opening his lecture entitled "Walking." This was an essay contrasting sharply with that simpler, younger paper of long ago, "A Winter's Walk," which Emerson had put into *The Dial.*

"I think that I cannot preserve my health and spirits, unless I spend four hours a day at least—and it is commonly more than that—sauntering through the woods and over the hills and fields, absolutely free from all worldly engagements. . . .

"I, who cannot stay in my chamber for a single day without acquiring some rust, and when sometimes I have stolen forth for a walk at the eleventh hour or four o'clock in the afternoon, too late to redeem the day, when the shades of night were already beginning to be mingled with the daylight, I have felt as if I had committed some sin to be atoned for—I confess that I am astonished at the power of endurance, to say nothing of the moral insensibility, of my neighbors who confine themselves to shops and offices the whole day for weeks and months, aye, and years almost together. I know not what manner of stuff they are of—sitting there now at three o'clock in the afternoon, as if it were three o'clock in the morning. . . . I wonder that about this time, or say between four and five o'clock in the afternoon, too late for the morning papers and too early for the evening ones, there is not a general explosion heard up and down the street, scattering a legion of antiquated and house-bred notions and whims to the four winds for an airing—and so the evil cure itself."

But Concord lacked the quality of explosiveness, possessed more solidity than lively vapor, dried itself year by year, yet was determined not to take fire or burn. The town was now long familiar with Henry's opinions, even his insults, and could not be influenced by them. His neighbors continued to live and work indoors and, if they walked, to do so in their own circumscribed fashion.

Alcott's friends, by this time, had realized that he could never strike a balance in the competitive system of the world Henry so plainly denounced, and they contributed to a life annuity fund to see him through. The smallest amount noted on the subscription paper was one dollar given by Henry Thoreau—or was this the largest amount, after all?

Henry, in times past, had himself circulated a subscription paper for a bereft Irish family, for he showed a readier humanity than most who professed all that he so explicitly disavowed. But when Dr. Bartlett came around asking contributions for a statue for Horace Mann, Henry declined, saying he thought "a man ought not any more to take up room in the world after he was dead. We shall lose one advantage of a man's dying if we are to have a statue forthwith. This is probably meant to be an opposition statue to that of Webster. At this rate they will crowd the streets with them."

Hawthorne returned to Concord once again. Henry went to see him and wrote to Sophia that he was "looking quite brown after his voyage" and was "as simple and childlike as ever." This was in July 1860, and in August Henry and Channing, most dependable of companions, made an expedition to Monadnock.

Channing had never camped out before, and now he found himself on the mountain in a drenching summer rain, watching Henry build a shelter of spruce boughs. As Henry wrote to Blake later, "This was a great deal better than going up there in fair weather, and having no adventure. . . . The genius of the mountains saw us starting from Concord, and it said, There come two of our folks. Let us get ready for them. Get up a serious storm, that will send a-packing these holiday guests. (They may have their say another time.) Let us receive them with true mountain hospitality—kill the fatted cloud. Let them know the value of a spruce roof, and of a fire of dead spruce stumps. Every bush dripped tears of joy at our advent."

Channing, it is likely, did not share all of Henry's enthusiasm. The two breakfasted on stewed mountain cranberries, explored the spurs, gullies, swamps, and rocks of the mountain, and looked not only *from* Monadnock but *at* it, as Henry had planned to do. The plan had been to spend a week, but Channing suggested that six working days made a week and brought the outing to a halt after five nights and six days.

Henry had surveying to do; he walked and paddled at Walden; he and Channing walked to the old places. Channing said, and Henry agreed, that "You don't want to discover anything new, but to discover something old"—to be reminded that such things still are.

Henry picked between ten and eleven barrels of apples from trees he had planted at the Texas house, most of them fourteen years previously. There was a fire at Mrs. Hoar's house—a slight blaze and more smoke. Two or three hundred men, Henry recorded, rushed to the house, cut large holes in the roof, and threw many hogsheads of water into it, although a few bucketsful, if well aimed, would have been enough. Then, the fun being over, the enthusiastic firefighters went away again. "They were very forward to put out the fire, but they take no pains to put out the water, which does far more damage. The first was amusement; the last would be mere work and utility."

Early in November Henry visited Inches' woods in Boxboro, not far west of Concord but hitherto unexplored by him. After he got home he reflected on the beauty of the oaks and suggested, "It would be worth while if in each town there were a committee appointed to see that the beauty of the town received no detriment. If we have the largest boulder in the country, then it should not belong to an individual, nor be made into door-steps."

A little later he went on: "But most men, it seems to me, do not care for Nature and would sell their share in all her beauty, as long as they may live, for a stated sum—many for a glass of rum. Thank God, men cannot as yet fly, and lay waste the sky as well as the earth!"

A man "pauses at the end of his four or five thousand dollars" —when he has saved that much—"and then only fears that he has not got enough to carry him through—that is, merely to pay for what he will eat and wear and burn and for his lodging for the rest of his life. But, pray, what does he stay for? Suicide would be cheaper. Indeed, it would be nobler to found some good institution with the money and then cut your throat. If such is the whole upshot of their living, I think that it would be most profitable for all such to be carried or put through by being discharged from the mouth of a cannon as fast as they attained to years of such discretion."

Henry was confined to the house when he wrote that, for on December 3, sometime after his return from Boxboro, he had caught cold and it had turned into what he called bronchitis. The third of December had not been especially noteworthy. He had measured some white oaks and talked with Sam Staples and the others about John Brown. The next day the first snow fell. Henry did not refer to his illness in his journal, but he had to depend on Channing to report the first freezing of Walden.

In March Henry was writing to Daniel Ricketson: "To tell the truth, I am not on the alert for the signs of spring, not having had any winter yet. I took a severe cold . . . so that I have been confined to the house ever since, excepting a very few experi-mental trips as far as the postoffice in some particularly fine noons. My health otherwise has not been affected in the least, nor my spirits. I have simply been imprisoned for so long, and it has not prevented my doing a great deal of reading and the like.

"Channing has looked after me very faithfully; says he has made a study of my case, and knows me better than I know myself, etc., etc. Of course, if I knew how it began, I should know better how it would end."

Harrison Blake and Theophilus Brown, a friend of the same inclination, came to visit and to talk, and Henry kept up his part of the conversation though, as he said, his pipes were not in good order. Alcott likewise hovered near in friendship, and had risen to new heights. He had become superintendent of schools (Sanborn was a member of the school committee) and was showing off his pupils and all the new inspiration he had introduced.

4. *The Far Journeys*

Thomas Cholmondeley, the English friend returned from overseas, had wanted Henry to accompany him to the West Indies; but that was before Henry's father died and he was needed at Concord. Now there was talk of having Henry go to the West Indies for a change of climate—or perhaps to Europe. His health did not mend as the spring of 1861 advanced.

His journal had little to say of expeditions outdoors, or of Walden; his walks were fewer and shorter. He was more likely to be reflecting on former observations, or writing of the kitten he could watch at home. Young Horace Mann, whose father was the educator and whose mother was Mary Peabody, sister of Elizabeth Peabody and of Sophia Hawthorne, came often to bring specimens for Henry to see, and to tell of things he had seen. Young Mann was a naturalist of increasing attainments.

On the third of May Henry wrote to Blake: "I am still as much an invalid as when you and Brown were here, if not more of one, and at this rate there is danger that the cold weather may come again, before I get over my bronchitis. The doctor accordingly tells me that I must 'clear out' to the West Indies, or elsewhere—he does not seem to care much where. But I decide against the West Indies, on account of their muggy heat in the summer, and the South of Europe, on account of the expense of time and money, and have at last concluded that it will be most expedient for me to try the air of Minnesota, say somewhere about St. Paul's. I am only waiting to be well enough to start. Hope to get off within a week or ten days."

On the twelfth of May, with young Horace Mann for companion, Henry began his long trip in search of health, stopping at Worcester to see Blake and Brown. At last he was to look on the Mississippi, the stream that outrivered all others, but his closer association on the trip was with the Minnesota River, on which he and Horace Mann made an excursion of some length to see the plains and the Sioux Indians, who, half naked, performed a dance for the benefit of the visitors and of the Governor of Minnesota. For Thoreau the harvest of this long journey, which in other days might have been considerable, proved sadly small. The inland air, of which so much had been hoped, could work no magic, and the sick Thoreau did not respond to the new scenes.

He was back home in July, and in August he was writing to Daniel Ricketson that he had been sick so long he had almost forgotten what it was to be well. He accepted an invitation to visit this New Bedford friend and sat for an ambrotype showing a sad, historic face. Ricketson foresaw no favorable end of his friend's illness. Even though Henry's spirits seemed much as usual and his appetite good, there was no ignoring his emaciation and bad cough. Ricketson was interested in a new kind of therapy and arranged to have a doctor who specialized in it to stop off in Concord to see Henry, but nothing came of this or any other venture of the kind.

In Concord Henry was slipping into his final illness. He ceased to write in his journal—as Emerson said, when he could not be outdoors he could not write—though he did occupy himself with his manuscripts. That October he managed a letter to

Ricketson: ". . . my faith in doctors has not increased. . . . Instead of riding on horseback, I ride in a wagon every other day. My neighbor, Mr. E. R. Hoar, has two horses, and he, being away for the most part this fall, has generously offered me the use of one of them; and, as I notice, the dog throws himself in, and does scouting duty."

Sophia Thoreau applied herself devotedly to the care of her beloved brother. She took over the writing of his letters, made him as comfortable as a tender woman could, sat to await his next word. She had seen him so long as he moved in and out of the family circle, the home attachment always one of the essential, deeply rooted things; she had watched and worried when he was known as an odd stick, through the stormy times, the Walden period, and now that he had become a sort of prophet she had him much to herself. His study bed was brought down to the front room and he lay there to receive visitors and to sleep or contemplate the hours away.

She knew him better than she could ever have hoped to know so odd a brother. When his walking was done and he rode instead, Sophia had ridden with him and he had showed her "some of his familiar haunts, far away in the thick woods, or by the ponds" which she found new and delightful. Now, when he had wakeful nights, he asked her to arrange the furniture so as to make fantastic shadows on the wall.

Not only his friends came and sent messages, but total strangers as well; and as for Concord—Concord was already anticipating his fame and acting on the anticipation.

Someone asked Henry what he thought of a future world and its compensations, and he waved the question aside: "Those were voluntaries I did not take." Aunt Louisa, that devout churchwoman, asked if he had made his peace with God, and he made his famous reply that he was not aware he and God had ever quarreled. "One world at a time," he said to Parker Pills-

bury, antislavery friend, who also broached the topic of a
future beyond the mortal span of earth.

Sophia, her heart sad but rising to the need of the tragic
hours, wrote Henry's last letter, addressed to an inquirer: "You
ask particularly after my health. I *suppose* that I have not many
months to live; but of course I know nothing about it. I may
add that I am enjoying existence as much as ever, and regret
nothing."

In January 1862, Bronson Alcott wrote to Daniel Ricketson
of Henry's declining state. "We had thought this oldest inhabitant of our Planet would have chosen to stay and see it
fairly dismissed into the Chaos (out of which he has brought
such precious jewels—gifts to friends, to mankind generally,
diadems of fame to coming followers, forgetful of his own
claim to the honors) before he chose simply to withdraw from
the spaces and times he has adorned with the truth of his genius.
But the masterly work is nearly done for us here. And our
woods and fields are sorrowing, though not in sombre, but in
robes of white, so becoming to the piety and probity they have
known so long and soon are to miss. There has been none such
since Pliny, and it will be long before there comes his like; the
most sagacious and wonderful Worthy of his time, and a
marvel to coming ones."

On the whole, that was well said. It was likewise to Ricketson that Sophia wrote later of Henry's final weeks. "His perfect contentment was truly wonderful. None of his friends
seemed to realize how ill he was, so full of life and good cheer
did he seem. One friend, as if by way of consolation, said to
him, 'Well, Mr. Thoreau, we must all go.' Henry replied,
'When I was a very little boy, I learned that I must die, and I set
that down, so, of course, I am not disappointed now. Death is as
near to you as it is to me.' "

Among Henry's visitors was Sam Staples, who, after he came

away, remarked to Emerson, "Never spent an hour with more satisfaction. Never saw a man dying with so much pleasure and peace."

On May 6, Judge Rockwood Hoar called with a bunch of hyacinths fresh from his garden which Henry smelled and said he liked. A few minutes later a friend came with a dish of jelly. Another two hours and, quite gently, Thoreau of Walden died at the age of forty-five, while his mother, Sophia, and Aunt Louisa looked on in sadness and tenderness.

5. *Elegy*

It was Thoreau himself, of course, who was to have the last word. But it was appropriate that Emerson, with his strong and loyal affection and his powers of expression unmatched for an occasion such as this, should have the first of all the other last words—the remarks of friends, critics, scholars, doubters, and followers. Emerson spoke them first in a funeral address, then made of this a biographical essay for *The Atlantic Monthly* and so sent it down the long aisle of years.

He looked not only into his heart and memory but also through the pages of his journal and culled from them some of the things he had written about Henry Thoreau as their two lives were running along so closely yet decisively apart in Concord.

Back in 1842 he had said of Henry's verse, "The gold does not yet flow pure, but is drossy and crude." Now he used these same words, adding, "The thyme and marjoram are not yet honey." Henry's poetry was never much, but his prose was better than Emerson's.

Far back in 1843 Emerson had noted with irritation how Henry praised "wild mountains and winter forests for their domestic air; snow and ice for their warmth; villagers and wood-choppers for their urbanity, and the wilderness for re-

sembling Rome and Paris." This too he repeated now, for
Henry had never abandoned this sort of expression.

In 1851 Emerson had written, "Thoreau wants a little ambition in his mixture. Fault of this, instead of being the head of
American engineers, he is captain of a huckleberry party," and
now he elaborated and rephrased the thought for the funeral
occasion: ". . . I so much regret the loss of his rare powers of
action, that I cannot help counting it a fault in him that he had
no ambition. Wanting this, instead of engineering for all
America, he was the captain of a huckleberry party. Pounding beans is good to the end of pounding empires one of these
days; but if, at the end of years, it is still only beans!"

Thoreau had attacked that old fraud ambition as no man
before him, but the myth still lived.

In 1853 Emerson had written that passage about Henry needing a fallacy to expose, and so on. He used these words again
but did not refer to "weary captious paradoxes." Instead he
turned the meaning a little and did justice to his friend's independence. "It cost him nothing to say No; indeed he found it
much easier than to say Yes. It seemed as if his first instinct on
hearing a proposition was to controvert it, so impatient was he
of the limitations of our daily thought. This habit, of course, is
a little chilling to the social affections."

But in new language Emerson gave credit to Thoreau's
genius for nature, his idealism, common sense, and understanding. He told how Henry had served as "attorney for the
indigenous plants," spoke of his patience, his way with animals. "Snakes coiled round his legs; the fishes swam into his
hand, and he took them out of the water; he pulled the woodchuck out of its hole by the tail, and took the foxes under his
protection from the hunters."

He told how Henry had gone to the Harvard library to
borrow books, only to be refused under a rule that permitted
the loan of books solely to resident graduates, to clergymen

who were alumni, and to some others resident within a circle
of ten miles from the college.

"Mr. Thoreau explained to the President that the railroad had
destroyed the old scale of distances—that the library was useless,
yes, and President and College useless, on the terms of his
rules—that the one benefit he owed to the College was its library—that at this moment, not only his want of books was
imperative, but that he wanted a large number of books, and
assured him that he, Thoreau, and not the librarian, was the
proper custodian of these. In short, the President found the
petitioner so formidable, and the rules getting to look so ridiculous, that he ended by giving him a privilege which in his
hands proved unlimited thereafter."

Emerson likewise quoted from *Walden* that appealing fable
of Henry's that so many attempted to construe literally: "I
long ago lost a hound, a bay horse and a turtle-dove, and am
still on their trail. Many are the travellers I have spoken concerning them, describing their tracks, and what calls they answered to. I have met one or two who have heard the hound,
and the tramp of the horse, and even seen the dove disappear
behind a cloud; and they seemed as anxious to recover them as
if they had lost them themselves."

When Henry himself had been asked about these losses he
had replied, "Have not you?" Even in the motorized age, generations later, there were to be those who seemed to hear dis-
tantly the baying of Thoreau's hound, the hoofbeats of his
horse, and perhaps a soft mourning of his turtledove.

Emerson concluded his address with these words: "His soul
was made for the noblest society; he had in a short life exhausted
the capabilities of this world; wherever there is knowledge,
wherever there is virtue, wherever there is beauty, he will find
a home."

Ellery Channing, never more consciously the poet, placed
tributes of words on his friend's coffin, among them these:

"Hail to thee, O man! who has come from the transitory place to the imperishable." What Lidian Emerson said, or any of the others, is not now remembered. The past began to close in quickly.

"Profound joy mingles with my grief," Sophia wrote later that same month to Daniel Ricketson. "I feel as if something very beautiful had happened—not death. Although Henry is with us no longer, yet the memory of his sweet and virtuous soul must ever cheer and comfort me. My heart is filled with praise to God for the gift of such a brother, and may I never distrust the wisdom of Him who made him, and who has now called him to labor in more glorious fields than earth affords!"

6. *The Voice Unstilled*

During his final illness, his journal ended and put aside, with new things to write, Henry had worked to prepare various papers for publication. He never ceased to call for his manuscript till the last day of his life, Sophia recorded. *The Atlantic Monthly*, James Russell Lowell no longer editor, had arranged for at least three of Henry's essays.

"Autumnal Tints" was one of them. When Henry had presented this as a lecture, some of his auditors seemed to think they had already observed the colors of which he spoke. He corrected this misimpression.

"Wild Apples" had a good deal of the tang of his life. Wild apples, he had written, "should be eaten in the fields, when your system is all aglow with exercise, when the frosty weather nips your fingers, the wind rattles the bare boughs or rustles the few remaining leaves, and the jay is heard screaming around. What is sour in the house a bracing walk makes sweet. Some of these apples might be labeled, 'To be eaten in the wind.' "

"Night and Moonlight" contained vivid memories: "Many

men walk by day; few walk by night. It is a very different season. Take a July night, for instance. About ten o'clock—when man is asleep, and day fairly forgotten—the beauty of moonlight is seen over lonely pastures where cattle are silently feeding. On all sides novelties present themselves. Instead of the sun there are the moon and stars, instead of the wood-thrush there is the whippoorwill—instead of butterflies in the meadows, fireflies, winged sparks of fire! who would have believed it? What kind of cool deliberate life dwells in those dewy abodes associated with a spark of fire? So man has fire in his eyes, or blood, or brain. . . . The potato-vines stand up-right, the corn grows apace, the bushes loom, the grain-fields are boundless. On our open river terraces once cultivated by the Indian, they appear to occupy the ground like an army—their heads nodding in the breeze. . . . The sweet fern and indigo in overgrown wood paths wet you with dew up to your middle. The leaves of the shrub oak are shining as if a liquid were flowing over them."

So ran this legacy of Thoreau's. Sophia, Blake, Channing, Emerson, Sanborn—all had a hand in editing or in the bringing out of Henry's writings in one form or another. Emerson edited a volume of letters and complained ruefully, when Sophia insisted on the inclusion of certain material, that she had spoiled his portrait of a Greek god. Thoreau, of course, had not wanted to be a Greek of any station, godlike or otherwise; he had meant to be only himself, forever, different from any other, even as different as might be possible through the exercise of complete sincerity and independence—Thoreau of Concord, Thoreau of Walden, and so with the passage of years it was to come about.

Soon the long shelf was filled. Everything, almost, that he had written was printed and bound between covers: *Cape Cod, The Maine Woods, A Yankee in Canada, Familiar Letters, Miscellanies, Excursions.* Harrison Blake made selections for four volumes from the journals, then at last all the journals came out. *Walden* and the *Week*, of course, had been on the shelf from the beginning.

When the journal was published in full, it was easy at last for anyone to look over Thoreau's shoulder, so to speak, and thus to discover passages of distinction, many a characteristic epigram and descriptive note of nature, and likewise much that was of interest to Henry Thoreau alone—a fact that should not have been surprising, though there was no telling what he might have made of the material if he had finally embodied it in a finished manuscript, perhaps in an ambitious work about Concord that Alcott referred to as an atlas.

In 1865, when six of Thoreau's volumes had been published, James Russell Lowell subjected them to critical attention and found Henry "to have been a man with so high a conceit of himself that he accepted without questioning, and insisted on our accepting, his defects and weaknesses of character as virtues and powers peculiar to himself." But Lowell insisted on gulping, whole hog, the peculiarities of economics and the social order that Henry had denounced. He sat on an opposite hill—but from that summit, which he assumed was the only proper outlook, did he enjoy a clearer or more distant view than Henry's?

It was true, as Lowell and so many others complained, that Thoreau turned his crabbed back on conformity; but when Lowell termed such perversities "defects and weakness of character," what did his complaint come to? The merits of the question must be left to a period or to an observer of greater objectivity.

Men in the mass, by habit and preachment, acted out their own contradictions which, bluntly stated, seemed more extreme and unnatural than Thoreau's. He believed that the one man must be protected from the million—but somehow the notion became generally accepted that the million must be protected from the one man, lest his thinking or example should corrupt them utterly. Thoreau believed in simple freedom as the final refuge of security for faith and being; a different generation rushed headlong to the view that men needed security first of all, and therefore that the first requisite of freedom was to do away with it.

Thoreau said that money was nothing, but was this more peculiar than the opposite belief, on which so large a part of the human race plainly acted, that money was everything?

7. *Walden Down to Date*

It is easy now to visit "Walden water," as Emerson called it, where he sat to read Goethe on a quiet afternoon and where Hawthorne walked and became lost. Walden is in a state reserve in memory of Thoreau, and the surfaced highway touches the pond, there is a concrete bathing pavilion for public use, and the holiday crowd of the same Massachusetts Thoreau so heartily denounced on occasion may whoop and holler there on any summer day.

Once in October Hawthorne bathed in Walden and wrote: ". . . though the water was thrillingly cold, it was like the thrill of a happy death. Never was there such transparent water as this. I threw sticks into it, and saw them float suspended on an almost invisible medium. It seemed as if the pure air were beneath them, as well as above. It is fit for baptisms; but one would not wish to have it polluted by having sins washed into it. None but the angels should bathe in it; but blessed babies might be dipped into its bosom."

Walden is now an abode of gregariousness and those who bathe in it make no pretense of being angels. A Concord guidebook reports that many a pilgrim visits the site of Thoreau's hut, though it is largely ignored by the thronging pleasure seekers who crowd the beach across the pond.

Emerson, Hawthorne and others loved Walden. They had, in a manner of speaking, Sunday thoughts about it—but only Thoreau had also weekday thoughts about it throughout the year in all kinds of weather, and night and day thoughts for all ages of man on all occasions in respect to Walden. Thoreau forgave the railroad (Hawthorne wrote that it was "a torment to see the great, high ugly embankment of the railroad, which is here thrusting itself into the lake"), forgave even the cutting of the trees in his own day because of the need of the Irish woodcutters, and he could see the glow of the Walden woods in their faces.

Not only is Walden so changed today, but all New England as well. Who will rally now to the sign of the shrub oak or find that tree dear and wholesome? The proper emblems have become concrete blocks and filling stations. There is little reverence for a tree or a plant that the chance of a few dollars' profit will not extinguish quickly and forever. The unwritten law is that nothing may endure unless it will pay.

There is nothing to climbing Mount Wachusett now; motor cars drive to the top, and once a year a great fuss is made about a race of antique automobiles to the summit, where, once arrived, no one seems to feel "infinitely removed from the plain," nor any other grand sensation whatsoever. Thoreau and Dick Fuller read Vergil and Wordsworth in their tent with Wachusett under them, but it is almost unnecessary to remark that such reading has hardly become a custom, nor is it so frequently come upon at lower altitudes.

Thoreau wrote: "Every creature is better alive than dead, men and moose and pine-trees, and he who understands it aright will rather preserve its life than destroy it." The poet, he declared, had best right in the forest. But the poet is forced into a tight corner today, and wild life is given, in effect, to the hunters and fishers, who, through their license fees, establish their right to destroy it. Public officials regard the life out of doors as a "crop" to be harvested by exploiters. In short, most creatures of forest and open country are worth more dead than alive.

In his time Thoreau sent specimens from Walden to Agassiz, but the considered faith of his life was that a rare fish should be in the pond and not in his hand or anyone's. It would have astonished him to know that wardens would one day liberate fish in Massachusetts streams so that anglers could come along a few hours later and catch them.

He would have been astonished too if he could have known that the Fish and Wildlife Service of the United States would one day spend $134,000 to collect "data on the amount of time and money that American sportsmen spend annually on hunting and fishing" and would deem it important and necessary to learn "the economic status of hunting and fishing" as a guide for the management of natural resources—in other words, to arrive at the value of wildlife by the money to be made through destroying it.

Thoreau thought that towns were not beautiful. They are uglier today, and the inhabitants are ruled by stranger values than he ever dreamed of. A teen-age boy counts the whole scientific age vain and wasted if he must walk three blocks instead of covering the distance in an automobile. It is no longer exciting to see a statesman or a general in the flesh, because such figures may be observed on television; but the sight of television "personalities" in the flesh is absorbing to the point of high sensation. Most aspects of small towns that outsiders admire are despised by the inhabitants, who replace them as quickly as practical with imitations of city modes. To look inward is not the fashion. The advertising man tells where to look; you can be happy, he says, only if you are like everyone else.

"How few ever get beyond feeding, clothing, sheltering, and warming themselves in this world," wrote Thoreau, "and begin to treat themselves as human beings—as intellectual and moral beings! Most seem not to see any further—not to see over the ridge-pole of their barns—or to be exhausted and accomplish nothing more than a full barn, though it be accompanied by an empty head."

The nature of the town and rural capitalism has changed, but not the length of man's vision; it is now a television screen he cannot see past, or a neon sign or tin roof he cannot see over.

8. *Afterward*

It was as if someone in the back of the hall had cupped his hands and inquired hoarsely, "What did he say?"

And it was as if all of them hastened to explain what it was that Thoreau had said. Many made it a point to tell it in their own way, making excuses for Thoreau at places where they could not claim he had agreed with them. Many had difficulties, or scraped them up, because consistency was so much more important to them than it had been to him—though his temper and direction had always been clear enough. Others were so fussy and slow that their words seemed dusty as his never had.

Outside, in the clearer air, things were different. While the critics labored, many men, even in far and strange places, read *Walden* and understood that it was neither radical nor conservative but only true; the question was how to take and use the truth of it. For everyone, at the very least, there was the individual beauty and tang of Thoreau's writing, and the tonic freshness of his insight and point of view.

Elsewhere, through the years, philosophers, moralists, and economists aimed for the universal and fell short, or, if they gained it, were too dry, remote, and involved for ordinary interest and understanding. Thoreau, appearing to aim only at Concord, struck so close to some of the important universals that the final issues lay exposed. Others wrote earnestly of

civilized man and the evils of competition, of the conflict between ideals and earning a living, or how to relate the best of
man to the possibilities of his environment. But Thoreau lived
in the many-sided fact of the matter and, writing, put words
and sentences into place so rightly that they could never afterward be budged—or ignored. If there was, or is, or may be, a
place for the one whole man in this teeming world, still with
due respect to the crowd, the many, Thoreau's writing sets it
forth with the vitality of a homely scripture.

In Johannesburg in 1908, a slightly built attorney who had
been born at Porbondar, India, in 1869, eight years after Thoreau's death, borrowed from the library of a jail where the
British had locked him up a volume containing "Civil Disobedience" and made it a sourcebook for a purpose that
changed worldly history. Mohandas K. Gandhi, like Thoreau,
had read and studied the Bhagavad-Gita in English. Back and
forth across the world this current of learning, insight, and
poetry had flowed as if preparing, by appointment, for a time
when Gandhi would meet Thoreau.

Gandhi was deeply impressed with "Civil Disobedience";
he translated some passages for a journal called *Indian Opinion
in South Africa* which he was editing, and printed longer ex-
tracts in the paper's English section. "The essay seemed to me
so convincing and truthful," he wrote years later, "that I felt
the need of knowing more of Thoreau." *Walden* and other
essays he read with eager interest, but "Civil Disobedience"
became for him a bedside book.

Here was a theme for the protagonist of the oppressed and
unarmed. "The State . . . is not armed with superior wit or
honesty, but with superior physical strength. I was not born
to be forced. I will breathe after my own fashion. Let us see
who is strongest. What force has a multitude? They can only
force me who obey a higher law than I."

One honest man locked up in the county jail could abolish

slavery in America—so Thoreau had written. In how many jails now Gandhi was to sit with his thoughts. "I could not but smile to see how industriously they locked the door on my meditations, which followed them out again without let or hindrance, and *they* were really all that was dangerous." The spirit of Gandhi imprisoned became a force so unquenchable that he was set finally free at last—and so was India, erect and free.

In Britain *Walden* became a text of the labor movement. In Russia Leo Tolstoy read Thoreau and drew nourishment for the great influence of his own creed of Christianity, poverty, and non-resistance. From Concord the horizon had become as wide as the circle of the globe.

John Burroughs, naturalist, sprinkled quotations from Thoreau through his first book like raisins in a cake, and not as a matter of preserving dry specimens. "A howling wilderness seldom ever howls. The howling is chiefly done by the imagination of the traveler." So quoted John Burroughs, and other naturalists frowned, for they preferred the dry specimens. It was a fashion to say that Thoreau was not a real scientist—he who preferred to hold a rare creature in his affections rather than in his hand—and Burroughs was down-graded as a "follower of Thoreau." Yet there were more and more followers of the same kind.

Thoreau, neither specialist nor absolutist, spoke most of all to the spirit and need of the common man. "I find that I can see the sun set from almost any hill in Concord, and some within the confines of the neighboring towns, and though this takes place at just about 5 P.M., when the cows come in, get to the postoffice by the time the mail is distributed."

So the common man: if we must go to the post office for the mail—the tax bills and circulars and newspapers—let us go first to the hilltop and see the sun coloring the sky. There is time, there is still time enough.

Thoreau said so much, to so many. He wrote at different times, on different impulses, suiting his expression to the place where he was, and to the season and the occasion. His words ran with his life.

"As I was entering the Deep Cut," he wrote in the early fall of 1851, "the wind, which was conveying a message to me from heaven, dropped it on the wire of the telegraph which it vibrated as it passed. I instantly sat down on a stone at the foot of the telegraph pole, and attended to the communication. It merely said: 'Bear in mind, Child, and never for an instant forget, that there are higher planes of life than this thou art now traveling on. Know that the goal is distant, and is upward, and is worthy of all your life's efforts to attain to.' And then it ceased, and though I sat some minutes longer, I heard nothing more."

Many another might have been the author of a passage like this, yet Thoreau wrote these words too, in a softer mood than usual, not differentiating himself from all the other walkers of the earth, alien or near, who listened for an unfinished message.

After having lived momentously, he lies buried, Thoreau of Walden, on a ridge in Sleepy Hollow cemetery at Concord, under a stone not large or heavy enough to keep down his fame. Even those who have voyaged far and counted the cats in Zanzibar or perhaps in regions remoter still may envy the eventfulness of his short life.

INDEX

❧ ❧

ABOUT THE AUTHOR

Thirty-six years ago Henry Beetle Hough and his wife, Elizabeth Bowie Hough (they had just been married), left the big cities and settled down on the island of Martha's Vineyard to edit and publish the weekly newspaper, the Vineyard Gazette. *They are still there. In 1940 Mr. Hough's* Country Editor *was published, reporting on their small-town life and work, and the critical comments on the book that pleased the author most were those that found qualities suggestive of Thoreau.*

In all, Mr. Hough has now written eleven books.* The present biography of Thoreau reflects also the major interests and direction of the life he and Mrs. Hough have lived on Martha's Vineyard. There they have acquired an abandoned ice pond as a wild-life sanctuary, and the Vineyard Gazette *is dedicated first of all to conservation in the spirit of Thoreau.*

Mr. Hough was born in New Bedford, grandson of a Martha's Vineyard whaling captain. He worked for a year in Chicago and for several years in New York City before his permanent transplantation to the country.

* The other books are: *Martha's Vineyard, Summer Resort; Country Editor; That Lofty Sky* (novel); *All Things Are Yours* (novel); *Roosters Crow in Town* (novel); *Long Anchorage* (novel); *Once More the Thunderer; Singing in the Morning; Whaling Wives* (with Emma Mayhew Whiting); *An Alcoholic to His Sons,* as told to Henry Beetle Hough.

MAY 1 0 __

DEC __ 1978

MAR 1 __

OCT 29 '78

DEC 20 '78

APR 2 1 1986

MAY 1 1 1987

DEC 1 4 '__

DE__ 1 __

MA O 6 19__

APR 6 1994

MAY 1 5 1995

SEP 1 3 80.

APR 1 4 '80

Nov 30 '81

MAY 9 1 '8__

MAY 22 '8__

DEC 18 '82

NOV 2 6 1984

JAN 14 '85

MAR 1 7 1986

FRANKLIN AND MARSHALL COLLEGE
PS3053 .H6 1970   010101 000
Hough, Henry Beetle,
Thoreau of Walden; the man and

0 1114 0056765 2